From Silent Film Idol
to *Superman*

"Do you remember I used to hold up the number board for you on *Sailors Don't Care* in 1928? You were one of my boyhood heroes."—director David Lean, letter to John Stuart, 1947

"Pictures of John Stuart, a hero in the silent twenties, the aquiline profile under the wavy hair looking devotedly into the face under the bob and the cloche hat, stir so deep a nostalgia for the innocent past. In a way his story embraces the story of the British screen between the wars."—critic Dilys Powell, *Silent Picture* magazine, 1972

"Although some films were virtually halted by sound, there were still popular idols: charismatic Ivor Novello, soon to return to the stage where he was worshipped; and dark, brooding John Stuart, who had the common touch."—David Quinlan, *British Sound Films: The Studio Years 1928–1959*

"John Stuart's performance is a very good one indeed, and his simplicity and sincerity atone for the histrionics of Cedric Hardwicke and Conrad Veidt."—*Era* review of *Bella Donna*, 1934

"John Stuart was an exceptionally good actor—just about the best we had in those years."—Kevin Brownlow, in his foreword to *Forgotten Stars*, 2013

Acknowledgments

My warm thanks to film historian Kevin Brownlow, who persuaded me to write about my father's work and helped me greatly as I did so. I am similarly indebted to my friend Brian McFarlane for giving me the benefit of his encyclopedic knowledge of British film and for his good-natured support.

I must thank Ronald Grant and Martin Humphries at their unique Cinema Museum in London for their help with providing many of the photographs. I am also grateful to Frances Iddon at the British Film Institute archive in Berkhamsted for her patient help in giving me access to my father's scrapbooks, which are housed there, and to the staff at the institute's Reuben Library on the Southbank.

Table of Contents

Preface

This book is about a star of the British cinema who happened to be my father. As such, it provides a uniquely personal portrait of an actor whose film career spanned six decades of the twentieth century, who appeared in 172 films, and who worked in every British studio of the time. He acted alongside many of the top stars and was directed by two of the cinema's great directors.

As a film enthusiast from an early age, I was fascinated to watch my father on screen while I was still living with him at home. After finishing at university, I started to interview him with the aim of writing his biography, but the project lapsed when marriage, children and a career as an editor in book publishing took over my life.

From Silent Film Idol to Superman: *The Life and Career of John Stuart* covers my father's film career in comprehensive detail. It also deals with the conditions under which he and his fellow actors worked, the pressures created by the fans and the film journalists, the changing nature of the stories on which films were based, and the lure of Hollywood to which many actors succumbed. It also examines his extensive work in the theater and in television.

I was fortunate to inherit from him five bulky scrapbooks, now housed in the archive of the British Film Institute (BFI). They proved an invaluable resource: a rich collection of film reviews, interviews and profiles, gossip columns in which he was regularly featured, and articles he wrote about the benefits and drawbacks of being a star.

I carried out further research mainly in two venues. The wonderful Cinema Museum in South London has a unique collection of photos, books, films and posters, extensive files on countless films, and runs of many of the film magazines, all of which I drew on. The BFI library on the South Bank of the Thames has a large and valuable collection of books about film and film history, which I was able to consult, and copies of many film journals relevant to my research.

I own just three of my father's silent films but have watched several others in the BFI viewing room. Sad to say, all the remainder are lost, although three reels of *Mademoiselle from Armentières* recently turned up in Australia. But from my own collection, I have been able to watch the vast majority of the talkies in which he appeared.

Although there are numerous books about the film world and its stars, the only direct competitor is my own, now out of print, *Forgotten Stars: My Father and the*

British Silent-Film World, some of which I have used in revised and extended form in the present book.

My father's film career was extensive. Some of his films are inevitably less worthy of attention than others or have only meager information available. These I have put in the "Other Films" section at the end of each chapter. But as he worked extensively outside the film studios, I have included two chapters on his life in the theater and one on his many television appearances, all of which broadened his experience as an actor and fed into his work in films. He kept less material for these parts of his career, but they have been included in order to emphasize the breadth of his work. These chapters are more cursory than the others and contain no images; these I have reserved for those chapters which deal with his life and film work. I have also left unillustrated "Part Two: The Background," which steps back from his career to explore the context in which he worked.

Unless otherwise stated, comments by my father are taken from *Caught in the Act*, published in 1971. In compiling this memoir, he drew on an extended 1964 interview about his film career with film historian Denis Gifford. Another major source has been *Michael Balcon Presents … A Lifetime in Films*, a detailed account of the work and memories of the producer who played a key role in the development of the British film industry. For quotations from other books, I have indicated the source within the text. Full publication details of these titles are set out in the bibliography.

The major television documentary series *Cinema Europe: The Other Hollywood*, created by Kevin Brownlow and David Gill, has been invaluable, providing a panoramic view of the growth of cinema in France, Sweden, Germany and Russia.

Introduction

My father John Croall was born in the nineteenth century, became a star actor in films for decades in the twentieth, and is all but forgotten in the twenty-first.

As John Stuart—he dropped our family name early on—he was a major player in the British cinema between the two world wars. He was handsome, charming, and feted for the consistently naturalistic style of his acting. During a career spanning nearly 60 years, he appeared in no fewer than 172 films, at one time more than any screen actor of his day.

He began work in the silent era and quickly became a matinee idol with a large fan club. He was mentioned in the same breath as American stars Rudolph Valentino, Ramon Novarro and John Barrymore. He turned down the offer of a contract from Paramount at a time when many British actors, directors and writers were being lured to Hollywood. He continued to be a popular star throughout the 1930s and into the 1940s. In later years he moved into character roles, creating a wide variety of parts, usually playing professional men such as detectives, doctors, solicitors and judges. He ended his film career in 1978 with *Superman*.

He was directed by two of the cinema's leading directors, Alfred Hitchcock and G.W. Pabst. In the film *Kitty*, he played a small but significant part in cinema history when he and Estelle Brody became the first stars to talk in a feature film in Britain. His pleasing tenor voice enabled him to survive the arrival of the talkies with comparative ease.

He starred opposite most of the leading British actresses of the time, including Fay Compton, Estelle Brody, Mabel Poulton, Betty Balfour, Lilian Hall-Davis, Madeleine Carroll and Gracie Fields. He also appeared with Hollywood stars such as Florence Turner and Virginia Valli and Continental luminaries Conrad Veidt, Brigitte Helm and Arlette Marchal. His romantic temperament, his natural affinity with women, and his ability to relate to them on screen, gained him a reputation as the ideal screen lover.

In the mid–1930s, he plunged fully into the theater, starring in West End plays and touring the provinces while continuing with his film career. At the end of the decade, he took a break from filming to lead a provincial repertory company in the northeast, appearing in 49 plays during three seasons. In his career, he made 123 appearances on stage, many of them on tour. After the war, he started to work in television, a medium in which he acted in 103 plays and series. Yet who, beyond my family, and students and historians of twentieth-century British cinema, would now even recognize the name John Stuart?

During his years on screen, the British film industry went through fundamental and often turbulent changes, most notably with the coming of sound in 1929. His career was typical of many other stars who rose rapidly to success but also experienced many setbacks. I hope his story will shed light on a period of film history which is gradually fading from memory, as well as on his remarkable and extensive career as a popular and much-respected actor.

PART ONE

Silent Idol

1

Childhood, School, War

My father came from a prosperous business background, with no hint of any artistic inclinations. The Croalls were a well-to-do Scottish family, whose money from the late eighteenth century onward came first from building and running mail coaches, and later from constructing the chassis for luxury cars such as Rolls-Royce. The firm John Croall & Sons, run by his grandfather Robert Croall, became the largest motorcar business north of the river Tweed.

His father, John Croall, who worked for the family firm, was considered a very handsome and eligible bachelor. His mother, Agnes Park, a tall and elegant woman, was said to be one of the most beautiful in Edinburgh. According to family legend, at dances at the Usher Assembly Rooms, her card would be full by the time she reached the bottom of the main staircase.

My father was the second of three brothers. He was born John Alfred Louden Croall at eight p.m. on July 18, 1898, at 14 Eton Terrace in Edinburgh New Town, an elegant three-story house just over Dean Bridge from the city center, and close to Dean Gardens.

When he was seven, the family moved to London, apparently on doctor's advice, as his father's health was none too good—though why London should be considered a healthier city than Edinburgh is not clear.

The Croall family in 1896. Front row: center, my father's grandfather Robert. Back row: second left, father John; third right, grandmother Emily.

7

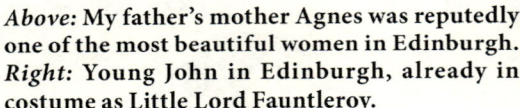

Above: My father's mother Agnes was reputedly one of the most beautiful women in Edinburgh. *Right:* Young John in Edinburgh, already in costume as Little Lord Fauntleroy.

They lived initially in a house in Hampstead, from where my father attended a prep school. A year later, his parents separated, partly because his mother was not happy with his father drinking with the workers in the family firm. His father moved to the East Sussex town of Eastbourne on the south coast, while Agnes remained in London with their three sons Robbie, John and Eric.

At nine, my father was sent as a boarder to Dunstable Grammar School in Bedfordshire, where his elder brother Robbie was already a pupil (as was Gary Cooper before he went to America and became a Hollywood star). My father remembered his liking for the stories of heroes: "Often with a problem of geometry before me, I would sit for the whole lesson with my thoughts roaming away through a crusade with Richard Coeur de Lion, or into the battle of Agincourt with Henry V."

He developed an interest in the theater, particularly Shakespeare, once selling his schoolbooks and playing truant in order to see a local production of *Hamlet*. On his return, he was called before the headteacher, who told him he should become an actor, as he was so keen on the theater, then gave him a caning and "sent him to Coventry" (ostracized him). So he began to act, playing small parts in school productions. "All through my school days, I was very keen on amateur theatricals, always taking part very eagerly in any show that my school put on."

At 14, he moved to Eastbourne College, which enabled him to see his father regularly during term time. In the holidays, he alternated between seeing each of his

At Eastbourne College he was a keen member of the Junior Rugby XV (front row, right) and later captain of the Senior XV.

parents. Although he was keen on athletics and rugby (he captained the first fifteen), he was by his own admission "scholastically hopeless." To his surprise, he did win a prize for French. "I had no idea of taking up acting as a profession. At this stage my ambition was to become a naval doctor." His first appearance on any stage outside school was in 1912, when he sang in a concert in a mission hall to help raise funds for those affected by the sinking of the *Titanic*.

After receiving a medal for being the smartest cadet in the school, he was under canvas on the annual Officers Training Corps summer camp when war broke out on August 4, 1914. The corps were immediately ordered to strike camp and return home. Patriotic fervor was rampant, and men signed up for the forces in great numbers. Keen to be involved, and dressed in his cadet uniform, he was allowed to help as an orderly at the Eastbourne military hospital. With Belgian refugees streaming over the Channel, one of his duties was "to take wounded Belgian soldiers along the seafront in a bath-chair, and sit there inhaling the sea breezes."

As the war continued, he shelved his idea of becoming a naval doctor, and at 17, like many others of his age, he decided to join the army. Being underage, he was rejected. At 19, he re-applied and joined the Black Watch. After training, he was sent to the Arras sector of the Western Front in France, as a second lieutenant with the second battalion of the Seaforth Highlanders. He saw several months' fierce fighting there, during which most of his colleagues were killed. In September 1918, he was invalided out with a bad attack of trench fever. He left the naval and military hospital in London on November 11, Armistice Day.

While in France, he had taken part in a battalion concert party, *Old Bill Gets a Blighty*, playing a raw recruit who ducked in terror every time a shell burst. It was this experience which sparked in him an ambition to act professionally. Then, while waiting in Scotland to be demobbed, he had the idea of staging a concert for the troops. So he became the battalion's entertainments officer, in charge of the regimental band, the pipes and the concert party, which was known as "The Duds." They put on several successful shows for charity; one was for the relief fund for the many lives lost in the Stornoway disaster in the Isle of Lewis harbor in the Scottish Highlands.

In 1917, at the age of 19, my father joined the Seaforth Highlanders to fight on the Western Front in France.

He was then faced with a choice of remaining in the army or returning to civilian life. His father wanted him to join the London office of the family firm, but after a brief spell there, he found it hard to adapt to the commercial way of life. So in the autumn of 1919, he decided, against his parents' wishes, to try his luck as an actor.

2

From Stage to Screen

"I was paid three guineas a day. As I was only getting three pounds a week on tour, I felt like a millionaire. I thought, 'I'll stick to films.'"

Film was still a young industry when my father entered it in 1920. At the beginning of the twentieth century, short, flickering films were shown at traveling fairs, in church halls, in vacant shop fronts and skating rinks. They also became part of music hall programs. Purpose-built cinemas only began to appear in 1909; by 1915, some 3500 cinemas had been built. Soon feature-length dramas started to be made in Britain.

Then the First World War had a devastating impact on the industry. In 1917, the arrival of conscription drained the studios of manpower, and film production virtually ceased. But audiences had already turned against the homegrown films, because of their inferiority to the American output. Hollywood was supreme in all departments—photography, technology, publicity, scripts, acting, directing. They had a more adventurous spirit, they had the stars, and they had the glamour. By 1918, at least 80 percent of films shown in Britain came from Hollywood. In 1920, of the 878 films available, only 144 were British; and by 1923, British films constituted only ten percent of the films exhibited.

After the war, the audience for this new form of mass entertainment was still principally a working-class one, very much the same people who enjoyed the music hall. As the director David Lean later observed, "You have no idea how the silent movies were despised by the middle classes. They were cheap entertainment for the poor."

In his memoir *Michael Balcon Presents*, the influential producer stated: "The war had virtually killed off British film production, and the Americans had taken full advantage to provide all the films the British cinema required." The companies avoided taking up controversial subjects; Balcon explained: "Film producers, during the years which saw women in Britain enfranchised, the American slump and the Wall Street crash, were making silent films on themes so little influenced by the march of world events. We were in the business of giving the public entertainment. We did not talk about art or social significance."

Before the war, as one observer put it, there was such a strong prejudice against the cinema "that some people would almost as soon confess to entering a gin-palace as a picture-palace." But during the 1920s, as films became more popular, the audience widened. Eventually three million people were going to the cinema every night, with women providing a majority of the filmgoers.

A growing middle-class audience lent the cinema more respectability. As one report loftily stated: "A fellow of an Oxford college no longer feels an embarrassment or an explanation to be necessary when he is recognised leaving a cinema." But such places were still seen by many as sinful, as "dim havens for courting couples" and "the recruiting stations of vice." According to the literary critic Walter Allen, films were "what the working classes, consuming fish and chips from greasy paper bags, watched in places called picture-palaces." The critic Iris Barry wrote: "It is strange that people are still a trifle ashamed of going to the pictures, and admit they do so apologetically, while they positively boast of going to the theatre." She argued that the great strength of the cinema was "that it caters for dreams more thoroughly, more generously, more convincingly than any other form of entertainment."

But filmgoing was not always a relaxing experience. There were complaints about people reading the titles aloud, or those who had already seen the feature letting others know about it. The cinema was a meeting place to discuss the day's events: people would talk freely to each other, and sometimes even to the screen. On occasions they were known to shout out "Slower!" so they could read the titles, and the projectionist would slow down the film. If the projector broke down, the audience would occasionally throw food at the screen.

In an attempt to attain respectability, and move away from the cinema's humble origins, the film companies concentrated on a narrow range of subject matter. Films emphasized Englishness, and often had idyllic countryside settings. This genteel output, heavily dependent on novels and West End plays for its stories, favored costume dramas, or melodramas dealing with the lives of the rich and privileged.

British films suffered in comparison with those produced in other countries. In Europe, notably in Germany, France, and post-revolutionary Russia, film was already seen as an art form by an influential minority, as it was in America. In Britain, few saw it in this light. As Balcon admitted: "We were making our contribution to what was no more than entertainment opium for the masses."

The British public much preferred to watch the livelier, brasher, more populist American films. According to George Atkinson, critic of the *Daily Express*:

> The bulk of our picturegoers are Americanised to the extent that makes them regard a British film as a foreign film, and an interesting but more frequently an irritating interlude in their favourite entertainment. They go to see American stars, they have been brought up on American publicity. They talk America, think America, and dream America. We have several million people, mostly women, who to all intents and purposes are temporary American citizens.

This was the context in which my father embarked on his new life. He began by changing his name to John Stuart, partly because it emphasized his Scottish background. The first few months looking for work were difficult. "I tried hard to gain a footing," he recalled, "but not coming from a theatrical family, I didn't know the ropes at all. My clothes began to look shabby, and I felt a bit desperate. I never knew where the next job—even the next meal—was coming from."

Although drama schools such as the Royal Academy of Dramatic Art and the Central School of Speech and Drama already existed, he apparently made no effort to apply for a place in one. But within two months, he landed a job as an extra at the

Old Vic, appearing on stage with the great actress Sybil Thorndike, who was playing Hecuba in Euripides' tragedy *The Trojan Women*. "It wasn't exactly an arduous part. I hadn't a line to say, and I hadn't a thing in the world to do, except to hold her very firmly by the arms as she tried to throw herself into the flames of burning Troy. What more could a stage-struck young man desire?"

He claimed that when he told an agent he had been "supporting" Thorndike at the Old Vic, the agent was impressed and immediately recommended him for a part in a touring production of *The Chinese Puzzle*, a new play by Marion Bower and Leon M. Lion, which was to start at the Theatre Royal in Windsor. The company was run by the Irish actor-manager Charles Macdona, who specialized in sending West End successes out on tour.

My father's foot was now firmly on the bottom rung of the theatrical ladder. He was earning £3 a week playing the juvenile lead in the first three acts, a Chinese servant in the fourth, and acting as an assistant stage manager. When the six-month tour finished, he had some photos taken for publicity purposes and "climbed the stone stairs to agents' offices for six solid months."

Eventually a break came, but not in the theater; it was on screen. The producer-director Walter West was looking for a young man to feature in his next picture, the melodrama *Her Son*. My father encountered him at a dinner party. "I didn't know who he was, but I felt him looking at me all through the dinner." West, having also seen my father on stage in *The Chinese Puzzle*, decided that this dark, handsome young man had "a film face," and that he resembled his wife Violet Hopson, who was to play the mother in *Her Son*. He offered him the title role of young Min Gascoyne, a minor but crucial character.

West had been an actor before turning to directing and setting up Broadwest Films. He was later to give Clive Brook his first screen role, and to provide Ronald Colman with an early opportunity. West recalled the conditions under which he directed one of his first pictures, *A Bold Adventuress*, in just ten days: "The plot was conceived in a little back office by candlelight, because my last shilling had long since been put in the gas meter. I, as producer, scenario-writer, electrician, and set designer, also played a leading part, whilst the carpenters, office boy, and secretary of the small company were also featured."

A big, astute and persuasive man, flamboyant and full of enthusiasm, West was a lover of horse-racing, and owned a string of horses. Believing them to be the key ingredient to appeal to the public, he featured them in many films about the sporting world, based on the stories of Nat Gould. According to Rachael Low in *The History of British Film 1918–1929*:

> The stories were as a rule simple and straightforward plots, unrealistic and contrived, but not too grotesquely melodramatic.... It was a world peopled with guardians, profligate sons, concealed identities, girls delightfully learning to love their husbands-of-convenience, and race-horse owners with their fortunes or their girl-friends for ever at stake, their horses for ever in danger of nobbling.

Broadwest released no less than ten films in 1920, seven starring Violet Hopson. The story was not always the main attraction: The magazine *Cinema Chat* called one film, *Under Suspicion,* "another Broadwest film which will show you some lovely frocks." Nor were the films of great technical quality: of *A Dead Certainty*, one of his "turf dramas," *Kine Monthly* noted, "The exterior scenes especially were either dim, flickery, or out of focus, and sometimes suffered from all three faults at once."

California-born Violet Hopson was the first screen actress in Britain to be systematically exploited as glamorous and well-dressed. Before the war, stars were not always identified by name in the credits, and some were known only by nicknames, initially supplied by the audience. They were not allowed to be interviewed or to make personal appearances.

In America, producers tried to keep stars' identities secret, for fear they would become well-known and demand much higher

His supposed resemblance to star actress Violet Hopson brought him his film debut in *Her Son* (1920) (courtesy the Cinema Museum, London).

salaries linked to their popularity. In their turn, the stars preferred to remain anonymous for fear that stage managers wouldn't hire them if they were known to be working in films. Mary Pickford, who specialized in child roles, was initially known simply as "Little Mary" or "The Girl with the Golden Curls," until producer Adolph Zukor decided to reveal her name. "I thought it would lift film from being a peepshow to a reputable level of entertainment," he explained.

With her dark hair, dark eyes and strong, handsome face, Hopson was labeled the "Dear Delightful Villainess." She played a sequence of villainesses before "reforming," and specializing in demure English heroines in early British films such as *The Vicar of Wakefield* and *Barnaby Rudge*. In the 1924 *Daily News* poll of Favourite British Film Stars, she landed in fourth place behind Betty Balfour, Alma Taylor and Gladys Cooper.

She had also set up Broadwest Films with her husband. In December 1921, *Motion Picture Studio* noted: "Despite her dramatic ability, Miss Hopson also possesses a keen business sense, a combination rarely found in a man, more rarely in a woman." It reported that her New Year's resolution was "to show the British public that a woman's influence, if exercised in the right direction, can be a tremendous benefit to British films." This was certainly a rare event in these male-dominated times, in which full voting rights for women were not to come until 1928.

In June 1920, at age 21, my father was summoned to West's studio in Walthamstow, North London. His scenes were to be shot in a single Sunday between two touring dates of *The Chinese Puzzle*. He recalled:

> The studio was a huge converted tram garage with a glass roof. It had very few mercury vapour lamps, so we used natural sunlight. It was very hot, like being in a conservatory. The camera was very static—they didn't have it coming in or going out. You heard it going, because the man was standing there winding the handle, like a hurdy-gurdy man. As soon as you heard that, you started. There was no dolly coming in to do a close-up and then pulling out again. It was a matter of lifting up the camera, tripod and all, and bringing it closer to the actor or actress. They just hoped the continuity would be all right.

He shared a dressing-room with Stewart Rome, now firmly established as a matinee idol. Tall and dark, handsome and aristocratic-looking, Rome specialized in playing quintessential English country gentlemen. When he was first given a film test, he was told he was too tall. "In those days there were no such things as close-ups," Rome explained. "An actor was seen in his entirety or not at all, and there was evidently too much of me to get comfortably into the picture." Promoted as rugged and manly, he was voted second to Charlie Chaplin in a 1915 magazine popularity poll. Shortly after the war, he was said to be receiving 600 fan letters a week, and by 1921 he was Britain's most popular screen actor. As my father remembered:

> He was a big star, and I was very impressed that he condescended to share his dressing room with a complete beginner, and very kindly showed me how to do makeup, as I didn't know a thing about it. In those days you used a yellow no. 5 stick, which made you look as if you had yellow jaundice. Actors and actresses used the same makeup. There were no hairdressers in the studios: the women had to have their hair done in a local hairdresser's. Nor were there any makeup people: one had to do it oneself. There were no doubles, no stand-ins; it was all very do-it-yourself.
>
> I didn't have to read for the part. There was no audition or screen test: We had just one or two rehearsals before shooting. West just said, "You do this and then you do that," and so I did it. Some directors I worked with later were more meticulous, and would rehearse more. When it came to the acting, I just tried to be as natural as possible, which I think is the great secret, to be real. I tried to be myself, I didn't act at all.
>
> We shot two interior scenes, and some exteriors of me playing in goal in a football match. I was paid three guineas a day. As I was only getting three pounds a week on tour, I felt like a millionaire. I thought, "I'll stick to films."

As happened to many stars in these early years, my father's breakthrough came as a result of his looks rather than any proven talent or experience. For a young novice actor, this was a great opportunity, since it enabled him to work with the public's two favorite screen stars.

Because of their great popularity, *Her Son* was publicly shown much sooner than usual, being released less than two months after my father completed his day's filming. As the *Evening News* reported after its first screening: "The Pavilion in Piccadilly Circus was swamped by crowds of women. The storm of applause at the end showed they were pleased with the picture, and so were all who saw it, judging from the general enthusiasm, and the presence of a crowd of 'fans' outside, waiting to see

Miss Hopson … come out of the theatre."

Her Son is one of the few of my father's silent films to have survived. Like so many of the period, it was based on a stage play, written by the prolific Horace Annesley Vachell, who at one time was compared to John Galsworthy. It's a complicated tale of love, motherhood and adoption, set in 1900 when, one title explains, "the bachelor girl was a social curiosity." Good finally triumphs over evil—or, as the final title has it: "Time has laid its gentle finger upon the memories of tragedy and error, pain and sorrow, and the mists of years have vanished in the dawn of a new day."

Stewart Rome was sometimes criticized for his expansive on-screen gestures, but in *Her Son* he acts with restraint. Violet Hopson's acting is heavy-handed, with a fair amount of head-clutching and expressions

A publicity shot for *Her Son*.

of wide-eyed surprise. My father tackles his half-dozen brief scenes with the two stars in a cheerful, energetic but unaffected manner. They were, according to *Studio*, "delighted with his fresh and natural performance." His first reviews in the trade press were brief but positive: "John Stuart fits into the picture well" (*Kine Weekly*) and "He appears to advantage" (*Bioscope*).

A French critic writing in 1921 accused British actors of having the wrong temperament for films, suggesting there was no race in the world to whom showing their emotions was so repugnant. My father, with his dark good looks and obvious rapport with the actresses who played opposite him, was one of the actors whose performances clearly refuted this idea. Invariably cast as the young hero, he had no trouble conveying the appropriate emotions. On the evidence of his ten surviving silent films, and the consensus among critics, he was a strikingly natural actor, who managed to avoid the histrionics in which many of his contemporaries indulged.

The easy, unforced style that he displayed in *Her Son* proved a valuable asset in his subsequent early work. He was given a decent variety of roles which went well beyond the conventional juvenile leads, and included a racing-boat pilot, a Canadian rancher, a Cornish fisherman, a Welsh musician, an Irishman and a shop assistant. No doubt it helped that no accents were required in those silent days.

His debut had clearly impressed his director: "West then told me he had another picture coming along shortly, and would I be interested? I loved it: It gave me a great feeling for films." *The Great Gay Road* (1920), directed by former actor Norman McDonald, was an adaptation of the novel by Tom Gallon, several of whose stories became the basis of films after his death in 1914. Popular novels were a much-used source at the time: In 1922, some 70 films, almost a quarter of the output, fell into this category.

The film again starred Stewart Rome, here playing against type as a "ragged and tattered gentleman tramp," and giving a performance described by *Pictures* magazine as "masterly." My father played Rodney Foster, a supporting juvenile role, opposite his first screen sweetheart, Pauline Johnson. He made little impression, his acting being described as merely "pleasant" and "without serious fault."

That same year, he appeared opposite singer–stage actress Moya Nugent in the subplot of a Victorian melodrama, *The Lights of Home* (1920). It was directed by the Swiss-born actor Fred Paul, who directed 65 films during the 1920s. A medical student and then a journalist before turning to acting, he appeared in 80 films, most notably playing the lead in *East Lynne*. His best-known film as a director was the wartime screen version of Oscar Wilde's *Lady Windermere's Fan*.

The Lights of Home, based on a popular Victorian stage melodrama, was a tale of love and betrayal among Cornish fishing folk, with more than a whiff of *Romeo and Juliet* about it. "Here's one that will ring up a new record on your cash register!" was the film company's message to the exhibitors. My father was cast as the good-natured hero Philip Compton, a young fisherman who elopes

As the young hero in *The Lights of Home* (1920), a story of love and betrayal among Cornish fishing folk.

with his girl, then returns to clear himself of the charge of murdering his wicked rival.

The film was shot in Cornwall, known as "England's natural film studio," at Polkerris and Coombe Beach, and in Fowey and Menabilly House, where Daphne du Maurier later lived and found the inspiration for Manderley, the house in her novel *Rebecca*. In one scene, my father reportedly had to "rescue the heroine from a dizzy crag near Fowey in the face of a strong breeze and heavy seas." This was his first experience of location filming. "Fortunately the sun shone all day," he recalled, "and we had quite a big audience watching us, including many trippers." *Referee* thought his playing was "excellent" and *Kine Weekly* said he put "a good deal of convincing feeling into his part."

Soon afterwards, he made four "song films," an odd, short-lived genre which involved acting out stories based on popular songs such as "Home Sweet Home" and the Victorian parlor song "The Village Blacksmith," to accompany the publication of a book of songs. Each film took just two days to shoot. My father appeared in *Home Sweet Home*, played the young lover for the Irish song heard in *Eileen Allanah*, and the greengrocer's assistant in *Sally in Our Alley*. One critic wrote that in the last two, "he sustains both roles, one comedy and one dramatic, in fine style." The *Motion Picture Studio* reviewer noted: "In *Eileen Allanah* his expressions were splendid; in *Sally in Our Alley* he acted as a coster, and took to the part as to the manor born. I am quite sure he will make a name for himself. He is so natural, and his lover-like actions were very real."

However, after a promising start with this initial flurry of parts, he struck a bad patch. With no immediate offers in sight, he decided to work as an extra, spending four months doing "crowd work" on several films at Islington and Twickenham studios. At such times he drew comfort by recalling his first acting experience with Sybil Thorndike at the Old Vic. "It was Miss Thorndike's wonderful enthusiasm and obvious love for her work which made me still more determined to win through," he explained. "Whenever I am feeling disconsolate and hopeless about things now, I just think of all the hard work and disappointments Miss Thorndike had to face at the beginning of her career, and I feel wonderfully encouraged."

Other Films

He also took part in 1921 in half a dozen "Leaves from My Life" films, a series of short crime dramas. The titles were *Something in the City*, *The Stolen Jewels*, *Belle of the Gambling Den*, *The Notorious Mrs. Fagin*, *The Case of a Packing Case*, and *The Man Who Came Back*.

3

An Emerging Star

"In *Little Miss Nobody* John Stuart is very natural and pleasant as the lover, and plays with a lightness that is, as far as we know, to be found in the work of no other British juvenile lead."—*Motion Picture Studio*, 1923

After this temporary setback, my father's fortunes changed, and he began to appear in leading roles. *Land of My Fathers* (1921), based on a Cambrian legend about the Welsh national anthem, was billed as "A Stirring Drama of Love and Sacrifice." He was cast as David Morgan, a famous young Welsh violinist who loses his memory and becomes involved in a love tangle with two women (Edith Pearson and Yvonne Thomas). For the first time, there's a brief biography of him in *Kine Weekly*, where he is described as "a thorough-bred Scot, whose abilities as an all-round athlete stood him in good stead" during the filming.

Land of My Fathers was directed by Fred Rains, the father of actor Claude Rains. In these silent years, many actors and directors came from the music halls. Originally a slapstick comedian in short films which he directed himself, Rains was also a music hall performer, a composer and a busy character actor in films; he played a tramp in *Land of My Fathers*. He was, my father said, "a terribly good director, and very sympathetic. He'd never ask you to do anything he couldn't do himself."

The critics liked the film and approved of my father's performance: *Kine Weekly* praised his "very natural study of a young man, who wins one's liking despite his rather graceless behaviour," while *Bioscope* reckoned "he played the part to perfection." He was also praised for the convincing way he handled the violin. One reporter wrote, "Stuart says he was very careful to watch the first violinist at the various restaurants he visited prior to the filming of his violin scenes." To get the handling of the instrument correct, he was given private lessons by the celebrated violinist Malvina. "It seemed to work all right because people said, 'I didn't know you were a violinist,' which was rather a compliment."

He also noted: "We had a three-piece band playing off the set to help set the mood, which was especially good for the love scenes." Film screenings were of course accompanied by music, initially from a piano, an organ or a three-piece band. A news item of the time stated: "Music now plays such an important part in the presentation of films that the services of well-known composers are being enlisted when the musical settings for new films are being arranged."

During the filming in Aberystwyth, my father came perilously close to drowning:

In the 1921 film *Land of My Fathers*, he played the famous Welsh violinist of Cambrian legend.

As the hero I'd been shanghaied by two villains who were fishermen. They took me out to a boat about five miles out in Cardigan Bay, and threw me overboard. Fred Rains and the cameraman were in a little motorboat standing by to pick me up. But its engine broke down, so there I was, flapping about in the sea, getting numb with the cold, and fearing I'd never be able to swim to the boat. There was a pretty high sea running at the time, I must have been crazy to do this scene, even though I am a good swimmer. Fortunately they got the engine going, picked me up just in time, and revived me with half a bottle of brandy. It was an anxious moment, and Fred Rains was very upset about my being stuck in the water.

The local paper reported: "Only his strong swimming and endurance enabled Mr. Stuart to keep afloat in heavy seas, impeded as he was by his clothes."

Making screen adaptations of novels was seen as a good way to promote British films, with stories which, as *Bioscope* put it, "show Britain as it has been pictured by its own great writers." But as film historian Brian McFarlane noted, the adaptations were often unadventurous, and had "a characteristic tendency to be awed by or to trade on the prestige and popularity of the source novels."

My father's next film made use of Compton Mackenzie's pre-war novel *Sinister Street*, a semi-autobiographical work in which the hero passes through school, Oxford and sleazy London low life. Immensely popular but controversial when first published before the war, it prompted Henry James to call Mackenzie "the greatest talent of the new generation." The film was directed by the Australian George Beranger, another actor turned director. Born in Sydney, he had toured Australia in

Shakespeare, then moved to Hollywood, where for seven years he worked as D.W. Griffith's assistant director and appeared in *The Birth of a Nation*, *Intolerance* and *Broken Blossoms*.

My father played the hero Michael Fane, "a chivalrous youth with high ideals about how women should be treated, and with monkish tendencies." This was his first major part, for which there was apparently considerable competition. It was made at Elstree Studios (otherwise known as "Hollywood without the palm trees and sun"), where he found the facilities decidedly primitive. "The dressing rooms were like an army hut. In the tiny studio there was only room for one set, so they had to keep taking them down."

Mackenzie came over from his Channel Island home in Herm to collaborate on the screenplay. My father reportedly "had a long chat with Fane's creator, who told him many points about the character which are not included in the book." As he watched the rushes, Mackenzie was horrified to see one of his characters riding on horseback down a country lane to join a tea party, dressed in the full regalia of the Welsh Guards. When he complained that he should be in civilian dress, the producers allegedly told him: "You have to understand, Mr. Mackenzie, that the cinema audience wants romance."

Film Renter felt that my father "acted in capital style"; another paper reported, "John Stuart is restrained and real in his fencing with life." But his performance was not widely admired. *The Times* criticized his playing of a climactic scene in which, on learning of the infidelity of the woman he loves (Maudie Dunham, a big star of the day), "he staggers backwards and forwards for an appreciable time, and then, after breaking a few ornaments and tearing down some heavy curtains, he lurches from the room like a drunken man. It was all very tragic, but it scarcely seemed true." The *Evening News* concluded: "John Stuart, although a very promising film player, is hardly experienced enough for such an exacting part," while *Kine Weekly* noted, "John Stuart as Michael is exaggerated and artificial. He has been badly handled, for he has real promise if better directed." My father later explained: "Beranger was an Australian, and didn't understand the English side of the story. He made us over-act a lot."

After *Sinister Street,* he confessed to a reporter that being "so steeped in the Compton Mackenzie atmosphere, I was glad to have a little respite between productions." He found "just enough time to indulge in a little theatre-going and hunting" before starting on his next film. This was the generally disappointing *The Little Mother* (1922), a tale of life in the Canadian backwoods. Director A.V. Bramble was a modest man with a modest talent. Another actor turned director, his work was generally uninspiring, although he was sometimes praised for his thoroughness with detail and the beauty of his sets. He was known principally for his all-round efficiency.

In the title role was Florence Turner, one of America's first movie stars to be known by her own name (the very first was Florence Lawrence). At first, she was simply called the "Vitagraph Girl" by the studio which signed her in 1906. She then became the most popular American screen actress of the day, specializing in "pathetic-unattractive" parts.

An early example of Shakespeare on film shows her as Viola in *Twelfth Night*, her expressive features topped by a mop of pre–Raphaelite-style hair. She was a woman of many talents and great versatility, who also wrote screenplays and directed films. In 1913, she moved to Britain and set up her own production company, Turner Films. She performed in the music halls and made several films during the war, including a version of Thomas Hardy's novel *Far from the Madding Crowd*, playing the heroine Bathsheba Everdene.

The Little Mother was a story of a kind then popular in America, one which (according to *Film Renter*) "is assured of a warm welcome by the majority of kinemagoers, who thoroughly enjoy a play in which sentiment—frequently near to tears—predominates." My father played Turner's son Jack, a rancher in the backwoods. In one scene he had to fight with the villain in a saloon. "We fought nearly all day to get the scene right," he said during the filming. "I was so stiff the next day I could scarcely walk. I have not yet become accustomed to the heavy boots and furs I have to wear. Wearing them in a temperature somewhere below zero is all very well, but under the strong studio lights, furs are hardly essential to keep one warm."

The film was criticized on several counts by the *Kine Weekly* reviewer, who disliked "its air of false and overstrained sentiment." He continued:

> [Its] hopelessly stilted sub-titles … are most ridiculous when they seek to be most impressive, and far more likely to create laughter than tears. Only a very unsophisticated audience is likely to accept the story at face value. Mechanically, A.V. Bramble's work is just adequate; dramatically, it is a record of lost opportunities, very little attempt having been made, by careful characterisation, to get over the emotional effect aimed at.

Studio complained, "The director has spared no pains to ladle out the sentiment in such liberal quantities that the picture almost becomes a burlesque."

But the critics liked my father's performance: "John Stuart is good, but he has little chance with the poor material at his disposal," wrote the *Studio* critic. *Picture Show* stated approvingly, "His acting was something of a revelation. He played so easily, without a trace of self-consciousness—he is the ideal type for romance." Yet despite his positive notices, he felt he was still very much a novice. He observed, "Every new film teaches me how much I've got to learn." He professed himself a great admirer of Turner's technique and also said of her, according to the *Daily Record*: "As regards second mothers, I couldn't have a nicer and sweeter one than her." However, her reviews were lukewarm. "The acting is not of a very high standard," *Studio* noted. "She has done better work."

During a break in the filming, my father (accompanied by Turner) returned to Scotland for the first time since he started in films. He made appearances at a number of Edinburgh cinemas, visited friends from his boyhood, and attended the Cinema Carnival in Glasgow, where he and his film mother joined in the dancing. "It's so nice to get back to Edinburgh that I shall not want to go south again," he told her.

Another 1922 film was *A Sporting Double*, written and directed by Arthur Rooke, another former stage and screen actor. As Will Blunt, the hero and son of a coal mine manager, my father has to repay a debt in order to win the girl (Lilian Douglas). He does so by placing a large bet on the outcome of that year's Derby (won by Captain Cuttle) and the Cup Final (Huddersfield beat Preston). The film includes footage of both events, to give it authenticity.

My father recalled a difficult moment during the filming of a football scene. "For the Cup Final—it was actually the semi-final—I had to stand at the players' entrance and as the camera rolled clap each player on the back as they emerged from the dressing room. Was my face red! I was very embarrassed." But according to one light-hearted report, he enjoyed his day at the Derby: "On Epsom Downs, Stuart found so much of interest apart from the racing that every time the director wanted him to take part in a scene he had to send out a search party for him. Usually he was found to be listening attentively to the wonderful tales of the tipsters. Stuart did not follow their advice, however, and won on the day's betting."

Several scenes were filmed in Batley in Yorkshire, apparently with a particular eye on northern audiences. Once again he is involved in a fight scene, and an especially demanding one. He jumps from a bridge onto the deck of a barge, where he struggles with the villain (Terry Cavanagh). "We fought so hard that we eventually landed in the river," he said soon after, "but even that did not stop us. We floundered about in the muddy water for some time, and on reaching the riverbank continued our fight there. We were both breathless and black and blue by the time we finished, for owing to re-takes and close-ups the fight took us one whole day to film. But the director Arthur Rooke says it is some fight."

The *Times* reviewer agreed: "John Stuart is a pleasing hero, and seems to revel in an unorthodox fight with the villain that is as realistic as anything of the kind that has been seen in a film. The villain is very severely handled, and this alone should make the film popular with the average audience." His other notices are extremely positive. *Bioscope* mentions his "pleasing easy style," *Studio* notes his "very fine acting," while *Picture Show* observes: "John Stuart has fine handsome features, and moreover he possesses all that charm and manliness which is so essential to the making of a popular artiste." The *News of the World* went further: "His acting is very fine. Undoubtedly, although he is one of the newest, he is one of the best juveniles of the British screen."

His next film, *If Four Walls Told* (1922), was based on a popular play by Edward Percy and directed by Fred Paul. Filming again in Cornwall, where the story was set, he suffered another accident. As the young hero Ned Mason, he had to run through the water in heavy boots and jump into a lifeboat being launched. Unfortunately, he missed the boat and cut his chin. The weather then held up filming for three weeks, during which he was reported to be "writing a film story which he hopes to sell to an American firm." There is no further reference to this unexpected sideline.

If Four Walls Told was the first film in which he played opposite Lilian Hall-Davis, whom he remembered as "a very sweet person and a very good actress, a joy to work with." The most glamorous and graceful of all the English female stars of the period, and at one stage the biggest, Hall-Davis was an elegant, instinctive actress. Her contemporary Joan Morgan called her "a very neat, beautifully groomed, simple girl, not at all sophisticated, and quite conventional."

Born in London's East End, Hall-Davis later attempted to cover up her origins, changing her birthplace to Hampstead and adding a hyphen to her surname. A taxi driver's daughter who became a beauty queen, she made her screen debut as a child. For a while she was Hitchcock's favorite actress: She gives a sympathetic, understated portrayal of a woman caught between two men in *The Ring* (1927) and displays an attractive restraint and natural ease in the title role of his rural comedy *The Farmer's Wife* (1928).

During the following year, my father was greatly in demand and made no less than seven films, a mixture of costume dramas and contemporary stories. It was also a time when he made his West End stage debut in a sensational new Somerset Maugham play.

Of the films, the short *The Mistletoe Bough* (1923), the first in the "Gems of Literature" series, was a slight story set during the civil war. In it, my father played his first aristocrat, Lord Lovell, and wore a dashing Cavalier costume. Cast as his new bride was charming and petite Flora le Breton, a popular star of mixed English, French, Scottish and English blood who was labeled "The English Mary Pickford." Her beauty was, according to one critic, "of the Dresden-doll type." Le Breton had appeared in several revues as a singer and dancer before entering films. She was in the first color film made in Britain, *The Glorious Adventure*, starring the society beauty Diana Cooper.

My father was re-teamed with Le Breton in *Little Miss Nobody* (1923), again playing her lover. A farce set in a Scottish castle, it was directed by the prolific Wilfred Noy, the uncle of the actor Leslie Howard. This was one of seven films my father made with the rising young actress Gladys Jennings. One critic wrote of her, "She has a great frank beauty, the embodiment of the nice English girl. We mean of course the pleasant, but thoughtful, participator in life, not the leggy lipstick flourisher."

The film earned my father the cover slot on *Motion Picture Studio*. The magazine includes many fascinating small ads from actors seeking work ("Milton Rosmer invites offers," etc.). Surprisingly, most of them provide their home address. The magazine's critic commended my father for his performance as a penniless young man: "John Stuart is very natural and pleasant as the lover, and plays with a lightness that is, so far as we know, to be found in the work of no other British juvenile lead. He gets better and better in every picture."

Many of these silent films were just photographed stage plays. Most of the actors came from a theatrical background, as did many of the producers and directors. Cinema was seen as a decidedly inferior medium but useful commercially. Gladys Cooper was dismissive: "All you really need is a face that photographs well, and a good director." John Gielgud, then a young actor, recalled a considerable degree of snobbery; filming, he said, was often seen merely as a way of earning extra money to pay your taxes: "You had to take it on the chin, shut your eyes, and think of England." Ralph Richardson agreed: "Films are where you sell what you have learned on the stage." But Noël Coward begged to differ: "I believe there are still some theatrical people who regard contemptuously everything connected with films. I am not one of them."

My father's next film was *The Loves of Mary, Queen of Scots* (1923). This was the first screen version of her tragic story, which had already been widely used by novelists, playwrights and poets. Its writer-director was the American Denison Clift, who had started his film career writing scenarios for Cecil B. DeMille, the founding father of American cinema. A former short story writer, novelist and playwright, Clift was one of several American directors brought to Britain in the hope that they would ginger up the home industry's reputation.

According to the actor-director Harold French: "The American directors who came over here were generally on the skids; it was last-gasp stuff." But if this was true of many of them, Clift was an exception, and made a considerable impact. "No money will be spared to satisfy the public with the highest standards of artistic workmanship," he announced. He was described in the press as "brilliant … an intensely vital man who sizzles with efficiency," his technique "irreproachable." The *Star* critic put him at the top of the list of directors working in Britain, noting, "He has done so much to raise the tone of British pictures."

My father was said to have landed the part of young, handsome George Douglas through agent Sidney Jay. It is not clear whether Jay had been his agent previously, nor whether he continued to represent him. Douglas falls in love with Mary and later helps her escape from Lochleven Castle. The queen was played by Fay Compton, sister of the novelist Compton Mackenzie. This was the first of three films in which she starred with my father. Soon to be acclaimed in a poll as Britain's second most popular actress (Gladys Cooper was the first), she had made her screen debut in Oliver Goldsmith's *She Stoops to Conquer* and appeared in films of Arnold Bennett's *The Old Wives' Tale* and Oscar Wilde's *A Woman of No Importance*.

Both those films, and the 1922 *A Bill of Divorcement*, were directed by Clift, who spoke glowingly of her talent: "She has all the qualities to make her one of the greatest film actors, not only of Britain but of the whole world." The critic S.R. Littlewood underlined a key factor in her success, suggesting her value "is expressly that she is utterly different from the ordinary Hollywood film type, and that she conveys something of the repose, wilful poetry, beauty, and silence of our island home." She greatly admired Clift's skill, stating in her memoir *Rosemary: Some Remembrances*: "He taught me all I know of film technique, and a definite understanding of it that will enable me, I hope, to develop further."

In order to rescue Mary, in one scene my father had to climb the walls of Stirling Castle, without a double; he repeated the exploit in Edinburgh, watched by the press and a large crowd of spectators. Pictures in the *Daily Mirror* show the "athletic young actor" in action. He also had to be able to fence, as the part called for him to fight four duels. Although he had taken lessons at school, he now had some refresher sessions with Felix Bertrand, a well-known fencing master, who had an academy in London.

My father needed to be skillful as he faced expert swordsman Gerald Ames, a burly and athletic actor playing the part of Bothwell. Ames had represented Britain at the 1912 Olympic Games in Stockholm. My father explained to a journalist the difficulty of making a fight look realistic on screen: "Every movement must be memorised and then executed slowly enough for the camera to follow, with the apparent abandon of a desperate fighter." While rehearsing one duel, he fell and for a while was unable to get up because his chainmail armor was too heavy. His injury list

JOHN STUART
with
FAY COMPTON
in
"THE LOVES OF MARY QUEEN OF SCOTS."

My father, playing George Douglas in *The Loves of Mary, Queen of Scots* (1923), had to call on his fencing skills in the scene in which he saves Mary (Fay Compton).

included a deep cut on his nose, a wound on his knuckles, and a gash on his forearm.

The Loves of Mary, Queen of Scots was an ambitious film involving hundreds of extras; Clift shot some scenes in places where Mary had lived. He also filmed exterior scenes at Holyrood Palace, where Rizzio was assassinated, and in and outside several castles, including Lochleven and Fotheringay, as well as Stirling and Edinburgh.

In the program for the premiere, held at the Marble Arch Pavilion, Ideal Films made large claims for the production:

> The aim has been not to *teach* history, but to *make* it—film history. The object has been not merely to transcribe a blood-stained page of history, but to present in vivid and dramatic form what was one of the most picturesque and impressive dramas ever staged in real life. None can fail to be stirred by the playing of the lightnings of passion and jealousy around the head of the beautiful young sovereign, or to be moved to pity by her utter helplessness in the grip of a fate she seemingly could not control.

The critics were impressed. The verdict of *Cinema*: "Regarded as historical pageantry, the production strikes a new note in film artistry." *Bioscope* enthused, "Never has Britain's treasury of historical relics been so freely drawn upon as in this superbly mounted picture, which might almost be described as a screen museum of the period. It is undoubtedly one of the most conscientious historical pictures ever made."

Yet much of the acting is absurdly over-the-top, the editing is poor, and the fight scenes chaotic. Fay Compton plays several of her scenes with regal restraint, but in others she is infected by the histrionics of many of the other performers, especially Gerald Ames. She, like many of her contemporaries, had a stage background, and such actions—grimacing, hand-waving, breast-beating—were rooted in the theater's methods of portraying character's emotions in order to project them successfully to the audience. Yet my father provides a calm center within the frenzied action, notably in Douglas' scenes with Mary. At one point, Clift wanted his performance to be less calm: "This scene is too flat," he told my father. "I want you to get it up on the roof, not keep it down in the basement." Happily, he managed to resist this instruction.

He was now described as the "white hope" of British films, an actor who has "set the flapper hearts beating wildly." *Picture Show* stated: "John Stuart is one of the most versatile artists on the British screen. He is tremendously popular, perhaps one of the reasons being that in physique he is manly and athletic, and in feature so typically British." *Studio* was equally enthusiastic:

> The rise of John Stuart has been steady and consistent. It is due partly to his natural attributes and personal charm, but much more to his serious regard for his work and his faith in himself. He has acquired in the last two years a real versatility and a growing strength. ... Unassuming, young, the very opposite of effeminate and thoroughly English in character, appearance and sentiment, John Stuart must now be included among the screen assets of the country.

Girls' Magazine put him on its cover, describing him as "one of the best juveniles of the British screen."

Clift also directed *This Freedom* (1923), based on the novel by A.S.M. Hutchison, whose most successful work was the novel *If Winter Comes*; the previous year it had been the best-selling book in America, and immediately filmed in Hollywood. Billed as "The Drama of a Very Modern Woman," *This Freedom* was a controversial film, seen as anti-feminist by the women's rights movement, which was still campaigning for all women to have the vote; Rebecca West was one of its critics. It showed the degradation that could hit a family when a mother chooses to go to work rather than stay at home and bring up her children. "I'm going to keep my freedom.... I'm going to be what a man can be.... Why shouldn't I? ...Why shouldn't a woman?" ran the publicity.

In his biggest part yet, my father played Hugo Occleve, the dissolute son of Fay Compton and Clive Brook. "A wastrel and a drunkard," Occleve blames his behavior on his mother's absence during his childhood. "It was my first character part and an unusual one; I always seemed to be drunk," he recalled. During the filming, he claimed to be "a total abstainer," who had to observe men drunk in order to be convincing. "When one has never been drunk it is awfully difficult to get a good sway into one's walk," he told a reporter.

Motion Picture Studio suggested he gave "an excellent performance," while *Studio* noted that "he has already forged his way to the front rank of British actors." Another critic observed that his part "is very creditably performed. It seems he put a great deal of quiet study into his role, and he has his reward, in that he has been swept into some prominence."

The suavely handsome Clive Brook went on to have a lengthy stage and screen career. He usually appeared as a true gentleman, the stiff-upper-lipped hero and embodiment of moral rectitude. It was fancifully put about that he went to bed wearing a neck brace in order to keep his chin up. He came comparatively late into films at the age of 32 in 1920, after war service (he was wounded and invalided out of the army). He became ferociously busy, sometimes making two films concurrently. After just one year, he revealed to *Picturegoer*, "I have played four heroes, two villains—one a sportsman, the other a viscount—a Victorian poet, and two sympathetic parts." His leading roles included Sydney Carton in *A Tale of Two Cities* and Rawdon Crawley in *Vanity Fair*.

He and my father appeared together again in *Reverse of the Medal* (1923), one of a series of short two-reel pictures. It was directed by George A. Cooper, who was also an actor, reporter, film editor and playwright. In this war film, dubbed "a gem" by *Motion Picture Studio*, my father played Brook's son, a keen air pilot. The paper noted that "he acted superbly." While they were filming, Brook told my father that he was leaving Britain for Hollywood the following week. "I was very excited for him, but I also felt how lucky he was," he recalled.

A slump in the film industry in this period compelled him to return for a time to the stage, making his West End debut in Somerset Maugham's new play *Our Betters*. He was recommended to the director Stanley Bell for the part of young Lord Bleane by Fay Compton, a favor which he would always remember. On arrival at the theater, he was taken aback when Maugham eyed him up and down and asked him bluntly: "Well, young man, you look the part, but can you act?" He joined a top-quality cast that included Constance Collier, Margaret Bannerman, Ronald Squire and Marion Terry. Described as "a bitter comedy of hate," Maugham's withering attack on contemporary society, and especially on the amoral American women who marry into the aristocracy and then shamelessly take lovers, caused a sensation.

It took my father a while to adjust to being on stage again. During rehearsals, he found he was restricting his movements to "camera limits," and that even after numerous rehearsals he was still tempted to hold his position "until after the

In 1923 he was in great demand, making seven films.

close-up—which never came—had been registered." He had the only love scene in the play, but his role was considered poor; the *Daily News* reported, "John Stuart looked well, but had nothing to act." Another critic noted that he "played a none-too thankful part quite excellently."

Opening in September 1923 at the Globe, the play ran for 550 performances. During its 16-month run, he still managed to fit in film work. "I have no intention of deserting the screen for the stage," he told a journalist. "On the contrary, of the two I much prefer film work." But filming in the daytime and playing on stage in the evening was hugely demanding, especially as he also managed to find time for publicity work.

It helped considerably that most of the film studios were in easy reach of the West End. On one typical day, he worked in the studio in the morning, appeared in the matinee at the Globe, made a personal appearance at a cinema, returned to the theater for the evening performance, and afterward presented the prizes at a fancy-dress carnival. His energy and stamina seemed boundless. "It means hard work, but what is hard work when one is ambitious? It is only when one has no work that one has cause to grumble." He cited hard-working Fay Compton as an inspiration: "All the young and ambitious can learn big lessons from her and Sybil Thorndike as far as work is concerned."

A few weeks into the *Our Betters'* run, he wrote a piece for *Motion Picture Studio* called "Stage and Screen Comparisons." In a section on voice production in films, he offered some useful advice to his fellow actors: "Speak your lines, not lip them, because if one doesn't speak naturally on the 'take,' how can it look natural on the screen?" On technique, he observed: "Repose is, of course, common to both arts, and most essential and effective in each, particularly on the screen." It was a skill that seemed to come naturally to him.

During the run of *Our Betters,* he worked on a film version of one of the best-loved

His role as Lord Bleane in Somerset Maugham's play *Our Betters* (1923) marked his West End stage debut.

plays in the theatrical canon. The publicity for *The School for Scandal* (1923) emphasized the many famous theatrical names associated with Richard Brinsley Sheridan's classic play: Ellen Terry, Mrs. Patrick Campbell, Owen Nares, Henry Ainley and others. To give it relevance to the present time, it suggested Lady Teazle's desire to be smart was "as any flapper in the twentieth century." Director Bertram Phillips, who had reportedly "approached his difficult task in a spirit of utmost reverence for the great work," was happy to make "many new friends for the famous old play."

But according to *Picturegoer*, Phillips provoked a debate about whether such stage works could, or even should, be translated to the screen: "He was accused by some of possessing courage and enterprise; by others of hardihood and audacity; and by a few of impudence." Phillips said:

> Let it be conceded that the screen is not simply a means of popularising or picturising the great things of literature; and that Sheridan, as Sheridan, cannot be screened at all. Yet literature and the drama are undoubtedly popularised by the screen; and a plot, characterisation, and atmosphere can be made the basis of a photo-play with due reverence and regard to the original. Hundreds of people, who in ordinary circumstances would never see the play acted, or even read it in cold blood, will inevitably become interested in it for the first time.

Lady Teazle was played by Queenie Thomas, a Welsh actress married to the director. Basil Rathbone, with his sharp saturnine features (Dorothy Parker described him as "two profiles pasted together") and clear, menacing voice, was ideal casting for the urbane hypocrite Joseph Surface. He had started on the stage and had played Romeo and Cassius in Stratford and Prince Hal in London before going into films in 1921. The following year, he made his Broadway debut. Rathbone continued to move between stage and screen throughout his career, gaining international stardom as the movies' Sherlock Holmes.

My father's performance as his brother, the reckless but open-hearted Charles, was generally liked, prompting *Kine Weekly* to conclude: "John Stuart gives a very pleasing rendering of Charles Surface, and enlists the sympathy as is intended." *Motion Picture Studio* observed, "His naturalness is in itself splendid, and it is another of the successes of this rising young juvenile. ...As for the play itself, one may be thankful that no American has translated it, with the inevitable anachronisms."

He followed *Our Betters* with something completely different. *Sumurun* (1925) was billed as "The Wordless Play from Tales from the Arabian Nights," staged at the London Coliseum by Ernst Matray, who as an actor had worked with the great director Max Reinhardt. My father replaced the German film actor Walter Rilla as Nur-al-Din, a merchant, the only speaking part. He seemed a strange choice for the role: "I'd never done anything of the sort before, but I was determined to take on anything for the experience," he recalled. Having duly browned up, he spoke a five-minute prologue ("to capital effect" said the *Stage*), then joined in the play-ballet. His inexperience showed when the leading dancer, the German Maria Solveg, came whirling toward him, and he let her slip to the floor and injure her head.

A change now took place in his personal life. In January 1924 at Marylebone registry office, he married Jeanne Irene Lagrene, a slim, blonde Frenchwoman of his own age, who came originally from Amiens. It was what he described later as "an over-the-garden-wall romance": they were neighbors in London's Belsize Park. Photographs he took show her stylishly dressed, caught with his father outside his Eastbourne house, and also in Regent's Park. Because of his crowded work schedule, the honeymoon had to wait until the following year.

Returning to the screen, he took an unchallenging role in the melodrama *A Daughter of Love* (1925), working again under the direction of Walter West. It's a moralistic story about young Dudley Bellairs, who defies his family by falling in love with and marrying the illegitimate daughter of a "fallen" woman (Violet Hopson) seduced by a doctor ("Come and see the snaps in my surgery"), played by Jameson Thomas. Despite the intense social disapproval of her disgrace ("Love was her sin, knowledge was her betrayal," read one title), love finally conquers all, and the doctor acknowledges his bad behavior. Hopson gives a steady but dull performance as the mother. My father's acting is very relaxed: he shows considerable aplomb on the cricket pitch as a batsman, driving and cutting in style. (He and Alfred Hitchcock were among the founder members of the Kinema Cricket Club, which played against teams such as the Grenadier Guards and the Hampstead Nomads.) He also displays great warmth in the courtship scenes with the young woman he loves, played by Ena Evans. One reviewer calls him "the fans' hero."

The film of Sheridan's famous stage play *The School for Scandal* (1923) gave him a rare opportunity to appear in a classic.

He conveys the same feeling in *We Women* (1925), a light-hearted but banal story in which he stars alongside Billie and Dollie, two celebrated vaudeville stars. The Stoll publicity people suggested that the film "will prove of the greatest interest to women and girl patrons of the cinema." It charts the ups and downs of life for two young women, who are being pursued by two men around various London locations (a Soho restaurant, a jazz hall, a gambling saloon, a skating rink, a cinema studio). One man clearly has wicked intentions, the other, Michael Rivven, is the virtuous, trustworthy hero, played by my father, who gets his girl in the end. It's a sympathetic role, but again not much of a challenge. Director W.P. Kellino, a former music hall acrobat and circus clown, started by making slapstick shorts, then moved on to homely comic films. My father thought him "a very nice fellow, and a good director too."

His film profile continued to grow. *Picture Show* described him as "The Idyllic Lover and the Strong Silent Hero." For his ease in period costume, he's listed with Rudolph Valentino, Ivor Novello, George Arliss and John and Lionel Barrymore as "emphatically amongst the masculines who can wear fantastic clothes and get away with it." He also revealed that he has had "several tempting offers to go abroad."

With the limited opportunities available in Britain, and the industry often in the doldrums, many leading stars chose or were forced to work on the Continent. Ivor Novello made two of his early films in France. Stewart Rome starred in some Continental films, including *The Prodigal Son*, which was shot in Iceland, and an adaptation of Balzac's novel *Ferragus*. The versatile Miles Mander also crossed the Channel many times, playing in films made by German, Danish and Swedish companies. Adrian Brunel and Graham Cutts were among the directors who filmed extensively in Germany, France and Italy.

Such moves were not always popular with the British press. Betty Balfour starred in several French, German and Hungarian films. Fluent in French, she was very popular in France. But a *Picturegoer* writer criticized her decision to work in Europe: "It's a pity she makes films abroad, for they partly stifle her very British genius." Lilian Hall-Davis made several films in Germany, France and Italy, gaining an international reputation by playing a lead role in the Italian epic *Quo Vadis?* before establishing herself as a leading star in Britain.

The film industry flourished in Germany, where 600 films a year were being made and a million cinema tickets sold every day. Several of the films in which the British stars appeared were directed by the actor–theater director Georg Jacoby. They were filmed either at UFA (Universum Film AG), Europe's top film studio just outside Berlin, founded to make propaganda during the First World War and known as Germany's Hollywood; or at the Emelka studio on the outskirts of Munich, home of the second largest Continental film company, which had the facility of building sets on a large scale.

It was a moment when British and European companies were finding it very difficult to find markets big enough to pay for their production costs. Of the 420 films made in Britain in 1922, fewer than ten were sold to the United States. In order to compete with the Americans, British companies decided to work cooperatively with others in Europe, to amalgamate their financial and artistic resources. A good example of this collaboration was *Venetian Lovers* (1925), an Anglo-German production in which my father starred. Its co-director Frank Tilley, the former editor of *Kine Weekly*, explained the rationale:

The real cause of the failure of British film production is to be found in the fact that the enormous size of the American home market gave that country such an enormous advantage, in being able to spend huge sums on films and still recover that cost out of her own market, that not only England but the rest of the world would either have to find some means of acquiring a market which approximated to that of America, or give up film production entirely as an economic impossibility.

In a speech on "Experiences in German Studios" that my father gave to the Film Artists Guild in Britain in the summer of 1928, he stated, "There's always a welcome to British actors in Germany, and the field is a profitable one." His remark was based on experience, for he had recently achieved considerable success making films in Germany in both the UFA and Emelka studios. "British films weren't exactly looked on with great favour by the public," he remembered. "So they were trying to start an international link-up, with mixed casts."

The first was *Venetian Lovers*. Shot partly in Germany, on location in the Alps, and on the Lido in Venice, it was co-directed for Emelka by Tilley and Walter Niebuhr. A truly international affair, it featured four British actors, two German, one French, one Austrian, one Italian and one Serbian, as well as an Italian cinematographer, the aristocrat Baron Giovanni Ventimiglia, who was also a well-known painter.

My father received a wire from German film producer Frank Seitz inviting him to play Bob Goring, and star opposite Arlette Marchal, then the top actress in French cinema. The cast also included Margaret Schlegel, a leading actress at Berlin's Reinhardt Theatre; the Vienna Opera star and dancer Maria Mindzenty; English actor Hugh Miller, and Georg H. Schnell, a famous Shakespearean actor, best known on screen for his role in the film classic *Nosferatu*.

Tilley explained the benefits of such international cooperation: "At a cost for which one could not even produce a film in England, we have a first-class film, with the advantage of half the cast being British, and with the further advantage of putting promising artists like John Stuart into really big pictures which will circulate practically all over the world." A *Star* reporter visiting the set observed: "Direction is going on in four languages—English, French, German, and Italian—without any confusion or difficulties," and added hopefully that "Stuart will help to prove that it is not necessary to rely exclusively on Los Angeles for film stars."

Shooting began in the Emelka studios. In a *Pictures and Picturegoer* article, my father reported: "The sun is shining and it's holiday time in Munich—all bunting, bands and beer barrels." A photo shows him and Hugh Miller sitting outside a café sharing a drink with a "fair fraulein," a star of the Munich Art Theater. During the filming, there was an extraordinary coincidence: he and the German assistant director recognized each other, and it turned out that during the war, the German was a machine-gunner whom my father had captured in the trenches at Arras.

A brief paragraph about my father in the *Stoll Herald* is typical of the more gushing journalism of the day: "Yes, this is England's white hope all right. Though he's as dark as night to look at, and just as mysterious, he is now breaking many hearts in Germany, where he is taking the juvenile lead in this new film, which is creating such a sensation in all the papers. No! I don't know anything about his birth-place, only that his eyes are brown, because I've looked into them." A month later, another piece had a similar tone: "Who is there who still maintains Englishmen aren't actors? They conquer every country they go to, and John Stuart is an example."

The general feeling was that the film was disjointed, with the many rapid changes of scene preventing any real character development. In Munich, my father narrowly escaped injury while filming a scene in which a mob storms a hotel and fight on the staircase. The staircase gave way, seriously injuring several extras, while he and Hugh Miller hung precariously onto a beam. In Venice, according to the *Weekly Dispatch*, "a detachment of special film police not only restrained intrusive onlookers, but also acted 'bits' for the story with professional ease."

On the Lido in Venice with his first wife Jeanne Lagrene, enjoying a delayed honeymoon during the filming of *Venetian Lovers* (1925).

During the filming, his wife Jeanne joined my father for their long-delayed honeymoon. One of his photo albums, labeled "Venice—Honeymoon," includes snaps of them together. Alongside one snapped on the Lido, where she is dressed stylishly and sports a fashionable bob haircut, another picture catches them in bathing costumes in the water, with Jeanne perched on my father's shoulders.

His performance impressed the Germans, for halfway through the filming he was offered a part in another German film, *Bachelor Wives* (1925). Franz Seitz, Emelka's principal director, apparently chose him because he found it impossible to fill the role with an American actor. As the only non–German in the cast, he needed an interpreter throughout the filming, for which exterior scenes were shot in Milan and Vienna. He relished the experience of working in such a well-appointed studio: "I shall look forward to going back to Germany one day," he said on his return, adding pointedly, "if I haven't gone to America in the meanwhile."

Other Films

He appeared as a motorboat pilot in *The Extra Knot* (1922), a film in the one-reel "Sporting Twelve" series. In it, he had to undertake another fight. In the comedy short *Constant Hot Water* (1923), he played "a modern young man who gets into trouble by entering the wrong apartment." Gladys Jennings co-starred, George A. Cooper directed.

In *Claude Duval* (1924), the story of the notorious highwayman in post–Restoration Britain, he was simply hired for his fencing skills. A press report referred to "a duel strenuously fought between John Stuart and A.B. Imeson, with Fay Compton as an interested onlooker."

In 1924, he starred opposite Queenie Thomas in two films directed by her husband, Bertram Phillips. In the crime story *Her Redemption*, a gambler kills his wife's twin sister by mistake. *The Alley of the Golden Hearts* told the story of a lonely squire who throws a New Year's party for his villagers.

He was in the comedy *His Grace Gives Notice* (1924), in which a butler saves a lord's daughter from eloping with a married man. It was written by Una Troubridge, the lesbian partner of Radclyffe Hall, whose book *The Well of Loneliness*, about such a relationship, was later judged obscene. He also appeared opposite character actress Mary Jerrold in the two-hander *Parted* (1925), the second short drama in the "Twisted Tales" series, directed by Canadian actor Alexander Butler.

4

Alfred Hitchcock
and Maurice Elvey

"John Stuart is very easily the best leading man in British pictures."—*Daily Chronicle*, 1926

During the 1910s, France was clearly the dominant European country for cinema. But in the 1920s, it was Germany, with its visual style known as expressionism, which became pre-eminent. In Britain, cultural life, including film, had scarcely been affected by such influences. Yet the quality of British films began to improve in the mid–1920s, notably because of the work of directors Alfred Hitchcock and Maurice Elvey.

While filming in Germany, my father heard that Michael Balcon, who had recently set up Gainsborough Pictures, wanted to cast him as Hugh Fielding, one of the two male leads in the studio's next film, *The Pleasure Garden* (1927). The director Frank Tilley had recommended him for the part. Always keen to bring on new talent, Balcon had hired as its director "a plump young technician" to make his debut as a director.

Alfred Hitchcock was born in 1899 in Leyton, then part of Essex. The son of a greengrocer and fishmonger, he was a film fan from a very young age. As a boy, he had been taken to the music hall and to watch short films shown in skating rinks. From his early teens, he became a true enthusiast, giving himself an education in cinema: He read the American trade papers rather than fan magazines, and saw many of the early French and German films. He loved especially the work of the Americans Cecil B. DeMille and D.W. Griffith, including the latter's groundbreaking *The Birth of a Nation* and *Intolerance*.

His first job in the film industry was designing and writing titles for the American company Famous Players–Lasky, which had just opened a London studio in Islington. When he took on the role of art director, director George Pearson noticed him: "a very friendly young man who in the studio always seemed oblivious to his surroundings, deep in thought, pondering." When Hitchcock moved to Gainsborough (co-founded by Balcon and director Graham Cutts in 1924), he quickly made his mark. "He was little more than a boy," Balcon recalled, "but he attracted my attention at once because of his passion for films and his eagerness to learn."

Hitchcock soon became involved in many areas of the work, as art editor, set designer, scenario writer, production manager and sometimes several of these roles simultaneously. As assistant director to Cutts, he was even sent out to turn the camera now and then. By the time he came to direct his first film at the age of 25, he had already worked in various roles on 21 features. His method was to put himself forward whenever there was a vacancy. "I'm sure that if he never actually swept the floor at the studio, he would have been ready and willing to do so," Balcon observed.

Hitchcock was an inhibited young man: At the age of 22, when he wrote his first feature *Woman to Woman*, he had never had a drink or gone out with a woman. But he showed talent as an art editor in his use of an innovative storyboard technique on that film, on which he was the assistant director. As a result, Balcon felt he was ready to make his directorial debut. But he knew the British distributors who helped finance the studio's work were wary of backing untried talent: "It was not easy to get a young man launched in so important a job."

Balcon was also conscious of the technical limitations of British studios. His solution was to launch Hitchcock in Germany, whose film industry had remained active, despite the country's postwar problems. The plan was for Hitchcock to shoot the film at Emelka and on locations around Europe, including Lake Como. His cinematographer was Baron Giovanni Ventimiglia, while his assistant director was Alma Reville, whom he was to marry soon afterwards. Already respected within the industry, she had worked her way up from tea girl to editor to director's assistant, and was from the start of their collaboration an invaluable and trusted sounding-board for his work.

Hitchcock had already been to Germany and worked alongside German technicians as designer, scriptwriter and assistant director to Cutts on *The Blackguard*. He was impressed with the German cinema and the work of masters such as Fritz Lang and F.W. Murnau. He admired in particular their emphasis on telling the story visually, with a minimum of titles: Murnau, whom Hitchcock had watched at work, had managed to make *The Last Laugh* with Emil Jannings without a single title.

The screenplay of *The Pleasure Garden*, his debut feature as director, was written by the experienced Eliot Stannard, the first of eight he wrote for Hitchcock. Balcon chose Miles Mander to play the other male lead alongside my father. A former sheep farmer, Mander had tried aviation, motor racing, writing and film renting before turning to acting and directing.

To improve the film's chances in America, Balcon initially cast the American star Marguerite de la Motte, who had made her name playing opposite Douglas Fairbanks in his swashbuckling films. But in the end he brought in another Hollywood star, Virginia Valli, a striking and popular player at Universal who was then at the height of her career. Dark-haired and sad-eyed, she specialized in melodramas, in roles that tended toward the saintly or the innocent; one critic described her approvingly as "one of the screen's few womanly women." For the second female part, he chose Carmelita Geraghty, a promising 19-year-old on the brink of Hollywood stardom.

Faced with this American contingent, Hitchcock was in a cold sweat, hoping they wouldn't realize he was a mere beginner. His relative innocence was revealed when the young actress cast as a native girl refused to do a swimming scene because she was having her period. Ventimiglia had to explain to the young director this biological fact, of which he was quite unaware. A local German girl was hastily brought in as a replacement.

The Pleasure Garden tells of the contrasting behavior toward their men of two London music hall chorus girls. One is virtuous (Valli), the other a gold-digger (Geraghty), while both display the bobbed hair and cupid-bow mouths then fashionable. The title originally came from a warning given by one of the chorus girls to a newcomer, about men who "buzz round a stage door like flies on something sweet…. The stage is their pleasure garden, and we girls are the flowers in it. We're really here for show, but some of the public don't keep to the paths."

Their two men represent Good and Evil, with Mander clearly slated as the bounder. Balcon described him as "a thin, elegant man with the eyes of a ferret." Hitchcock later observed: "It's a mistake to think that if you put a villain on screen, he must sneer nastily, stroke his black mustache, or kick a dog in the stomach." But in 1925, he had not yet learned this lesson. Mander, complete with bow tie, mustache and sneer, provokes the girls' dog to bark at him, while my father gains the dog's affection, even rolling on the floor with him. When the two of them are sent to work "out east," my father succumbs to a fever, Mander to drink, the native girl and a bad attack of jerky acting. When Valli, who gives a sympathetic and restrained performance, arrives and discovers her husband's infidelity, he tries but fails to murder her, and duly gets his comeuppance.

My father instils a breezy spirit into his laid-back, well-mannered, but innocent character. It was not a particularly challenging role. Yet as *Kinematograph Weekly* observed: "John Stuart has little to do but does it well." It's one of his most engaging performances, in which his physical ease and unforced charm are much in evidence in the early scenes in London, notably in the warmth of his relationship with Valli. But he's also suitably restrained in his scenes out east, when she comes to nurse him back to health. Asked by a journalist about working with her, he said, in his usual diplomatic way: "I must say I found her exceedingly charming." He was invariably careful not to criticize his co-stars.

Hitchcock later described the essence of the director's job as "the assembly of pieces of film to create fright." But with *The Pleasure Garden*, that was not yet his aim. It's a relatively simple, even banal story, but one told with humor, and with several Hitchcockian signature themes, including voyeurism—it opens with male members of the audience gazing lasciviously through binoculars at a row of chorus girls' legs—and male violence toward women. By personally creating a storyboard, he was already demonstrating his talent for conveying information visually, notably in a scene where the two young women undress for bed in their lodgings.

In the middle of filming, Hitchcock sensed that the story was too straightforward a melodrama and rearranged certain scenes. His aim was to emphasize more starkly the difference between the relationships of the two couples by using the kind of cross-cutting technique he had picked up from his observation of the German cinema. Unusually, and a sure sign of the confidence of the man described by one fan magazine as "the youngest director in the world," his credit came at the start of the film, and consisted of his handwritten signature. "Actors come and actors go," he asserted, "but the name of the director should stay clearly in the mind of the audiences."

Ronald Neame, who was to be his assistant cameraman on his first sound film *Blackmail*, described him as "very autocratic but also mischievous." My father, who was later to star in another Hitchcock film (the 1932 talkie *Number Seventeen*), had a warmer memory of him:

> I was sorry when *The Pleasure Garden* finished. Hitch was a delight to work with. As an actor you usually knew where you stood with him. He never wasted words. Certainly in those days he was not a temperamental director. He never shouted or stormed, nor did he try to show you exactly how he wanted a particular scene to be played. If he disagreed with your interpretation of a character he would quickly suggest an alternative approach, or point out a motive which you may have overlooked. In this way he inspired confidence and respect.

Hitchcock later described *The Pleasure Garden* as melodramatic, but felt "there were several interesting scenes in it." Balcon certainly admired it, telling his young protégé that it had the look more of an American than a European film—a remark intended as a compliment—and immediately hiring him to shoot another one in Germany. This was *The Mountain Eagle*, now sadly lost, a melodrama set in a mountain village and filmed in the Tyrol and at Emelka.

But despite favorable advance reviews, exhibitors were dubious about both films, fearing that English audiences would be puzzled by Hitchcock's weird camera angles and Germanic-style lighting. One of Gainsborough's partners, C.M. Woolf, was convinced the films had no commercial appeal.

So while *The Pleasure Garden* was shown to the trade in March 1926, it was not released until January 1927, following the success of Hitchcock's next film, *The Lodger*, of which *Bioscope* wrote: "It is possible

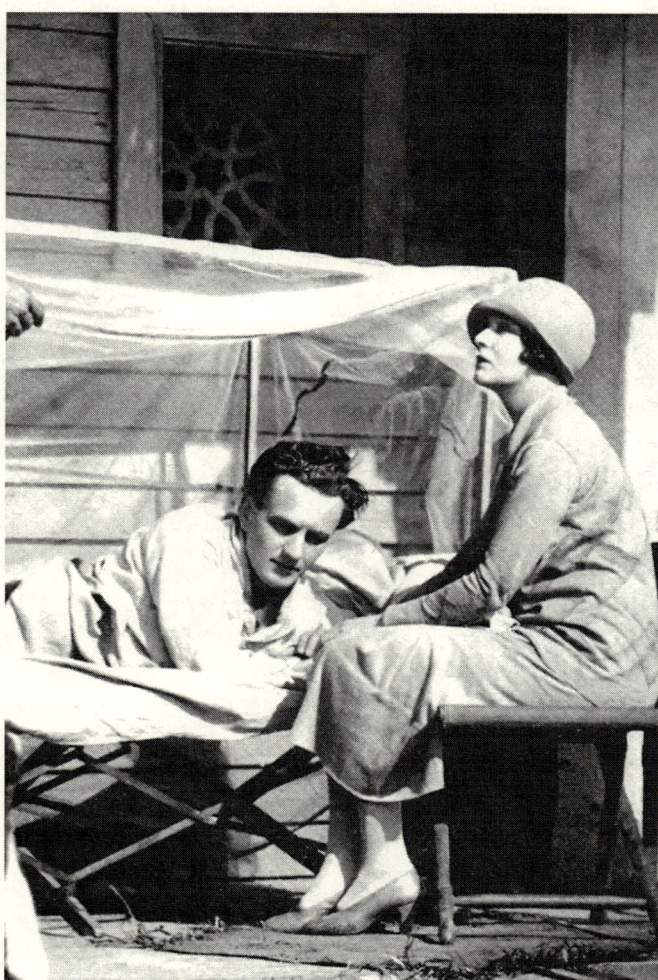

Playing opposite Hollywood star Virginia Valli in *The Pleasure Garden* (1927), Hitchcock's debut as a director.

that this film is the finest British production ever made." His debut film *The Pleasure Garden* also received rave reviews in the mainstream press. The *Sunday Express* reported that Hitchcock had directed it with "remarkable power and imaginative resource ... The technical skill revealed was superior to that shown in any film yet made by a British producer." The *Sunday Pictorial* described it as "the most hopeful event in home film-making in the last seven years."

Hitchcock was a discovery: "He definitely arrives in one stride" said the *Sunday Herald*, while the *Daily Express* announced, "Mr. Hitchcock is an inspiring young man with a master mind, who gives genuine encouragement to those optimists who believe in the eventual prosperity of the native British film industry.... His work is of a uniformly high quality; there are times when it is great, times when the onlooker says to himself, 'That is perfect.'" In the *Observer,* Ivor Montagu praised his skill with narrative, his naturalism and the realism of his characterization.

The specialist film press was equally enthused, with *Bioscope* noting, "The admirable acting and masterly production all combine to make this a film of outstanding merit." Iris Barry in the *Spectator* felt that Hitchcock had "astonished everyone with his freshness and power," though she had one reservation: "*The Pleasure Garden*, though saddled with a crude and tasteless story, had an adult air, was often gracious to the eye, and sometimes to the fancy." *Kine Weekly* gave a similar warning as to its moral tone: "It is not a picture for family halls, as the effect generally is sordid." When the film was released in Germany, *Film Kurier* critic called it "a warning to all chorus girls to dance modestly and chastely through life, in order to end up like this film's heroine, who gets an honest and faithful husband."

With the film scene in Britain still dominated by American imports, there was agitation for more British films to be made, and their quality to be improved. The emergence of a director so obviously promising as Hitchcock was seen as a good omen.

On my father's return from Germany, the *Edinburgh Evening News* observed: "After making a big hit in *Venetian Lovers* and *The Pleasure Garden*, with this reputation he acquired honour in his own country, and since his return from Europe he has been one of the busiest actors in the British studios."

He acted for the third time with Fay Compton in *London Love* (1926), which began his association with Gaumont. Described by the *Evening News* as "a highly successful melodrama for the unsophisticated," this was a romantic story about an East End flower girl who becomes a film star in order to raise enough money to pay for her lover's legal defense in a murder trial. Compton was cast as "a jaunty little East End flapper," my father as her sailor lover Harry Raymond. Miles Mander and Moore Marriott were also featured.

Although the film was admired, it was not, according to *Kine Weekly*, a suitable vehicle for Compton. "She is suited to more mature and less melodramatic parts, but she does her best," the critic suggested.

The film was directed by Manning Haynes, who was considered promising, even highbrow. Formerly an actor who worked in the theater with Herbert Beerbohm Tree, he had come to notice after filming short stories by the popular W.W. Jacobs. According to *Picturegoer*, Haynes "had vast technical knowledge, and a flair for bright comedy and strong drama." A magazine reporter watched his meticulous approach on the set of *London Love* at the Gaumont studios in Shepherd's Bush: "He has a quiet method of directing, and infinite patience, it seemed to me. To get a scene exactly right he will rehearse over and over again before the cameraman starts to turn." The *Star* also approved of his work: "He has the cinematic sense, which enables him to present the points of his story to the best possible effect, in contrast to the flat results usually achieved over here in Britain." He was, the writer suggested, "among the younger school of directors to whom the struggling British industry looks for hope and comfort as to the future."

During the making of silent films, music was often used to get the actors in the right mood. This might be played live off-camera by a three-piece band, with the star actors being asked for their preferences. One reporter visiting the *London Love* set noticed that Compton used music played on a gramophone to help her with the emotional scenes. But my father was, unusually for him, happy to do without it on this occasion. "I'm very sensitive to music," he observed. "I love having it playing in the background, especially in a romantic scene. It's a great help."

His qualities on screen are summed up in the *Daily Telegraph* review: "John Stuart is the handsome hero to the life, and there is always something sympathetic and boyish about him." The quirky magazine *Girls' Cinema* positively swooned in adoration: "No wonder all his feminine followers lose their heart to him. If they met him in real life they would be even more enamoured, for apart from his good looks he has a charming personality. His hair is dark and boasts a wave, while there's a whole wealth of humour in his dark eyes."

During the shooting, the cast had the novel experience of working in three media simultaneously. In "The Making of a Film," the BBC experimented by broadcasting live on the radio the shooting of a scene from the studio in Shepherd's Bush. The event was also being captured on camera for a cinema newsreel.

That experiment was in March 1926. In May, work was interrupted by the General Strike, called to give nationwide support to the miners in their dispute with their employers. Many actors opposed it, and actively helped the government in its efforts to keep normal life going; Laurence Olivier, for instance, worked on the London Underground. My father was also among the quarter-million volunteers who actively helped the government. Enlisting as a special constable, he was supplied with an armband and truncheon, and detailed to guard Lots Road power station in Chelsea.

He treasured those few days as a rare moment when he was able to escape his screen persona. "I spent many hours playing darts with men who cared nothing, and knew less, about film stars," he recalled. "They regarded me as a human being. It was a kind of near-heaven." He kept the certificate he received, signed by the prime minister Stanley Baldwin and the home secretary William Joynson-Hicks. It stated: "We desire on behalf of His Majesty's Government to thank you in common with all others who came forward so readily during the crisis and gave their services to the country in the capacity of Special Constables."

Otherwise there was rarely much of a gap between his pictures. *Picturegoer* observed: "Almost as soon as a film has been finished he has been booked up for another one." This was due in part to his willingness to accept small parts in short films. "If there was a lull I thought there was no harm in accepting such parts, as long as it was a good script. It didn't hurt me, and I went straight back to the big roles."

His work-rate on screen was phenomenal. Despite occasional spells of unemployment, after six years he had made 23 features and 20 shorts, averaging seven films a year. His qualities were approvingly noted: "Only those who have an unlimited amount of determination or enthusiasm eventually win star laurels," ran one feature. "Of such stuff is John Stuart made. He has that inborn spirit of adventure-with-success-as-a-goal that makes screen stars of good-looking and talented young men." He himself had no illusions about his celebrity status. "I don't think there's any such thing as being established permanently as a lead in films," he told a journalist. "All the time you've got to keep learning, work like the devil, never relax, and never be satisfied."

A *Picture Show* writer summed up the quality of his acting: "John Stuart is another star who shows a masterly grip on himself when up against things. His bright expression changes as if by magic, the light dies out of his eyes. He tackles a tense situation as if he is facing the whole gamut of life's most unpleasant emotions: disillusionment and horror follow one another in dramatic force."

This was a response to his performance in *Mademoiselle from Armentières* (1926), directed by Maurice Elvey, who was now to play an important part in his career. Elvey (real name: William Seward Folkard) was for a while considered by many to be Britain's top director: in an international poll in 1927, male voters placed him fourth behind Rex Ingram, D.W. Griffith and Cecil B. DeMille, but ahead of Hitchcock, who was in fifth place. The country's most active director, Elvey had the longest career, making over 300 feature films as well as numerous shorts between 1913 and 1957.

Stage-struck in his youth, he became a stagehand and then an actor, working in the theater with the influential director Harley Granville-Barker. In 1911, he founded the Adelphi Players and gained considerable theater experience, staging plays by Ibsen, Strindberg and Gorky, and the first English production of Chekhov's *The Seagull*; with Barker, he also co-produced Shaw on Broadway. He switched to films in 1912; by the end of the First World War, he was known particularly for his facility with location work and crowd scenes, and for biographical films such as *Florence Nightingale* and especially *Nelson: The Story of England's Immortal Naval Hero*, which *The Times* called "one of the best things that English producers have attained…."

Elvey likened the job of a film director to that of a conductor of a symphony orchestra: "Somebody else has written the music, and the technicians have to play it," he said. He was a director of huge energy and enthusiasm, who during the 1920s made an astonishing 20 films a year. Not surprisingly, they varied greatly in quality, in part because he rarely worked to improve a script, but simply shot it as written. He was mocked for using a portrait of himself to introduce his films. But he was an imaginative director, who relied on unusual camera angles and skillful editing to emphasize dramatic points and keep the narratives flowing.

According to his fellow director Victor Saville, Elvey "had a wide knowledge of music and a sensitive feeling for the emotional. He had started in films so early that his technical know-how was authoritative—he knew exactly how to make a platoon of soldiers look like a company." In 1924, when the British industry briefly closed down, he went to America and made five films for the Fox Corporation.

Films based on the First World War were still popular in Britain at this time. *Mademoiselle from Armentières* marked the first film of Elvey's partnership at Gaumont-British with Saville, who co-wrote the script with him. After being severely wounded at the Battle of Loos, Saville had worked as a film distributor and a cinema manager, and with Michael Balcon produced *Woman to Woman*. Also involved was Gareth Gundrey, the company's head of scripts, who was remembered by David Lean as "bright and intelligent." He was an appropriate choice, given his war experience: he survived the battle of Passchendaele, but was wounded just before the armistice and had to have a leg amputated.

Gaumont-British described *Mademoiselle from Armentières* as "a soldier's story of the last war," dedicated to "the author and composer Thomas Atkins, who composed his song to the accompaniment of marching feet on poplar-lined roads." The story, conceived by Saville and set in wartime France, concerns British soldiers and the mythical mademoiselle (Estelle Brody), a "lady of uncertain age and doubtful virtue" immortalized in the popular song, which had many bawdy versions.

The central story is framed by an opening scene set in the present day, in which the soldier hero Johnny (Stuart) and his young son watch a military band playing "Mademoiselle from Armentières," and by a final one in which the father tells his boy, "And that's how I came to meet your mother." Gaumont emphasized the wartime background of the 50-strong cast: "The fact that every man engaged in the film except one saw military service in the West is an assurance to the public that it is not being offered a travesty of the conditions under which the bloody combat was fought and won."

Elvey had recently had a popular success with the naval melodrama *The Flag Lieutenant*, advertised immodestly as "The British Film Masterpiece of All Time." He had achieved a spectacular success with his handling of crowds and battles, and with an impressively large set replicating a fort in the desert. For *Mademoiselle from Armentières*, for which he originally planned to film scenes in France, he had a French village built near Andover in Hampshire, said to be the biggest U.K. film set yet created. The interior scenes were shot in Lime Grove Studios in Shepherd's Bush, a glass-sided building resembling a large conservatory.

Elvey employed 500 extras, including a regiment of real soldiers, and to create atmosphere, he made his principals speak French on the set. A surviving reel, with French subtitles, shows hundreds of soldiers marching up the line to the front, followed by shots of life in the trenches. The film achieves a strong degree of authenticity, the enacted scenes being interspersed with War Office footage of the actual conflict. Elvey shot it in just 28 working days and assembled and edited it in three weeks.

He made the film as a response to King Vidor's *The Big Parade*, a recent spectacular American hit about the ordinary men and women involved in the war, which established John Gilbert as a star. Elvey was accused by the critics of plagiarizing one especially striking scene from the American film, when the heroine clings to a truck and to her lover as he marches to the front. The scene is remarkably close to the one in the American film, but Elvey strenuously denied the charge, later commenting acidly: "I thought it was about time people realised that Britain had something to do with the Great War." The main story starts with the scene of the alleged plagiarism, which demonstrates Elvey's bold use of Russian-style montage and cross-cutting.

My father had to re-live his months in the trenches in France, an experience which must have been stressful, but also perhaps valuable in helping him to inhabit the part. Most of the film has been lost, but in 1978 Chris Long, a film researcher, discovered three reels in the Australian National

As the soldier hero in the successful war film *Mademoiselle from Armentieres* (1926). The role echoed his experience on the Western Front in 1918.

Film Archive. In one of the surviving scenes, my father comes under fire, is badly wounded, captured by the Germans, and finally reunited with the heroine. In these scenes, he conveys powerfully the young soldier's fear, anguish and despair. On the set, Elvey told a visiting journalist, "John Stuart and Estelle Brody have immersed themselves thoroughly in their roles, and just played a dramatically beautiful and tense episode with a fine shade of feeling and delicacy."

Brody, cast in the title role, was a virtually unknown actress, plucked from the cast of a musical comedy at the Gaiety in London. She was a New Yorker, but because of hostility to the American influence on the British film industry, for publicity purposes she was said to be French-Canadian. After moving to Britain in the 1920s, Brody had worked in London's West End theaters. Film director Thomas Bentley liked her vivaciousness and offered her a supporting role in *White Heat*, after which she landed the *Mademoiselle from Armentières* lead. To her great surprise, she found herself instantly acclaimed as a bright new star and a natural in front of the camera. The critics liked her spirit and charm, *The Times* deciding that she "acted with attractive simplicity." *Picturegoer* declared firmly: "She is one of those stars who are recognisable as major luminaries from the very moment of their first appearance."

A big box office success, the film ran for several months in cinemas around

With his co-star Estelle Brody, a relative newcomer, who played the mythical mademoiselle in *Mademoiselle from Armentieres.*

the country. It was the most profitable British film of 1926, and the first British war film to secure a release in America; it was also sold to 14 other countries. It was very well received by the press, with *Bioscope* describing it as "a convincing and realistic picture of trench warfare." The *Westminster Gazette* stated, "It gains its stirring effects by sheer subtlety and restraint," and *Picture Show* called it "one of the most soul-stirring pictures of the year." It moved even the flintiest of filmgoers, the *Yorkshire Post* reporting, "It commanded the ungrudging applause of a Yorkshire audience not easily conjured to enthusiasm."

The battle scenes were particularly liked, with Elvey, who used real-life footage, being praised for his technical skill and bold handling of the life of the soldiers at the front. Critic Iris Barry was especially enthusiastic: "Mr. Maurice Elvey ... has burst forth resplendent with the simple, heartfelt *Mademoiselle from Armentières*. There is at last a breath of intelligent animation and lively purpose about the English studios; and bright ideas, long banished therefrom, are coming into fashion." The *Daily Mail* saw it in overtly patriotic terms: "This picture alone disproves forever the silly legend that we cannot make first-rate productions in England. It does more than that. It definitely proves that a first-rate film such as this can be all the more enchanting when it is genuinely English."

At the trade show, a band played a dozen or so popular wartime songs—including "Good Bye-ee," "Tipperary" and "Keep the Home Fires Burning"—which in the view of one critic "enhanced the film by 80 per cent." The showing prompted the *News of the World* to comment: "This has been a great and happy week for British films. Five big ones have been trade-shown, and all along new brilliances, improved techniques, and better-than-ever ingredients of real entertainment were noticeable. Our film-makers are getting into form at last."

For the opening night at the Marble Arch Pavilion, there were 3000 applications for 1000 seats. Audience reaction to the hero was summed up in a piece of doggerel published in *Picture Show*: "Johnny comes from Edinburgh / Makes a hero good and thorough / His audience were moved to cheers / By Mademoiselle from Armentières." At one performance, a woman was so shocked by the scene in which Johnny was wounded that she fainted and had to be carried out of the cinema. This turned out to be his mother Agnes, now an ardent supporter of his career.

Along with Elvey and Brody, my father made many personal appearances to publicize the film, including one at the Angel cinema in Islington in North London, where it was reported: "Mr. Stuart, who must have captivated all the ladies in the cinema, in a low, pleasant voice remarked that he was no speech-maker." On another occasion, he and Brody joined day-trippers on a boat journey down the Thames and out to Clacton and Margate, during which he entertained the passengers by singing and playing the banjo.

The press was effusive about his performance. The *Guild Cinema* critic wrote: "John Stuart does about the best bit of screen work of his career"; the *Daily Mail* thought that the love passages were so lit with sincerity that they required no subtitles at all. *Picture Show* spelled out the actor's popular appeal:

> John Stuart has made a remarkable hit in one of the most soul-stirring pictures of the year. This fine young star is one of the most modest of men in private life. He has a great sense of humour, and there are few stars that have so many friends, both on the stage and off it. He combines that happy combination of being an extremely popular hero with the female fans, and also popular with men. He is well-built, athletic-looking, and essentially British; but with all this he has a strong romantic temperament which enables him to get right in to the skin of his part. He has the knack of becoming the real person whose fortunes he is following on the screen.

My father later observed: "Maurice Elvey knew how to handle me, and I knew I was safe in his hands. I've been very lucky with my directors, most of them were easygoing. But occasionally you'd get one who blew his top." His performance prompted *Picture Show* to put him on its cover. More importantly, it gained him a three-year contract with Gaumont-British.

Later in 1926, he signed up for the leading role of a coastguard in *The Creeping Tide*, "a tale of the good old smuggling days on the Devon and Cornish coasts," to be filmed in the West Country by a new company, British General Film Enterprises Ltd., which said it wanted to encourage young directors. They began filming in Lulworth Cove in Dorset, but after a week the money ran out. The company claimed there was a dispute about ownership of the story, and that the film had only been suspended. In fact, no more was heard of it.

Elvey handled him again in *Hindle Wakes* (1927), a popular screen subject, which the director had already filmed in 1918, and Saville would film as a talkie in 1931. The source play was written by Stanley Houghton, one of the Manchester School of playwrights who brought a new realism to the theater. He had initially worked in the cotton trade and as a journalist on the *Manchester Guardian* while trying to break into the theater.

The story deals with a woman's right to self-determination, exemplified by Fanny (Estelle Brody), a Lancashire mill girl, and her defiance in the face of convention: "I'm a woman and you were my little fancy," she explains to Alan Jeffcote, the mill owner's son (my father); she refuses to marry him after their illicit seaside weekend together is revealed. It was a bold stance for the time. When the play was first staged in 1912, it was hugely controversial; posters appeared on the London Underground asking, "Should Fanny marry Alan?"

Technically the film was seen as a landmark in British cinematography. The lighting and camerawork had absorbed a great deal from practice in Hollywood and Berlin, and had improved dramatically from the static and unimaginatively lit pictures of the early 1920s. Much of it was shot on location in the seaside resorts of Llandudno and Blackpool, with hundreds of locals recruited for the crowd scenes. The results were impressive.

One scene featuring hundreds of couples dancing around the Tower Ballroom in Blackpool was said to be the biggest interior crowd scene yet filmed in Britain. For this, my father and Brody danced together on a raised platform which was moved around the crowded ballroom. In another exhilarating scene, they hurtle together down the switchback in Fun City on the pleasure beach, with the cameraman riding in it backward while shooting their excited reactions.

Elvey shot other scenes in a large cotton mill in Eccles, where the real mill girls with their bobbed and shingled hair were filmed at work at their spinning machines. Praising them for adapting quickly to the camera, Elvey observed: "Of course the factory girls go to the cinema so many times that they really know something about it."

A *Daily Mail* reporter watched him shooting one scene in a billiard room, where "Taking!" rather than "Action!" was the cue to begin. In the subsequent article, Elvey is pictured with the director's trademark tools, a cigar and a megaphone. The article gives a glimpse of his method, and the actors' contrasting techniques in a silent film:

> Mr. Elvey vigorously acted each bit of each actor's part, explaining exactly what he wanted and why. Then each actor rehearsed again and again, the director commenting and correcting, or heightening a gesture or glance. All being prepared, there came the usual cry for the glaring lights and the whistle signal, which tells cameramen and actors alike that the real business of shooting has begun. Mr. Norman McKinnel, when speaking, only formed his words with his lips, but Mr. John Stuart cried his words loudly in a hush that comes when a scene is really being taken, as soon as Mr. Elvey had prompted him.

The action takes place during Wakes Week. The wakes, as the first title on the screen explains, is the week "when the bond slaves of Cotton know the ecstasy of freedom," which in this case they find during the annual works outing to Blackpool. Brody was the chirpy and independent Fanny, but my father's role as the mill owner's son was less interesting, as *Bioscope* noted: "John Stuart makes the best of Allan Jeffcote, a part which cannot but be a very thankless one."

His other reviews were only modest, and he was overshadowed by his spirited co-star, whose performance was generally seen as her most accomplished. "She is strong, simple, and genuine," *Picturegoer* decided. "It is the technique of an artist who *feels* the material." But the two of them achieve a warm and attractive rapport in certain scenes, canoodling on the seafront and riding the Big Dipper; their acting is lively and natural. My father is similarly convincing when trying to woo back his fiancée after his illicit weekend, but less at ease in the climactic scene with his father. Often he seems most comfortable when acting a scene alone with a woman, when his romantic temperament comes to the fore.

An unusual mixture of realism and melodrama, *Hindle Wakes* was praised for answering the charge that British films never dealt with the lives of ordinary people. *Bioscope* noted: "The story is somewhat sombre and pessimistic, but it is one well calculated to appeal to every class as a true picture of ordinary people. Mr Elvey and his company have presented a strong and convincing picture of the everyday life of the working classes, and its truth and sincerity ensure its position as one of the outstanding pictures of the year."

Hindle Wakes deftly portrays the class differences between workers and management at the mill, and was one of the few films to recognize the changing status of women. Elvey pinned his patriotic colors to the mast, declaring, "We should show now once and for all that the British can make films as good as anyone else. I have just come from two years' film work in Hollywood, and I know that we can do the work as well as they can."

The critics agreed with him. According to the *Daily News*, "Technically it is equal to the best work America sends us." No one was more enthusiastic than the *Picturegoer* critic, who felt the film "achieves a truly national flavour, something as British as roast beef, the open-hearth fire, or the weather," a film which "at long last gave my country to me, where I had given up hope of finding it—on the screen."

My father was judged to have reached the first rank of screen actors: "With the possible exception of Ivor Novello, he is now Britain's most popular male star," one reporter observed. When cast and crew arrived in Llandudno to film some of the exteriors, the *Liverpool Echo* noted that the party included "Mr. John Stuart, the new film 'find,' who is expected to rival even Ramon Novarro as a screen lover."

This fanciful idea gets some backing from *Picture Show*, which states: "Faces without brains do not make men fortunes. John Stuart is not only strikingly handsome, but he is a strong character." It then asks: "Who is Your Favourite Screen Lover?" and lists ten contestants: Ricardo Cortez, Douglas Fairbanks, Richard Dix, Adolphe Menjou, Ramon Novarro, John Barrymore, John Gilbert, Ronald Colman, Ivor Novello—and John Stuart.

While Elvey was completing the picture, the BBC broadcast a radio item giving a rare glimpse inside Elstree Studios and into the working methods of certain directors. According to *Cinema*: "It must have provided entertainment for every brand of listener except the sniffy ones. There was E.A. Dupont's Napoleonic gesture getting across in vocal form. The silvery tones of Alfred Hitchcock directing the real he-manliness of Carl Brisson. Maurice Elvey leading John Stuart and Estelle Brody up the straight and narrow paths of accurate osculation."

He received his best notices yet in 1927, when he starred with Lilian Hall-Davis in another war picture, *Roses of Picardy*, again under Elvey's direction. He played Lt. Skene, an ex-officer returning after the war to the village of Hondebecq on the Flemish border, where through his eyes we see what really happened. The film was based on a trilogy by R.H. Mottram, but principally on the prize-winning novel in it, *The Spanish Farm*, which caused a stir when it had been recently published. A non-conformist and a poet as well as a novelist, Mottram based the trilogy on his war experiences in France and Flanders. John Galsworthy described it as "unlike any war book I have met with." Gaumont-British advertised their film adaptation in a double-page spread as "A Drama of Intimate Human Emotions played against a Background of Graphic War Realism," calling it "the greatest story of the war yet written … a war film for men and women … a drama of great poignancy—and a picture more brilliant in technique than *Hindle Wakes*. It is unquestionably Elvey's greatest."

Victor Saville later called it "one of the most moving films I had to deal with." Part of the story is set during the Big Push of August 1918, which happened to be the exact moment my father was invalided out of the conflict. His acting was widely acclaimed: "A remarkably good performance in an extremely exacting part," observed *Kine Weekly*. The *Star* declared, "His portrayal of Skene gets to the heart of the character"; the *Catholic News* thought his performance "masterly": E.A. Baughan wrote in the *Daily News*: "His acting would lift any film from the commonplace, and we may congratulate ourselves on possessing a British actor equal to, if not surpassing, any of the American stars."

The indomitable heroine, the daughter of the Flemish owner of a farm in Flanders, was played by Hall-Davis. Typifying the implacable spirit of the village amid the carnage of war, her character sacrifices herself for the shell-shocked British officer hero, Skene. *The Times* thought her performance one of "exceptional reason and dignity," and the *Manchester Dispatch* announced, "She must be hailed as one of the greatest emotional film actresses of the day." On the set in Nice, she was amused to overhear the technicians, unaware that she understood French, making critical remarks about her acting, and deciding that this was obviously her first picture. "These are the little things that dispose of any small conceit an artist may possess," she remarked to a visiting journalist.

Films about the recent war continued to be popular, as audiences struggled to understand the reality of a conflict that had begun in such a jingoistic spirit. Elvey and Saville exploited this with *Roses of Picardy*, a title which reflected a well-known song that was once sung in every drawing room and on every concert platform. It told the story of a Flemish family in Flanders, and how their life was affected by the war.

While some of the graphic trench scenes were filmed in Hounslow, much of the film was shot in the south of France. Elvey used to go there with his unit every winter, to shoot exterior scenes for his films in the Riviera sunshine. On this occasion, Saville heard that a picturesque French village built for another film had been left standing on the back lot of the Rex Ingram studios in Nice. He leased it for a month and hired both French locals and Russian émigrés to play the English troops.

In *Roses of Picardy* (1927), he teamed up with Lilian Hall-Davis, an actress of great emotional power.

The director Michael Powell, then 21, was working there as an assistant on another film. While watching the filming, he was impressed by the efficiency of the operation and Elvey's dynamic presence. In his autobiography *A Life in Movies* he observed:

> [Elvey] arrived with every shot worked out. Shells burst, buildings collapsed, a 1917 bi-plane swooped down along the street, the pilot's gunner firing his machine-guns over the panic-stricken peasants; in four days they had wrapped the whole job up. Elvey was no remote controller, he was in the thick of it, imposing the tempo on the action, getting what he wanted the first time, working to a plan and a slender budget.

This was Elvey's 101st feature, and his intention, he said, was not to glorify war, but "to show the opposing armies for what they were—just non-professional soldiers keen on doing their job, but equally keen on getting it over." The film begins with a coach party of present-day tourists arriving in the village during a tour of the wartime battlefields. According to their guide, "This is the village of Hondebecq. It was occupied by the British. Nothing much happened here." The camera then turns to my father's character, through whose eyes we then see in flashback that in reality a great deal happened there, and that the local population endured much suffering.

Elvey was scrupulous in his planning and execution, as Jympson Harman, critic of the *Evening News*, pointed out:

> British producers are not out to dally over picture-making. Maurice Elvey and his co-operators are examples of this new economy. *Roses of Picardy* has probably set up a British record for the early public presentation of a full-dress film. The acting began on 17 January and was finished by 5 March. Editing the film and matching the negative took only another five weeks, and now, only three months and a week from the beginning, the film is ready for showing. Elvey is seldom more than a day or two out on the estimate.

The film was advertised as "a brilliant British triumph, breathing British sentiments—those sentiments which have given her world supremacy." The press echoed this patriotic theme: "Miles ahead of U.S. efforts," was the view of the *Evening News*; the *Observer* critic wrote: "Brings British achievement abreast of the American"; the *Daily Sketch* stated: "This film will go to the heart of woman in a way that no other has done." *The Times* thought it "a film of uncommon psychological integrity," and congratulated Elvey on "its freedom from hysteria and its steadily proportionate treatment of incident and character." *Picture Show* put my father and Lilian Hall-Davis on its cover.

Elvey called it his favorite film, while my father later described it as "without doubt my favourite part." It went into general release in Armistice Week, and on Armistice Day the two of them watched it in London at the Super Cinema in Charing Cross Road. The audience was a very special one, consisting of 300 limb-less ex-servicemen who had just attended a Memorial Service for the Fallen in Saint-Martin-in-the-Fields.

The many favorable reviews sent my father's fan mail soaring, and prompted

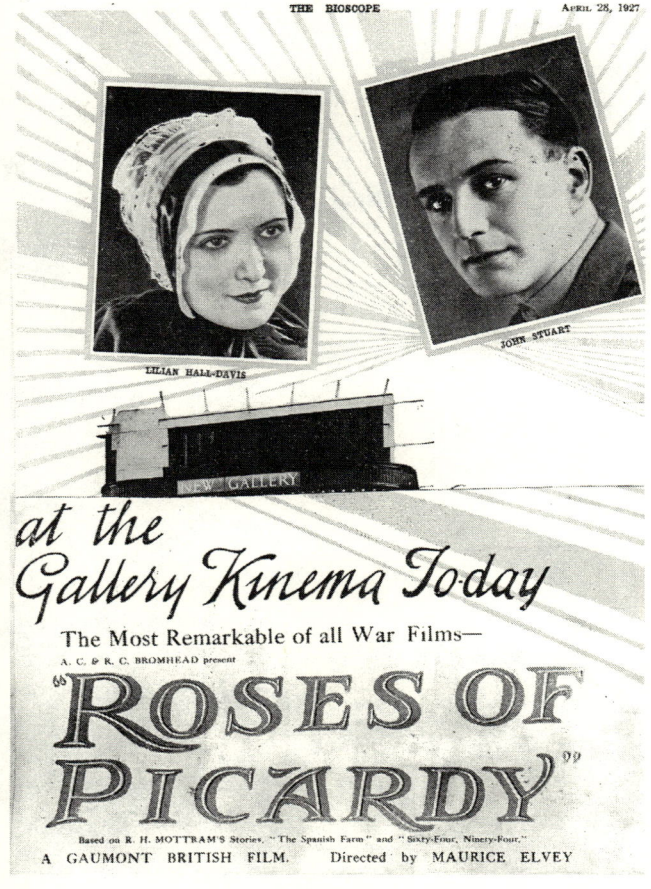

Roses of Picardy **was widely praised by the critics.**

the *Daily Chronicle* to declare, "He is very easily the best leading man in British pictures."

Other Films

My father appeared in *Back to the Trees* and *The Woman Juror* (both 1926), entries in a new series of two-reel "featurettes," comparable to dramatic sketches in the theater. Gaumont explained: "They are not potted dramas, but complete and perfect little plays—the short stories of the screen."

In the short *Curfew Shall Not Ring Tonight* (1926), an English civil war drama, my father played a cavalier facing a firing squad. He is rescued by the heroism of his fiancée. Directed by Frank Tilley, it was based on a celebrated ballad created by 16-year-old Rose Hartwick Thorpe, and was a favorite poem of Queen Victoria.

He also signed up for five shorts in a series directed by Maurice Elvey, *Haunted Houses and Castles of Great Britain* (1926), covering *Herne the Hunter, In Feudal Days, Kenilworth Castle, Baddesley Manor* and *The Tower of London.*

5

Britain or Hollywood?

In 1926, only 26 British feature films were released, compared to 103 in 1919. The British companies attempted to boost the home product by appealing to patriotism. For *London Love*, Gaumont claimed in its publicity: "No excuse needs to be offered for this British film: in staging, technique, and dramatic value it is as good as one expects of a good American film, and it has the added advantage of its British sentiment and characterization."

Soon afterwards, to try to help the badly struggling industry, the Cinematograph Films Act of 1927 was passed, leading to what became known as "quota quickies." In the previous year, British producers had contributed a mere five percent of the films shown on British screens. With the film business reportedly facing extinction, the new law was introduced to restore its fortunes and counter the American dominance.

The main aim of the act was "to secure the renting and exhibition of a certain proportion of British films." It called for a quota of five percent of British films in the first six months, which was to rise to 30 percent by successive stages over the next eight years. The rush to provide the films resulted in many new companies being set up, studios being re-equipped, and new staff being taken on. The result was a mini-boom. The number of films rose from 26 in 1926 to 128 the following year, and there was suddenly a shortage of studio space.

But some critics felt the industry was not yet distinctive or British or good enough to deserve such support. The experienced director George Pearson campaigned against the bill, arguing that it would result in a glut of poor films that would nullify the attempts to improve the quality of the output. He was proved right: most of the films produced during the decade that followed were quickly made on shoestring budgets, with scant attention being paid to the script or the technical quality. Often made in just ten days, they were unpopular with audiences and exhibitors alike, and brought the industry into disrepute.

Not all the quota quickies were bad; some were enjoyed and made decent profits. But in general, their quality was poor. The documentary filmmaker and critic Basil Wright later argued that the act produced "a great dreary mess of tasteless, ill-made films which debased the spectators if they didn't send them to sleep."

Exhibitors were only obliged to show them for a certain percentage of their opening hours, so many theaters ran them in the morning. There were stories of them being shown to empty cinemas; the manager of the Empire Leicester Square was prosecuted for screening one in the morning while the cleaners did their work. The new act prompted the *Evening Standard* to ask, "Where are we to find the stars?" and to include as illustration cartoons of my father, Ivor Novello, Lilian Hall-Davis, Jameson Thomas and Isabel Jeans.

Shortly after the act was passed, my father responded to the act's critics with remarks that flew in the face of reality, telling the *Edinburgh Evening Dispatch*: "Since this quota system has been established, those who prophesised a deterioration have been proved wrong. Every home studio is in full activity, and we are producing 100 per cent quality every time. This year may be considered the renaissance of the British film industry, and we are steadily forging ahead to international supremacy."

Despite the acclaim he received for his fine performances in *Mademoiselle from Armentières* and *Roses of Picardy*, several of his next films were of a disappointingly poor standard. He was clearly not happy with the parts he was being offered. "The contract system has its drawbacks, as you have to play any role given you," he complained. Although he worked with Maurice Elvey on three more films, they were vastly inferior to those they had previously made together.

The Flight Commander (1927), billed as "Britain's Biggest Thrill Melodrama," was a ludicrous tale set in the Far East, about a native uprising fomented by a gang of communist agitators. As the pilot hero John Massey, my father saved British residents from a dastardly Bolshevik plot. Elvey had a mock Chinese village built at Hendon aerodrome in North London and hired 600 men, mostly ex-soldiers, as extras. Also in the cast were Estelle Brody, Cyril McLaglen, John Longden and Alf Goddard. But the film's main interest was in Alan Cobham, a national hero after his recent round-the-world flight, who played himself in the title role.

My father's main scene with Cobham was a traumatic experience, and one he would never forget. It involved going up in an open two-seater plane with Cobham, who also acted as the cameraman. "From Croydon aerodrome to the Brooklands one in Surrey, we stunted about the south of England with an automatic camera on the tip of one of the wings," my father explained calmly to a journalist. "Filmmaking is sometimes no sinecure, but the variety of experience is unique and fascinating." But having never flown before, he was, he confessed later, absolutely terrified.

The action of the film was supposed to take place in a tropical climate, so he was wearing only cotton clothing. He became bitterly cold as the plane reached 12,000 feet in stormy conditions.

> I was supposed to be dropped by parachute into a village. The camera was strapped to one of the wing-tips. Sir Alan said: "As soon as I raise my hand, go through the motions as if you're about to make a jump." I was so frightened and shivering with cold that I could hardly get out of my seat, and after doing that I quickly got back into it.
>
> On returning to earth I had to be lifted from the plane and thawed out next to a car radiator. But all my agony had been in vain, because when the scene was shown on screen, I looked so frightened it couldn't be used. So it was re-taken in the studio, where all I had to do was jump out of a stationary plane onto a mattress. This was then cut in with a shot of a real parachute making a descent.

Despite the far-fetched plot, he got decent notices, the *Evening News* praising a particular quality in his acting. "He knows how to express sentiment like an Englishman—mainly by repression. You can understand why Americans will

never be able to imperson-
ate Englishmen successfully
on the screen." Estelle Brody
played a missionary's daughter who falls in love with my
father. It was a role that was
thought too intense for her
particular talents.

Another Elvey film,
co-directed with Victor Saville, *The Glad Eye* (1927) was
adapted from the popular
French stage farce *Le Zèbre*.
Once again my father played
opposite Estelle Brody, supported by Jeanne de Casa-
lis, Mabel Poulton and 50
members of the Lido Lady
chorus from the Gaiety Theatre. The film was enjoyed
by some critics for its polish
and slight sauciness, but the
Kine Monthly reviewer felt
it had "lost most of its point
in being transferred to the
screen."

My father and Humber-
ston Wright play two flirta-

He endured a traumatic experience while filming *The
Flight Commander* (1927) (courtesy the Cinema Museum,
London).

tious husbands, Maurice and Gaston, "who invariably betray any departure from
strict truth by respectively plucking at the trouser seam and by fidgeting with the
tie." The winking they indulge in for the publicity posters was ominous. This was my
father's first comedy, and he looked, according to one critic, "very much like a fish
out of water; he seems unhappy in farcical comedy." This was to remain a failing.

He fared little better in the melodramatic crime film *A Woman in Pawn* (1927).
It was directed by Edwin Greenwood, who was also a stage director, actor and
screenwriter, and co-starred Gladys Jennings and Lauderdale Maitland. My father
plays James Rawdon, a ruined stockbroker blamed for killing a crooked financier who has designs on his wife. The story centers on the theme that the love of
money is the root of all evil. *Bioscope* stated, "John Stuart gives a well-considered
rendering of a rather indefinite character," but *Cinema* saw things differently: "He
shows a tendency towards repetition in his mannerisms." He himself was appalled
by his performance and made no bones about it. "I regard my work in this film as
awful," he announced. "I was woefully miscast, and I would like the public to know
that it is not my fault." It was an uncharacteristic outburst, reflecting his obvious
frustration.

In a supporting role was Chili Bouchier, who had entered films as an 18-year-old. Born Dorothy Boucher, she decided to change her name to Bouchier because it sounded more French and glamorous. She got her break by answering a tantalizing newspaper advertisement which read: "We Make Film Stars. Price Three Guineas." In fact, the company made commercials for the cinema, but her work attracted the interest of Herbert Wilcox, who cast her in the wartime story *Mumsie*. She then played a bathing beauty in *Shooting Stars* and a skeptical gum-chewing cockney in *Palais de Danse*.

In *A Woman in Pawn,* she made enough of an impact for the press to dub her England's "It Girl" (the equivalent of Hollywood's sex symbol Clara Bow), "The Baby Vamp" and "The Brunette Bombshell." As she recalled in her memoir *Shooting Star*: "They draped me in slinky dresses, gave me a long cigarette holder, and swung great ropes of pearls around my neck. I didn't know what 'It' meant at the time. I thought it just meant *joie de vivre*. I became England's first sex symbol, only the word 'sex' was taboo in those days."

My father was now so busy that a new film of his was being released almost every two months. According to *Girls' Cinema*, "His services are so much sought after that he doesn't get breathing space between pictures, let alone holidays." Not surprisingly, there were times when he longed for a break. In June, he told the *Glasgow Evening News* that he planned to come up to Edinburgh at the first opportunity: "After I've looked up my friends, I'm going to bury myself in the lonely Highlands, forget all about such things as lights and cameras, and rest my mind and body in the solitude."

In August 1927, *Picturegoer* had reported that a handful of stars—including Lilian Hall-Davis, Jameson Thomas and my father—had been "secured on contract against American temptation." But the *Daily Express* complained soon after that the Americans "have kept their search for men stars at fever pitch, and incidentally given a chance to every decent-looking Englishman that happened along."

My father was one of those being courted. In 1928, he was said to have had many offers from Hollywood, but refused them all. "He means to work for British films only and help make us the world leaders of the film industry," ran one report. R.B. Marriott, film critic of *Era*, praised him for his patriotism, observing admiringly, "When success came he did not go to the land that appeared to offer better opportunities … like so many Britishers have done."

By 1924, there had been a considerable exodus of British film people to Hollywood, as *Picturegoer* noted: "Every department of American screenland is rich in artists over whose birthplace floated not the Stars and Stripes, but the Union Jack. Producers, actors, actresses, camera men and scenario writers, technical and art directors, and clever child players—you will find a little of Old England in every branch of the industry." As Cedric Hardwicke tartly observed: "God felt sorry for actors, so he created Hollywood to give them a place in the sun and a swimming pool. The price they had to pay was to surrender their talent."

So many European actors tried their luck in Hollywood during these years that they were known as "the Foreign Legion." One of the early emigrants, Clive Brook made an astonishing 35 films there in five years before the advent of the talkies.

From Hollywood he observed: "Pictures in England are not good. We are hampered by lighting, by old favouritisms, and by the fact that our intellectuals scorn the cinema." The *Daily Renter* despaired of the situation:

> It doesn't matter which way you turn, there doesn't seem the slightest hope for anybody possessing screen talent in this country. The few artists we do possess who are popular with screen patrons have nothing done to publicise them in any way. I don't blame anyone if they leave this country to seek their fortune abroad. They couldn't do worse than here, because some of our producers seem blind, and the pity of it is that the moment these people leave to get a regular job elsewhere, you hear the same old moan that America is collaring our players. The plain fact of the matter is that America has the ability to recognise talent and take a chance with it. That's more than we do.

It was hardly surprising, then, that many British stars decided to improve their financial and professional status by decamping to the Californian dream factory where, as Michael Powell put it in *A Life in Movies*, "formidable figures with strange names were building a vast industry, where orange groves and avenues of pepper trees were being bulldozed to make way for Hollywood and Vine and the Brown Derby." The major studios (Paramount, Famous Players, MGM, United Artists) were in full flood, with MGM claiming to have "more stars than there are in Heaven." Forever on the lookout for European talent, they were ready to spend large sums to secure the services of the most promising actors and directors.

Few British actresses tried their luck in Hollywood. According to Phil Lonergan, writing in *Picturegoer*, they had to face certain prejudices on the part of American producers: "It has been a common fallacy of Hollywood to characterise them as too cold, too expressionless for American pictures. Producers felt that British women lacked the fire and vivacity of Scandinavian, Slavonic, German, and Latin people."

Hollywood was attracting many European directors, from Italy, Germany, Russia and Scandinavia, but few English directors went there. So why, asked Adrian Brunel in *Film Weekly*, should there be such a difference, when there were British directors who would show themselves to be as good as the Americans if they had the kind of conditions and studios available in Hollywood? "The matter with us is that we are hampered, crippled and deterred by our colossal inferiority complex—in fact we are definitely hypnotised into actual inferiority. We stand numb, senseless and irresolute—like a row of chickens staring at a chalk line."

In a 1928 *Film Weekly*, Mabel Poulton made a withering attack on the typical British director's inability to give fruitful assistance to young actresses compared with his counterparts in Hollywood:

> Does he study the girl? Does he analyse her best points and endeavour to bring them out by careful lighting, by perfect casting, and sympathetic direction? Does he observe her shortcomings and experiment with her, avoiding her faults and cultivating her assets, until she learns her own power, and develops her own "type," as American directors study stars? In nineteen cases out of twenty he does nothing of the kind.

British writers were keenly sought by Hollywood, though many were highly critical of a place which Henry Miller described as "a dictatorship in which the artist is silenced." British writers were among those earmarked to test this view. In July 1920, Jesse Lasky announced, "Practically all the best-known playwrights and authors of England are about to turn their talents into the field of the movies, and many are coming to America within the next six months to learn screen drama writing." He cited Bernard Shaw, J.M. Barrie, Somerset Maugham, H.G. Wells and Arnold Bennett among his potential British catch.

This was his dream, but the reality was less impressive. Shaw rejected an invitation from Sam Goldwyn, stating mischievously: "All they talk about is art, whereas all I want to hear about is money." Highly critical of Hollywood, he turned down many offers, including one of a million dollars for the screen rights to all his works. "People complain that my plays are all talk," he said. "If they were turned into films, people would complain they were all pictures."

Barrie declined to go to California; Ben Travers also refused Hollywood's blandishments. Edward Knoblock was there for a while, but later shared his jaundiced view of the place: "What was lacking was any knowledge of the real world beyond a fantastic land of theatrical romance. Reality was always sacrificed for pictorial effect, and plausibility was thrown to the winds if a sequence could produce a thrill."

Elinor Glyn stayed for several years, and later summed up the fate awaiting writers snared in the Hollywood web:

> All authors, living or dead, famous or obscure, shared the same fate. Their stories were re-written and completely altered, either by the stenographers and continuity girls of the scenario department, or by the assistant director and his lady-love, or by the leading lady, or by anyone else who happened to pass through the same studio; and even when at last after infinite struggle a scene was shot which bore some resemblance to the original story, it was certain to be left out in the cutting-room, or pared away to such an extent that all meaning which it might once have had was lost.

Other leading English writers were to be lured to Hollywood in the following decade, including J.B. Priestley, Hugh Walpole, Aldous Huxley, Anthony Powell and P.G. Wodehouse. They were soon disillusioned. Walpole's view of the place was typical: "No wars, no politics, no deaths make any effect here. We are all on a raft together in the middle of a cinema sea, and nothing is real here but the salaries."

In September 1928, E.A. Baughan wrote in the *Daily News*: "Brian Aherne and John Stuart can hold their own with American stars, but they have not had the advantages of American direction and intensive boosting." In January 1929, *Kine Weekly* published a feature headed "Britain's Twenty Best Stars—Comparisons with American Favourites—Are They as Talented and Good Looking?" It was an issue that continued to be debated throughout the decade as several stars, mostly men, made the Atlantic crossing, then faced accusations of disloyalty for deserting their home country.

The temptation was considerable. In summer 1928, my father was interviewed in London by the two biggest stars in the Hollywood firmament, Douglas Fairbanks and Mary Pickford. She was the most powerful woman in Hollywood, who could insist her name appeared above the title in her films. Known as "America's Sweetheart" or even sometimes "The World's Sweetheart," she was still identified with "Little Mary" roles, often playing parts half her real age. For years she had been trying to change this situation. She declared,

I want to grow up on the screen. I am sick of Cinderella parts, of wearing rags and tatters. I want to wear smart clothes and play the lover. For this I am looking for a really suitable partner—a young Adonis who can make love as beautifully as he looks—one who would capture the heart of every woman in the audience and make every man admire my choice. I have a sneaking hope that this ideal partner may come from England.

In 1928 he met Mary Pickford and Douglas Fairbanks in London, to discuss a role for him as Pickford's screen lover (courtesy the Cinema Museum, London).

Then my father met the famous couple. Asked how he looked in a mustache, he offered to send them some photos with examples. Fairbanks said they would watch *Roses of Picardy* before deciding, but asked him if he would come to Hollywood if they found a suitable story for Mary and him to play in. My father agreed. But then news of the meeting leaked out. The press immediately began speculating about who this Adonis might be. My father seemed to be in the running: "John Stuart Likely Choice" and "Edinburgh Man as Mary Pickford's Partner?" ran typical headlines. But Brian Aherne and John Longden were also considered likely candidates.

My father was then forced to comment publicly. "I am not getting too worked up about it, for in this work it doesn't pay to be too hopeful about any of it," he explained, adding carefully: "I have always wanted to go to America, not to be there permanently, but merely to gain experience, to see how film work is done out there." Back in Hollywood, Mary Pickford was said to have "stolen him for her leading man." But the report proved premature: To his regret, though he had sent the photographs, he heard nothing further of the idea.

His next film, *Smashing Through* (1928), was a motor racing drama filmed on the Brooklands racetrack. It was directed by W.P. Kellino, and co-starred Eve Gray, an experienced stage actress who alternated between leading and supporting film roles. The *Daily Film Renter* decided, "The chief acting honours go to John Stuart, who gives an impressive rendering in the part of the hero Richard Bristol." The filming had its dangers: a stationary car in which he was sitting began to roll down a hill, resulting in the skin being torn off one of his hands. On another occasion, one

With co-star Eve Gray in the motor-racing drama *Smashing Through* (1928).

of the cars skidded and crashed through barriers, injuring a number of extras. Some had to be taken to hospital.

Kellino also directed him in the comedy *Sailors Don't Care* (1928). Scripted by Eliot Stannard, it was sold as a tale of "two very jolly tars and an elusive parlour maid." My father, cast as Slinger Woods, and Alf Goddard competed for the affections of Estelle Brody. Filmed aboard a real "Q" boat used in the war, it was written, Gaumont announced, "to catch the rollicking atmosphere of life on the ocean wave." The "clapper boy" on the film was David Lean. Twenty years later, after my father had written to him to ask if there might be a part for him in *Oliver Twist*, the director replied: "Do you remember I used to hold up the number board for you on *Sailors Don't Care*, etc., etc., etc.! You were one of my boyhood heroes. I never dreamt

I should live to see the day when I should receive such a letter from you of all people!"

My father reached a nadir with director Maurice Elvey's poorly received *Mademoiselle Parley Voo* (1928), a blatant attempt to cash in on the success of *Mademoiselle from Armentières*. He and Estelle Brody were cast as a team working in a postwar revue, he playing a manager, John Smith, she a chirpy star. The *Daily Mail* thought he was "always a little stilted"; *Kine Weekly* decided, "He is not well cast as a revue producer, and is inclined to over-emphasise his facial expressions." E.A. Baughan in the *Daily News* wrote: "The story is poor, the characterisation undeveloped," noting "the earnest endeavour of John Stuart to make something of a hero who is always jealous and otherwise futile."

Recently he had stated

Life on the ocean wave with fellow sailors Alf Goddard (left) and Humberston Wright (center) in the comedy *Sailors Don't Care* (1928).

firmly: "I will never leave England for America or other foreign studios." Despite this pledge, he now went to Germany for five weeks as part of an artist exchange scheme, to star in *Yacht of the Seven Sins* (1928). The film was made by UFA, Europe's top film company and dubbed Germany's Hollywood, and helmed by the Austrian pioneering director Luise Fleck and her husband Jacob Fleck. In this efficient murder mystery set aboard a ship, my father stars as Kilian Gurlitt, a disappointed lover and would-be suicide, opposite Brigitte Helm, the ultimate German "vamp." Famed for her powerful, fascinating and enigmatic beauty, she had just starred in the famous futuristic Fritz Lang film *Metropolis*, and was here cast as a *femme fatale* dancer.

A short surviving montage of scenes shows my father in various moments of disappointment, drinking and smoking, with Helm displaying her elegant cocktail dresses and cupid's-bow lips. He confessed smoothly to one reporter: "Being vamped by Brigitte Helm is quite a painless process really!" He also suggested diplomatically: "Any one of the girls in a UFA crowd is pretty enough to be featured before the camera." He made this remark at a time when his marriage was coming to an end: he and Jeanne separated in 1928 and were divorced the following year. He never revealed the reason for the split.

The adventure story *High Seas* (1929), directed by Denison Clift, who also wrote the screenplay, was described by *Cinema* as "a hearty slice of action drama with a romantic flavour." It was shot as a silent film; with the advent of sound, it was turned into a talkie. My father was cast as Tony Bracklethorpe, the lover of his co-star Lillian Rich, "a fearless daughter of the sea," who saves his life in this action-packed story of "love, hate, mutiny and shipwreck." A dark-haired English-born actress who had made a name in Hollywood, Rich graduated from Westerns to star in Cecil B. DeMille's extravaganza *The Golden Bed* (1925), and specialized in playing *femmes fatales* in melodramas, in roles which involved a great deal of lolling about on tiger skins.

My father reverts to his natural, understated style of acting, managing smoothly the transition from romantic hero to rugged shipboard fighter, and back again. The *Bioscope* critic wrote, "He does well in the difficult part of the lover," and he was praised for providing "a typical Stuart creation, upstanding and restrained."

During the filming, he had a hard time physically. According to a *Star* reporter visiting the set, "John Stuart endured one of the most exacting ordeals a film star has been called on to undergo." After a fortnight spent filming on a tramp steamer in the Channel, the cast moved to the large, specially constructed life-size vessel at Elstree, reportedly one of the most spectacular sets yet built in Britain. On what was apparently the coldest night of the year, he was stripped to the waist, lashed to the mast and flogged several times. As the surviving shooting script states: "Tony is writhing in agony under the terrible blows. His back is cut and bleeding. His eyes are glazed with suffering—his lips twisted as he murmurs 'Oh God! Help me.'"

To protect himself, he covered his body in olive oil. The temperature was below freezing when they shot the scene, during which he was buffeted by a gale created by six airplane engines and continually swamped by torrents of cold water pouring out from 12 tanks. The shooting lasted several hours and required multiple takes. Eventually, half-fainting and numb with cold, he was carried to a tent and given brandy to revive him. "All in the cause of realism, I suppose," he remarked stoically, while being treated. But he caught a chill and was seriously ill in bed for three weeks with pneumonia.

Originally called *The Silver Rosary*, this was his third film directed by Clift. Elstree's replica ship involved 300 men, women and children as extras. An unusual element is the presence in the film of several black and Chinese seamen on board ship. Some scenes were shot in Cardiff docks, and Clift drew on the local population for his sailor extras—described in the film's titles as "chinks," "dagos" and "niggers."

The *Cinema* critic wrote approvingly: "Here is romance and villainy, love and hate, mutiny and disaster, with sentimental appeal and a succession of hearty action and vibrant drama." Clift was rightly praised for the realism of the shipboard scenes, though today the story seems ponderous and scarcely credible, with a sentimental ending in which the heroine is suddenly all-forgiving of my father's character, her former lover. As the title tells us: "Her eyes, dim with tears, meet his in the miracle and understanding of a great love that has been born of hate and sorrow and travail."

My father later criticized the quality of his acting during this period, which had done little to add to his reputation. "I walk in terror of becoming stereotyped in my work, so I eagerly snatch at any role that is a little bit out of the ordinary. I did a lot of films in which I was not satisfied with my work. I felt that I was developing too pronounced mannerisms, a smug expression, and getting into a stereotyped rut. People would say to me I was excellent, but behind my back they said the opposite."

In a marked change of focus, he was involved in a short film with a political message. In *Memories of the Great Sacrifice 1914–1918* (1929), he plays one of four former comrades (John Longden, Jameson Thomas and Jack Raine were the others) who meet again on Armistice Day, to drink to those who died in the Great War. Their toast is: "Please God there will be no other such war. Let all the strength we possess be used to oppose it. It is a debt we owe to those others who lie in Flanders fields." With real footage from the conflict shown through the men's eyes, the experience must again have evoked painful memories of the part he played as a 19-year-old in that horrendous conflict.

6

Fame and a Fan Club

"Two Hundred Girls Mob Film Star John Stuart—Escape in Disguise after a Scrum."—*Daily Chronicle* headline, 1928

In America, the 1926 death of Rudolph Valentino led to a discussion about those British stars who had "real sex appeal." According to *Picture Show*, "Matheson Lang and John Stuart were well up among the favorites." The *Daily Sketch* noted, "John Stuart has been called the English Valentino," while another reported, "He can get more publicity out of a smile than most people can get out of a year's hard work."

That year his status as a screen lover was confirmed when he twice made the cover of *Picture Show*, gazing into the eyes of Virginia Valli (in *The Pleasure Garden*) and Estelle Brody (in *Mademoiselle from Armentières*). He featured in a lengthy *Film Weekly* piece which asked its readers whether they thought the established British stars were as talented and good-looking as their American counterparts. In general, the readers thought they were, with my father, Ivor Novello, Betty Balfour, Mabel Poulton and Jameson Thomas seen as the five most popular stars.

According to *Girls' Cinema* magazine in 1923, "it was no wonder all his feminine followers lose their heart to him."

He was now, in one writer's words, "the Idyllic Lover and the Strong Silent Hero." *Girls' Cinema* launched a competition in a feature on "Romance on the Screen," listing the attributes of the stars: "Which of these types is the favourite of the Girl of Today? There is the soulful, passionate, tender lover played so well by John Gilbert, the curious mixture of Apache and dreaming poet typified by Ivor Novello, the impetuous lover portrayed by Ramon Novarro, and the sincerity of John Stuart."

The magazine linked his appeal to his declared patriotism: "It is with the

John Stuart
relies on
'OVALTINE'
for a
Good Night's Rest

Prices in Great Britain and N. Ireland,
1/1, 1/10 and 3/3 per tin.

P800A

FOR health and energy all day and sound sleep at night, 'Ovaltine' is unrivalled. This fact is borne out by a huge volume of unsolicited testimony given by people in every walk of life. Among the many appreciative letters received from members of the theatrical profession is the following from that popular 'star,' John Stuart:—

"After a hard day's work in a film studio, a good night's rest is essential in order to be fresh the following morning. When I am working on a film, I always take a cup of 'Ovaltine' on retiring."

'Ovaltine' is a complete and perfect food. It supplies, in correctly balanced proportions, every nutritive element required to build up body, brain and nerves. Make delicious 'Ovaltine' *your* regular daytim and bedtime beverage. *To drink i always—is to be always well.*

Like other stars, he lent his name to commercial products, including Ovaltine and cigarettes.

greatest pleasure that we find John Stuart standing by British pictures. His hair is dark and boasts a wave, while there's a whole wealth of humour in his dark eyes." Soon after this, he became the magazine's cover image and the subject of a two-page biographical feature. His appeal was such that he was persuaded to promote "the fine mellow flavour of Turf Cigarettes," while he did a similar job for Ovaltine and for Sarony cigarettes: "John Stuart blindfolded picks Sarony," ran the sales pitch.

Like other major silent stars, including Ivor Novello, Betty Balfour, Ben Lyon and Estelle Brody, he had a fan club. "Novello seems to have a serious rival in Stuart," suggested the *Sunday Express*, reporting on the 1927 formation of the John Stuart Friendship Club. (With its initials JSFC, it was sometimes mistaken for a football club.) Set up by a fan from Grimsby, Louise Johnson, with my father acting as president, it quickly attracted several hundred members. It charged half a crown a year, the money going to the Cinematograph Trade Benevolent Fund. On joining, members received an autographed portrait of my father, a badge with a thistle on it, and a quarterly magazine. They also got a full list of members, which provided "unique facilities for forming congenial friendships with others interested in cinema."

The club organized dances and competitions, and arranged charabanc outings, which my father joined. It was stressed, "The president takes a very real and personal interest in the club and its activities, and is at all times eager to have the opportunity of meeting members and their friends." Members were encouraged to make their voices heard in the film world. The club's brochure explained:

> The club was founded with the object of popularising British films and film stars, and, with that end in view, members are requested to make a special effort to see as many British films as they can, and to ask their local cinema manager to book films in which John Stuart is appearing. Producers, exhibitors, actors, and critics are all seeking to find out what the public wants. YOU are the public—here is your chance to say what YOU want—and do *not* want—in film entertainment. You are asked to help build the future British film industry.

There was also the John Stuart Players, an acting company formed so the members could stage productions. Film journalist Leslie Wood was hired to write and direct the plays, and there were early plans to take the productions on tour, to play in halls for local charities. The dances were held twice a year at fashionable London hotels, attended by other stars. Invitations to a John Stuart Dance at the Imperial Hotel in Russell Square offered members "A Riotous Carnival Night You'll Never Forget!" Members could dance the night away to the music of Tom Arnell and His Kingsway Revels, and mix with stars such as Madeleine Carroll, Eve Gray, Stewart Rome and the two guests of honor, Mabel Poulton and my father.

During the following months he seemed to be everywhere, making an extended tour of the provinces, attending cinema carnivals, fancy-dress balls and screenings of his films. The fan club's first issue reports him making no less than 32 cinema appearances in the last three months, and attending 11 dances. At the Cinema Ball at the City Hall in Cardiff, "between judging, supper and autographing, he danced a lot." At the Stage Guild Ball and Cabaret held at the Palais de Danse in Hammersmith, he was one of several stars who offered themselves as "professional dance partners." Once he made personal appearances at three large London cinemas in one evening, in Shoreditch and Bethnal Green, where he received "a terrific ovation" at each theater. He was seen by 6500 audience members watching *Roses of Picardy.*

The actress-writer Norah Baring came across him at a fan club dance given in his honor at the Westminster Palace Rooms, and wrote in *Picture Show*: "A friend and I cornered him amid a bevy of beauties. For John it was a marathon dance; that is to say, one partner after another. He enjoyed every moment of it, which is, I am sure, one of the secrets of his tremendous popularity. He does really like to be among his fans. He is one of the most easy-going and delightful people you could ever hope to find in films."

He aimed to answer personally the scores of fan letters he received, but found it hard to find the time to do so. In May 1929 from Elstree Studios, he wrote to fan club

MARCH, 1928   *The Picturegoer*

JOHN STUART

In 1928 *Picturegoer* praised the acting power of "this modern British young man."

member Miss Wingate: "I regret not answering your letter before but I have been exceptionally busy of late. I am very glad to hear the club is doing so well, and I am sure your work on its behalf is very much appreciated by all concerned."

Some of the members were fervent in their adoration. In the club's newsletter, one woman described a meeting with him as the happiest day of her life: "I was once introduced to the Prince of Wales, but the 45 minutes I spent with Mr. Stuart far exceeded the pleasure I derived from the former. I am certain all British film lovers (could they have the pleasure of meeting him) would fall at his feet. What a handshake, and what a charming fellow!"

Sometimes he had to endure more than a handshake: At one of the club dances, he was "mobbed unmercifully," and was compelled to hastily "melt into space." When he visited a cinema in London's East Ham, the local *Gazette* reported that "traffic was impeded, and the police had to curb the enthusiasm of girls who besieged him for his autograph." There was a similar scene when he re-opened the Clapham Pavilion Cinema, when he was again mobbed by women and had to be given police protection. "So enthusiastically was Mr. Stuart received by his cinema admirers," ran one report, "that the police practically had to carry him through the crowd back to his car."

"Two Hundred Girls Mob Film Star—Escape in Disguise after a Scrum." This

1928 headline in the *Daily Chronicle* was one of several similar ones that day, after he was set upon by fans as he left the Film Artists' Fair, held at the Foundling Hospital in Bloomsbury. As he emerged, "he was surrounded by cheering girls, who clasped him round the neck and seized his arms." He had to be rescued by four stewards and fellow actor Alf Goddard. The next morning, he said, "Several of my buttons were torn off, while my hat, handkerchief, and tie were snatched away, my pocket ripped open, and my coat torn, all apparently for souvenirs. I finally got away through a back door, disguised in an overcoat, muffler, and cap."

He was now seriously famous. In 1928, the *Sunday Express* reported: "Mr. Stuart has admirers all over the world, and his fan mail now averages several hundred letters a week." But in a newspaper article the following year, he suggested that he received a more modest total of around 100 a week, giving a breakdown of the kind he was receiving:

> Love letters, begging letters, letters of criticism, silly letters, nice letters, and letters asking for autographs and signed portraits. Then there are the letters from adolescents suffering from bad attacks of calf love for a two-dimensional film hero. They are melodramatic, passionate, and silly outpourings. Why do cinemagoers write to film stars? The reason is the same which urges small boys to stick pins in a sentry. It is to see if we are real!

His popularity with women was evident: In Grimsby, where he was said to be a household name, he was "besieged by ladies" after a showing of *The Glad Eye*. After a personal appearance in Halifax, he toured Mackintosh's toffee works where, the local paper reported, "all the girls turned out and cheered." He received scores of letters imploring him to hire the letter-writer as his secretary, which they invariably saw as a first step to film stardom. "If I hired all those who have offered themselves as candidates, I should have to take Bush House," he remarked.

Other letter-writers were more direct, with young women asking him to find them a part in his next film, "ranging from co-star to parlourmaid." One who wrote asking if she could be his secretary added

He spent many hours answering hundreds of fan letters and requests for a signed photograph.

none too subtly: "I have the best pair of legs under and over an office-stool." He dutifully spent many hours and several hundred pounds a year answering these letters, and having photographs printed to send to his fans.

Charity appeals also arrived in abundance, and took up many hours of his leisure time. He explained,

> At the risk of being dubbed a "tight-wad" I must of necessity turn most of them down, otherwise I should soon be penniless. Others do not ask for money but for time; they want me to make personal appearances, to open bazaars and fetes. Though I cheerfully sacrifice some of my leisure to answer such calls, one cannot continually be bowling the first ball at cricket matches or judging pretty-ankle competitions.

He had a seemingly exhausting publicity schedule, promoting both his own films and the industry in general. He was described in *Cinema* as "indefatigable in doing good turns to cinema people who are opening new supers," noting that "John certainly works hard and puts over a lot of good publicity for British films in the provinces by these visits."

He was often photographed out and about, opening cinemas and fashion exhibitions, judging carnival-queen and bathing-beauty contests, and endlessly signing autographs or posing with local mayors and other worthies. In Brighton, he and Estelle Brody were guests of honor at a dinner given by Gaumont at the Grand Hotel. They also attended a showing of *Mademoiselle from Armentières* at the town's Academy cinema, where they were mobbed by autograph seekers.

At some events, he was seen in unexpected costumes. He donned the full tartan for the Glasgow Kinema Club Carnival, and went as a Crusader Knight to the

Entertaining day-trippers on a Thames riverboat during a Gaumont-British publicity trip with Estelle Brody.

Chelsea Arts Ball, held in London's Hotel Cecil. He also undertook a steady amount of charity work, including a visit to a hospital where he participated in a pierrot show that he had arranged.

While visiting cinemas and halls in Staffordshire, he took the opportunity to vigorously attack the stereotypical and unreal portrayal of the English in American films: "The Americans depict the well-dressed Englishman as a man who always wears an eye-glass and generally makes a fool of himself. Don't let the whole world be Americanised any longer. We should not allow the American producers to belittle us as they do. We in the British film industry want to show the world what the Englishman really is."

His grueling schedule seems to have paid off for his career. By the end of the 1920s, according to the *Daily Express*, "his box-office popularity is enormous." *Film Weekly* noted, "He has probably a greater fan following than any British film actor." But there was a price to pay, as he admitted in a heartfelt article in *Picturegoer*: "The screen has cost me myself. Always I am John Stuart the actor. Sometimes I have to run away from crowds. The person that cinema-goers mob is the black-and-white shadow player. I love being a shadow on the screen, but sometimes I wish I could rid myself of my shadow double when the cameras cease to turn."

"The shyest star in film land" was one journalist's description of him. Another wrote, "Mr. Stuart does not like being interviewed for the press, and has a habit of slipping in the back way if he smells a journalist in the offing." But his publicity agent Billie Bristow, who had been a publicity manager for Broadwest Films before setting up her own press agency in Shaftesbury Avenue in the West End, was considered one of the best in the business. She ensured that he was constantly kept in the public eye.

The picture that emerges from his many interviews is of an unassuming, unstarry and sincere person. His easy, unforced manner charmed journalists, especially women. After his success in *Mademoiselle from Armentières*, Edith Nepean of *Picture Show* wrote,

> This fine young star is one of the most modest of men in private life. He has a great sense of humour, both on the stage and off the stage. John Stuart has that happy combination of being an extremely popular hero with the fans, and also popular with men. He is well-built, athletic-looking, and essentially British; but with all this he has a strong romantic temperament, which enables him to get right into the skin of his part.

Although journalists often described him as thoroughly English—"as English as roast beef" was how the *Sunday Chronicle* put it—he was proud of his Scottish ancestry, and made a point of emphasizing it, especially when making personal appearances in Scotland. He had his photo taken in full tartan for the Scottish press, confessing: "My great ambition now is to be able to wear the Stuart tartan for the screen." He held forth on the correct usage of the national costume, arguing that in films about Scotland, "few of the actors know how to wear a kilt properly, or how to walk in one to display it to the best advantage. Usually the kilt is put on so that it droops at the back and is too long or too short. The correct length is such that when one is kneeling, and in an upright position, it just clears the floor."

Somewhat surprisingly, in view of his apparent reticence, one journalist was allowed inside his "delightful flat" in London's Manchester Street. "It's just twenty yards from Sherlock Holmes's fictitious residence in Baker Street," he wrote. "Anything less like a West End flat it would be difficult to imagine. The interior resembles a country cottage, with heavy old oak beams, big open fireplaces, and a tiled floor to the dining room. It has been furnished in perfect taste, and one of Stuart's pet hobbies is searching for quaint antiques." In fact, he had a cottage in Cornwall, but only rarely found time to take a holiday there.

He was portrayed as an animal lover, the proud possessor of a wire-haired terrier "purchased for sixpence from a Gypsy, an intelligent little animal who usually follows his master wherever he goes." His athletic abilities were frequently stressed: he was "a keen footballer who plays for one of the best-known amateur teams in London"; he was "a fine tennis player"; and, rather more unexpectedly, "a horse lover who rode to hounds." He was also a founding member of the Kinema Club cricket team, and though the record shows him batting well down the order at number nine or ten, he was a reasonably skillful batsman, as he demonstrates in *A Daughter of Love*. "I am very fond of sporting pictures," he said after making that film.

Several interviewers were struck by his modesty and ability to criticize himself. One reporter observed after talking to him in his dressing room: "He has no false notions of his own capabilities, confessing: 'I did a lot of films in which I did not feel satisfied with my work.'" The much-feared Nerina Shute was another who was struck by his capacity for self-deprecation; in 1930, she painted a sympathetic portrait of him in *Film Weekly* for a series labeled "What I Think of Myself":

> For those who know John Stuart quite well there is something about him more attractive than anyone else in films. He is probably the most popular juvenile on the British screen, but his lack of conceit makes him simple and sympathetic. ...He loves to listen to the other man's troubles. You will find him chuckling at the remarks of an electrician or a carpenter. You will find him frowning with interest at the tale of a woebegone extra. He is more at home, if anything, with people like these.

It was a revealing interview, but one she initially found difficult. "I drew his confessions like so many teeth," she revealed. "It takes a long time to know him and understand his queer habit of helpless silence. He cannot and will not talk about himself. Everyone admires him. Everyone likes his work. But no one is jealous of his personality. It shows him

JOHN STUART CLUB.

John Stuart snapped on holiday in Cornwall.

His fan-club magazine caught him on a rare holiday in the west country.

in a false light. Yet he is only too anxious to change his nature. He longs to express himself. This inferiority business sometimes maddens him."

When she finally persuaded him to open up, after "hours of coaxing and several gallons of China tea," he was startlingly self-critical: "I'm so damned reserved!" he tells her. "People think I'm a fool, I suppose. I sit about like a lump of clay, and because I can't talk, they think I've got nothing to say. The trouble is that I can't help feeling that everyone else is more interesting than I am. I'd much rather listen. Words make me dizzy, like too many drinks, and I get so tangled up when I try to express myself that I feel like an ass. It's a terrible drawback." Needless to say, this was very different from the average star's self-portrait.

She even managed to get him to talk about the war, when so many of the friends he fought alongside in the trenches in France were killed. "He admitted that never in his life had anything hurt him so much as the death of these youthful comrades. He came back from the war a typical Scotsman, dour and silent. He never spoke of the things he had seen. Instead he built a wall of stone round his private emotions, a wall that has grown, it seems, with the passing of the years."

The article was headed "Why I Prefer Women," a title prompted by his thoughts about the opposite sex. "I like women far better than men," he told her. "I find them more understanding. It's a dreadful admission. I sound like a gigolo or something. I like them to be blonde and tall, with blue eyes and lots to say." He was cagey about his close relationships: "I've nearly got married several times, but there's only one woman I've really loved." Perhaps on the advice of Billie Bristow, in order not to disappoint his fans he never mentioned his wife Jeanne in interviews. As to his one true love, he only revealed her name on condition it would not be printed.

In an *Ideas* magazine piece he wrote, "So Many Women Want to Marry Film Stars," he warned of the dangers of gold-diggers, confessing: "I am afraid of women, I have had so many narrow escapes. Through my long connection with films I have had all sorts of experiences." But he hastened to reassure his fans that he was not a woman-hater. "On the contrary, I adore women. They are the orchids in the garden of life." He developed this theme in another piece, "The Kind of Women Men Like," listing their most desirable attributes as charm, the ability to dress neatly, and to be good listeners. But he also advised: "Don't be too clever and, if you are very clever, pretend sometimes that you are not."

The John Stuart Fan Club, described as "Britain's strongest and most active fan club," continued to thrive, with new branches being set up in Torquay and Hull, and membership standing at 700, including fans from all over the world and, rather surprisingly, stars such as Clive Brook, Ronald Colman and Stewart Rome becoming members. At a dance at the Westminster Palace Rooms, billed as "the largest film ball ever held by a fan club," he acted as master of ceremonies, introducing stars Mabel Poulton, Adrianne Allen, Chili Bouchier and Muriel Angelus.

What invariably struck his interviewers was that he refused to play the big star. "Adoration and success leave John unspoilt," one observed. "He is natural and unaffected, a keen worker, and what may be termed an excellent sport." Another wrote: "It is impossible not to like Mr Stuart personally, for one very good reason: he is an unsparing critic of himself. And you can't say that of most actors and actresses."

PART TWO

The Background

7

Working Lives

"We worked all hours for six or seven days a week, but nobody minded, because we were all too interested in our jobs."—Cinematographer Freddie Young

In the pre-union era of the 1920s—the Film Artistes' Guild was not formed until 1927—the actors' working lives were none too rewarding, especially compared to those in Hollywood. The hours were long, the conditions primitive, the noise from the camera and lights intense; all this made the stress they faced considerable. As Fay Compton observed in her memoir *Rosemary: Some Reminiscences*: "A day on the floor of the studio, under the hot and heavy arc lights and the glass roof, with quick changes of sets, permitting the cameraman to wind that little handle and release countless feet of film, means to the artist a day of intensive concentration and practically continuous nervous strain."

The pay was relatively poor, especially for character actors. The earnings of the stars varied greatly: While Lilian Hall-Davis was paid £150 a week at the height of her fame, Mabel Poulton earned just £20 a week, and then only when she was working. Publicity about the stars was still in its infancy, so work opportunities were limited. The uncertainty led several stars to work abroad on European films in between their engagements at home. Even the top stars could be out of work for several months, and those on contract were often desperate for them to end.

The larger studios such as Gaumont were run like a factory, with employees wearing white coats with colored piping on their collars—red for the camera department, blue for electricians, mauve for a director. The smaller studios were less rigidly organized, with the boundaries between tasks often blurred. George Pearson's studio had just 12 staff members: two carpenters, two electricians, two scene painters, two handymen, a property man, a cameraman, the director and his personal assistant. "We made everything, from A to Z, that the silent film required," he remembered in his autobiography *Flashback*. "There was no place for regimentation into water-tight compartments. No matter what the technical category of a workman, he would always be ready to undertake any job outside his own calling."

Many of the early studios had a glass roof, and relied on the natural light coming through to provide the right level for filming. The artificial lights they used regularly hissed, and had to be trimmed every minute or so. There were other, more bizarre interruptions, as in the Gaumont studio during the shooting of a scene of *Hindle Wakes*, when a mist crept in and filming had to be abandoned for the day.

The average schedule for a film was four to five weeks. Work in the studios normally began at 9:30 a.m. and finished at 6 p.m., but could sometimes go on into the early hours, making it difficult for the actors and crew to stay fresh. Twice in a week while filming *High Seas*, my father and Lillian Rich worked until four in the morning. With *The Glad Eye*, he and the other actors had to work 12 hours a day and right through the Easter holidays, in order to meet a deadline.

The eminent cinematographer Freddie Young, who began his career in 1926, recalled: "We worked all hours for six or seven days a week, but nobody minded, because we were all too interested in our jobs." But the long hours often took their toll. Clive Brook once worked for 13 hours without a break, during which he went through five fight rehearsals and a scene in which he was strangled. Finally, at 10 p.m., he fainted, was revived by brandy, then worked for another two hours. On another occasion, he was filming two films concurrently, which meant being in front of the camera for 18 hours a day.

In his autobiography, Michael Powell wrote: "You think silent films were silent! The only silent thing about them was the actors." In the studio, there was often excessive noise from the adjacent sets. Since these were silent films, soundproofing was considered unnecessary. Cinemaphotographer Jack Cardiff observed: "The camera made a merry whirring noise and the noise on the set as we worked could be deafening."

Actors had to create their own makeup, using as the basis a saffron yellow Leichner no 5 stick. Under the lights, it had an alarming tendency to melt during filming. Some established stage actors, such as Matheson Lang, Henry Ainley and Milton Rosmer, preferred to use heavy pancake stage makeup; Lang continued to plaster it on in an elaborate style when adopting a heavy disguise in films such as *Mr. Wu*, *A Romance of Old Baghdad* and *The Chinese Bungalow*. To accommodate the film stock being used, which had little sensitivity to the red end of the spectrum, the actors' eyes had to be shaded in a dark red, and the lips brilliant crimson.

"Make up is a serious business," Madeleine Carroll suggested in a magazine article. "Too bright a lipstick tends to look black when on film, but if applied too lightly it becomes white." Gladys Cooper recalled her feelings while filming *Bonnie Prince Charlie* on location in Scotland: "Going out with yellow film make-up on during daylight disgusted me," she said. There was no one on the set to supervise the players, as Chili Bouchier remembered in *Shooting Star*: "We girls changed the colour of our eye-shadow with our moods, and vied with each other to put on the best cupid's-bow mouth. Neither was there a hairdresser, which is why all actresses looked as if they were wearing a bird's nest on their heads."

Not surprisingly, the stars sometimes complained about these tough working conditions, which were contrasted with those to be found elsewhere. My father reported on the efficiency of the UFA studio in Germany after filming there in 1928: "It is the practice of the company to collect their stars at 6.45 a.m., take them to the studio where they are made up by a make-up specialist, dressed by an expert valet (who remains in attendance all day), and are ready to start work at 8.30, continuing with only half-an-hour for lunch until 7 p.m."

In the early postwar years, the stars generally had to work without knowing the story in any detail. After making *The Little Mother* in 1922, my father said: "Even the leading artistes are seldom supplied with a scenario to study, with the result that for the first few days they play in scenes without knowing the story—or why they are making love, or quarrelling, or fighting. If a film is adapted from a novel one can read the book, but usually films are so freely adapted that this is little guide."

The actors were often expected to provide their own clothes, and this created a further problem:

> Usually about a week before work on the filming begins, the artiste is sent a dress chart with orders for the clothes required. But it is extremely difficult to dress a character without knowing something of the story. It is not so difficult for the man as the woman, but how an actress manages to obtain the right clothes when the order vaguely states "Two afternoon gowns, three evening dresses, one walking suit, etc.," I'm sure I do not know.

Mabel Poulton revealed her way of coping with this kind of demand: "I beg, borrow, or steal clothes from patient and long-suffering friends," she explained. "At other times I go to Petticoat Lane and buy things from the market stalls there. I certainly keep my eyes well open and watch what the real article buys while I am there."

This was very much in the spirit of the advice given by Violet Hopson in *Hints for the Cinema Actress*, in which she wrote: "If you are cast for, say, a slum girl's part, get down into the slums for the atmosphere, don't wait around a West End restaurant, for you will never find what you are seeking there. It is only when you have come into direct contact with the types that you will be able to successfully represent them before the camera."

Some of the stars took more trouble than others to create their characters. Moore Marriott, feted throughout the 1920s as Britain's best character actor, went to extreme lengths to achieve authenticity. Before playing an engine driver in *The Flying Scotsman,* he worked for six weeks in the engine room at King's Cross station. For *Turn of the Tide*, based on the lives of Whitby fishermen, he spent a similar period on the trawlers with the men.

It was not unknown for the stars to be helped to find the appropriate emotion for a scene by being told a piece of bad news or, in the case of one actress, having rats released at her feet. They were regularly helped to get in the right mood by having music played as support. According to Michael Balcon, American star Betty Compson "was incapable of registering emotion without the aid of a three-piece orchestra (piano, cello, and violin)." Sometimes original music was provided: for *The Constant Nymph*, Basil Dean commissioned Eugene Goossens to write a suitably atmospheric piece.

Often the musicians were hidden from the actors, so that the music could take them by surprise. Sometimes they were allowed a say in the music to be played. Chili Bouchier remembered the set-up for her early films: "There was a rather seedy little musical trio to play our 'mood music,' and we were allowed to choose our own. I had 'Sweet Sue' for the jolly scenes and 'The Songs My Mother Taught Me' for the sad ones." When Gladys Cooper had trouble producing tears for an emotional scene in *Bonnie Prince Charlie*, Ivor Novello took over on the harmonium and proved more successful in helping his co-star than the studio musicians had been. Some studios even had a permanent orchestra on hand. "I have come to regard Wagner as my patron saint," Novello recalled. "Much of what I personally consider my best screen acting has been achieved under the influence of the 'Fire Music' from *Die Valkyrie* and the 'Liebestod' from *Tristan and Isolde.*"

But it was not always easy for the actors to hold on to the right mood, especially when working on location. Sybil Thorndike recalled playing Jane Shore in a *Tense Moments from Great Plays* episode, and filming on the banks of the Thames, "with people in pleasure boats jeering at me as I died with a cross plastered on my bosom."

Rehearsals for a scene were done in small sections on the studio floor, immediately prior to shooting. The actors had the problem of working on scenes in which titles would later be interspersed between the action, and so interrupt it. In a *Motion Picture Studio* article, my father advised: "Speak your lines, don't lip them, because if one doesn't speak naturally on the 'take,' how can it look natural on the screen?"

To supplement their income, many actors, even relatively well-known ones such as my father, obtained work as extras in crowd scenes in between other roles. It was physically tough going, as Nerina Shute discovered when she signed on for a day at the Gaumont studio where Maurice Elvey was filming the futuristic film *High Treason*. She and 300 extras—"out-of-work actresses, hard-up society people, ambitious young things with private incomes—suffered an endurance test of aching backs, trodden-on feet, and about nine hours of chairless weariness. It was one of the hardest day's work I have ever experienced."

Jack Cardiff, then a child actor, undertook such work with his acting parents between their stage shows. He recalled his experience on *The Loves of Mary, Queen of Scots*:

> The large crowd was paid off from a tiny booth set up in a field. The cashier could only see one person at a time through a narrow window. As the crowd filed past they would be handed a guinea, and move on. What the cashier didn't see was that the extras were re-joining the line, having disguised themselves—changing hats or spectacles or coats—and receiving another guinea! They were making a fortune until they were found out.

When children were recruited, as they were for *Wuthering Heights*, they were paid a shilling each to appear in one scene. But actors initially faced competition from non-actors: some producers used real policemen, until the Actors' Association complained, and the practice was banned.

The actors encountered directors with many different approaches to filming. Thomas Bentley kept a metronome running on the set, claiming its steady ticking kept his mind attuned to the tempo the scene required; if the tempo needed to change, the metronome would be adjusted. Other directors liked to keep up a running commentary through a megaphone, with beginners being told exactly what to do, movement by movement. Cardiff remembered the method of the director of *My Son, My Son*, in which he played a little boy: "What acting I had to do was simplified by the director shouting instructions through a long megaphone: 'Look over to Miss Hopson.... You LOVE her.... SMILE a little.... Take his hand, Violet.... Jackie, look up at her and SMILE.... More, son—that's good.'"

Director Anthony Asquith worked in a similar way: "I sometimes talked to my actors while they were performing," he remembered. "Some of them liked being talked to." It depended, of course, on what was being said, and *how* it was said. In his autobiography *Early Stages*, John Gielgud recalled working with Walter Summers on *Who Is the Man?*, in which he played a dope-fiend sculptor. "I exhausted myself acting in a highly melodramatic manner, inspired in my efforts by a piano and violin which played tear-compelling extracts from popular melodies. The director acted harder than I did, and exhorted me frenziedly through every take, waving his arms and shouting directions above the music being played."

Elissa Landi had a similar experience with a young director while making one of her first silent films. "I remember once, during a very emotional scene, he stood before me, wringing his hands and moaning, tears in his eyes. 'Take me away from this place!' he cried, while I, under the lights and to the whirring of the camera, 'registered' his despair. Curiously enough, I found this manner of being drawn out very effective, and responded readily to his gyrations. He was a very hard taskmaster, and used to wear us out with work, especially on location." But she preferred this approach to the director who showed no interest in the characters. "He deliberately does not tell you how you should *feel*, only the exact mechanics of the scene. 'Now look up, now look down. Look surprised. Hold it! Cut!' Never a reason why one should look up or down or surprised. No appeal to one's imagination."

Directors were not always well-behaved; sometimes they exerted personal pressures. George Pearson fell in love with Betty Balfour, and even offered to leave his wife for her, but she firmly rejected him. Occasionally there were more sinister passions in play off-camera. One leading director, Graham Cutts, had a reputation for promiscuity, fueled by a story that he once took two sisters into his dressing room during a lunch break. In a *Picturegoer* article, he was unusually explicit about his method of handling an actress:

> A director sets himself—dishonest fellow—to charm her gently and lead her deprecatingly, knowing all the time that soon he is going to rap out an order to her as roughly as a sergeant-major to a raw recruit, with the express intention of wounding her feelings in full view of the camera. Like a vivisector, he bares her tenderest feelings first, to make them writhe the more at the first plunge of the knife.

He was not the only director to try to take advantage of a female cast member. Mabel Poulton's unpublished work *Cockles and Caviare: A Story of Theatre and Film Studios* was originally written as a novel, about a poor young actress from the East End. But it's clear that it was actually an autobiography: on the original typescript, housed in the British Film Institute archive, she has changed "Jenny" to "I" in handwriting throughout. She tells the story of a distressing episode with a director she identifies as Thomas Bentley. While she auditioned for a part, he asked her to raise her skirts, insisting the role required her to show her legs. Since the part concerned was that of Little Nell in *The Old Curiosity Shop*, this was a distinctly un–Victorian take on Dickens' heroine. When filming ended, Bentley demanded that she show him some "gratitude." When she resisted his advances, he tried to rape her, and she fought him off. He then told her that her refusal would affect her chances of any future work with him.

The lives of the stars were by no means as glamorous and comfortable as the fan magazines liked to make out. Dorothy Boyd, who appeared in *The Constant Nymph* and Hitchcock's *Easy Virtue*, emphasized the reality: "Although filming is supposed to be full of thrills, it is often just the reverse," she wrote in *Picturegoer*. "The same not very interesting shot has to be taken over and over and *over* again, with a frightful hullabaloo of hammering, whistle-blowing, and bellowing from the technical staff, and domination from the director as the normal state of affairs. Film acting is a job like any other, except that it is fifty times harder, and more precarious and nerve-racking than most."

Filming could be a hazardous occupation in these silent days, especially for those actors who agreed to do their own stunts. Clive Brook's experience while playing the hero in the aptly titled adventure film *Through Fire and Water* was not unusual, if somewhat extreme. During the filming he went through a remarkable series of physical batterings for director Thomas Bentley: he was knocked down, thrown into the docks where he nearly drowned, set upon by the villains and nearly strangled, bound and gagged and left to burn to death, and finally shot.

The physical dangers were not confined to the men. Flora le Breton, while working on *A Gypsy Cavalier*, claimed to have narrowly escaped drowning when a coach in which she was traveling tumbled into the river. A picture of the incident in *The Times* suggested this was a publicity stunt, to which she responded: "Some people may be willing to flirt with death to get their names before the public. I am not." Estelle Brody got a thorough soaking in the Thames during the making of *Kitty*, first having to fall from a punt into the river, and the next day having a bucket of water thrown over her for the following shot. As one onlooker reported: "Her wetting was no fun, for she was shivering and badly chilled as, wrapped in blankets, she was whirled back to the studio and black coffee."

Elissa Landi too remembers a challenging moment:

> During the shooting of this particular picture I had once to sit in (and eventually lie in the bottom of) a water-logged boat, in the open air, for nearly two hours. It was early in March, and I was frozen. "Stick it, old chap!" the director yelled at me from the raft which held him and the cameraman. "Take it like a man!" He himself had stood up to his knees in water for the greater part of the day, so one felt it would have been the merest cowardice not to have stuck it.

The lighting in the studios was another source of danger for the actors, and could cause them severe problems. Where artificial lighting was used, the strong lights could generate an uncomfortable amount of heat. When Diana Cooper acted in *A Glorious Adventure*, an unsuccessful experiment with color, the heat turned her face and arms a shade of lobster, and her eyes smarted so fiercely she was unable to sleep at night.

Actors and technicians had to be very careful not to look directly into the arc lights, because when the glass was removed, the ultra-violet rays could cause temporary blindness. This was known as Klieg Eye, a particularly painful form of conjunctivitis, in which the moisture in the eye would dry up, and it would seem as if you would never see properly again. It was not an uncommon affliction—my father was one of the victims—and it was for this reason that Mabel Poulton insured her eyes, described in one paper as "those precious orbs that irradiate the screen," for as much as £30,000.

According to *Picture Show*, "John Stuart has no fears, and is willing to take every risk for ultimate success." He was certainly keen not to be typecast as the conventional romantic hero. "I like a part with plenty of action in it," he explained. "Walking around and looking pretty does not appeal to me in the least. The worst of having gained a reputation as a screen lover is that producers sometimes think I ought not to be given anything in the nature of rough stuff."

He certainly got his wish: during his first decade of filming, he was involved in a great deal of "rough stuff," all of which demanded courage, stamina and no little skill. Rarely using a double, he had at various times to demonstrate an ability to swim, fence, play cricket and football, and drive a motorboat, a racing car, and a coach and pair. As a *Foyer* magazine reporter pointed out: "John Stuart is by no means a weakling: he has a fine physique and is quite as capable of undertaking roles of action as any other actor."

8

Writers, Screenplays, Titles

"There is hardly a novelist today, however brilliant, who is capable of writing a good film story."—Noël Coward

At the start of the First World War, it was the fashion for movie producers to draw on well-known plays or recently published novels. Immediately after the war, the majority of films still had similar origins, and few original screenplays were devised. Of the 166 features shown in 1919, no less than 135 were based on plays or novels. Producers believed they stood a better chance of success using stories that had already achieved popularity, preferably recently. Sidney Gilliat, who began his career writing the titles for Hitchcock's *Champagne*, said, "Of the stories that were bought, made or unmade, most of them were old ideas such as Victorian melodramas."

One commentator warned that producers should "direct their attention to discovering a few more authors with brains and imagination who can write a good scenario. Unless something is done, the majority of the new British stars of the shadow stage will be out of work." Critic Langford Reed wrote: "I almost believe that some producers would have preferred adaptations of the Telephone Directory to the first original work, by an unknown author, that could have been offered them."

Garnett Weston was an Englishman with considerable experience as a writer in Hollywood. As production editor for Famous Players–Lasky, he also supervised many scripts by well-known writers. After a brief spell observing the scene in England, Weston wrote a fierce article for *Picturegoer*, in which he reported on his efforts to write scenarios for British pictures that were rebuffed by people with the attitudes he encountered:

My first shock came when I read the stock of material on hand for stories. A collection of old-fashioned, hackneyed plots, poorly contrived, badly written, uninspired and dreary tripe, was turned over to me for my opinion. Am I to believe that this wretched garbage represented the cream of English stories available for the screen?

I tried to infuse something of the modern trend of drama into my scripts. I failed, because I had to do with minds which mistook melodrama for drama, and drama for slush. Any attempt at a new psychology was looked upon with suspicion. People didn't act in that way—they always act in the same way. That is what I was told, and I suppose my informants were right—they always act in the same way—in English pictures. That is what is the matter with them.

Weston argued that the typical English producer goes to see the American pictures that have crowds queuing round the block, but learns nothing from them:

He comes back and criticises them with the stubborn English mind that refuses to change or bend. The youth of them, swift life, the new and vital and joyous things will pass him by. He goes back and makes more pictures from stories dug up out of the churchyards, where the heroes have side-whiskers and the heroines have hooped skirts. With these he fondly imagines that a new age will be beguiled and amused.

He also pointed out that, despite the passing of the Cinematograph Act in 1927 which gave the British industry such a great opportunity, it was the Americans who were making the films that were a hit with audiences. He concluded: "If the English picture is to get anywhere except oblivion, it must have a new deal all round. It wants new brains at the head of its story departments, and brilliance in place of dullness and mediocrity in the men responsible for selecting and preparing its output."

In 1920, Walter West offered £500 to "any author who can supply him with an original story suited to his requirements for filming." Disappointed at the resulting submissions, he too had to rely mainly on plays, novels and short stories, both classic and modern. But this certainly didn't guarantee quality. Playwright Reginald Berkeley provided the story for *Dawn*, the film about Edith Cavell starring Sybil Thorndike, and later wrote screenplays. At the end of the decade, he observed: "The great fault of British films is want of story, which will not be supplied by purchasing great British books and plays and then butchering them. The film industry has a bad name among serious writers, because they have seen so much good work bowdlerised and turned into shoddy."

There is no doubt that in that era, the quality of British scenarios was extremely poor, and lacked the universal appeal of those created in Hollywood. Original screenplays were comparatively thin on the ground in Britain, and often much inferior to adaptations. They were not an attractive proposition for writers: The pay was low, and the writers had little control over how their screenplay was used.

Noël Coward gave a more fundamental reason for declining such work: "I want to write words, not stage directions. As a dramatist, dialogue and its psychology are practically my sole concern." He observed that film writing "is an art in itself," adding that novelists "tear their hair out" when they see their work being cut or changed beyond recognition. "They don't understand the art of pictorial writing," he told the journalist Nerina Shute. "They deal with words, while we deal with situations. There is hardly a novelist today, however brilliant, who is capable of writing a good film story."

Reginald Berkeley suggested the original writer should play a more active role, that he should be taught film technique, and then be present in the studio throughout the film's production, to work collaboratively with the director. "He should have the power to make suggestions, just as the writer for the stage is entitled to give his opinion to the director during the production of a play as to the manner in which this or that detail is brought out."

In this respect, R.H. Mottram was treated unusually well during the making of *Roses of Picardy*. "Many an author, after selling his rights, hears no more about the matter," he said. "But the Gaumont company were kind enough to grant me every facility to see the principals and the scenery, and to be present at rehearsals. The scenario written by the Gaumont editor contains a larger proportion of my words than is usual with most authors."

Certain directors took on the task of writing the screenplay themselves. Denison Clift did this for *The Loves of Mary, Queen of Scots*; Arthur Rooke wrote *A Sporting Double*; Victor Saville co-wrote *Mademoiselle from Armentières*. Others also became involved. Fred V. Merrick was the younger brother of Maurice Elvey, for whom he produced a few films. With actor John Longden, he co-wrote Elvey's film *Mademoiselle Parley Voo*, and with others he worked on the story of *Roses of Picardy*.

Women were often allotted the screenplay assignments, though not in such numbers as they were in Hollywood, where up until 1925 around a quarter of the films were written by women. In Hollywood, one of the best-known and most respected was Anita Loos, author of the best-selling novel *Gentlemen Prefer Blondes*. She gave sound practical advice to aspiring screenwriters, such as: "Keep the star in at least 50 per cent of the scenes and keep the part sympathetic, for film favorites usually balk at acting a despicable character." Elinor Glyn, who published a series of books on writing, offered similar advice: "Keep Your Hero Clean. He may err—but his mistake should be the result of carelessness, thoughtlessness, mischievousness, or recklessness, but never the result of direct intent."

One of the busiest writers in Britain was Lydia Hayward (*His Grace Gives Notice*, *We Women*, *London Love*), who wrote more than 30 screenplays, among them the popular adaptations of W.W. Jacobs' short stories, including his famous horror story "The Monkey's Paw." Mabel Winifred Knowles, using the pen name May Wynne (*The Little Mother*), authored over 200 books, mostly girls' adventure stories or tales carrying a morally improving message. Lucita Squier (*A Daughter of Love*) was an American who had recently been to Russia to make a film for the Quakers about war relief. She subsequently traveled around the USSR with her Communist husband, and in between her travels worked for various British film companies as continuity girl or writer.

Plays were generally adapted with little regard for the essential difference between stage and screen. With many directors and producers coming from the theater, all too many films were simply celluloid records of stage productions. A typical example was Walter West's wartime version of *The Merchant of Venice*, which had Matheson Lang as Shylock. It was essentially a photograph of the West End production, with the same cast.

Shakespeare's plays were rarely filmed during the 1920s, and then not in their entirety. *Macbeth* and *The Merchant of Venice* were among those featured in the series *Tense Moments from Great Plays*, with Sybil Thorndike playing Lady Macbeth and Portia. A heavily condensed version of *The Taming of the Shrew* narrowed the play down to the central story, with Dacia Dean as Katharina and Lauderdale Maitland making a somewhat portly Petruchio. There was also a short of *Julius Caesar* featuring only Basil Gill as Brutus and Malcolm Keen as Cassius; and a nine-minute scene from *The Merchant of Venice*, with Lewis Casson playing Shylock. J.M. Barrie made a speech in Stratford, mocking the idea that Shakespeare could be a candidate for worthwhile adaptation.

There was the occasional foray into other stage classics, such as *She Stoops to*

Conquer and *The School for Scandal*. Other classics included Tennyson's *Becket*, with the leading stage actor Frank Benson in the title-role; Bulwer-Lytton's *Money*, starring Henry Ainley; Oscar Wilde's *A Woman of No Importance* and *Lady Windermere's Fan*, directed respectively by Denison Clift and Fred Paul; and Arthur Wing Pinero's *The Magistrate* and *His House in Order*, the latter starring Tallulah Bankhead.

Recent or current West End hits were also exploited, having the great advantage of ready-made characters and plots, with existing publicity and press reviews available to draw on. Plays that were filmed included Arnold Ridley's popular hit *The Ghost Train*, Oscar Ashe's long-running wartime musical spectacle *Chu Chin Chow*, and A.A. Milne's light comedy *Mr. Pim Passes By*. There was also *The Rat* and its two sequels, based on plays co-written by Ivor Novello and Constance Collier under the pseudonym David L'Estrange.

Several leading writers of the day were courted during the 1920s by British producers, but many of them saw film as a threat to their work. J.M. Barrie was among those approached. But in Britain, only his plays *The Twelve-Pound Look* and *The Will*, both starring Milton Rosmer, were filmed. American producers too were in pursuit of the best talent. Famous Players–Lasky, which had a base in London, was in negotiation with several leading novelists and playwrights, hoping they would come up with "original stories written specifically for the screen, with special consideration for its requirements."

Another playwright on the American list was Noël Coward, whose subversive plays *The Vortex*, *Hay Fever* and *Easy Virtue* were creating a sensation in the West End. But Michael Balcon got in first, buying the film rights to *Easy Virtue* and announcing: "The future of the cinema lies in the hands of the young writers, and Mr. Coward, as one of the most brilliant of them all, is a notable newcomer to British films." He saw this as a breakthrough moment for the industry: "British production has been reproached with making films on American lines, with having failed to develop a national characteristic as the Germans have done. *Easy Virtue* is the answer: a country-house play with county people."

Although Hitchcock was the director, the film stands up poorly today. There are a handful of neat Hitchcockian camera tricks, but the story is disjointed and without humor; the first half has nothing to do with the play, and the acting is often stiff and unconvincing. The film highlights the problem for the silent cinema when working with stage plays, but especially when the dialogue is crucial, as it was in the case of Coward. The titles are conspicuous by their banality, and lack the playwright's famous wit and sparkle. As Balcon later observed, there was an obvious and fundamental paradox to adapting plays for the screen: "It was doubly a mistake to lean on stage plays, because we were making silent films, so the plays were deprived of their very essence, the words!"

Much the same problem faced Adrian Brunel when he directed *The Vortex*. Coward's brilliant, acerbic dialogue was largely lost, the titles being facetious rather than witty, while visually the film's stage origins were all too apparent. The sharpness of the original was considerably sweetened for fear of the censor, so that the young hero's (Ivor Novello) plea, which was effectively "Mother, will you give up lovers if I give up drugs?" became "Mummy, will you give up going to teas and dances if I give up cigarettes and aspirins?"

Irish playwrights were also in demand. Sean O'Casey turned down an offer to write the dialogue for the last reels of the 1929 version of *The Informer*, but in the same year he sold the film rights to his play *Juno and the Paycock*, which became Hitchcock's second sound film after *Blackmail*. He also talked to Hitchcock about writing a screenplay set in Hyde Park in the course of a single day, but the collaboration collapsed; instead he wrote it as a play, *Within the Gates*.

Bernard Shaw was an early enthusiast for silent films, an interest which arose out of his passion for photography. Recognizing early the potential of the medium, in 1914 he suggested films would "form the mind of England. The national conscience, the national ideals and tests of conduct, will be those of the film." He believed films would have even more impact than the invention of printing: because films told their stories to everyone, including the illiterate, so that "the cinema is going to produce effects that all the cheap books in the world could never produce."

But he refused to allow silent films to be made of most of his plays, declining to become what he called "a dumb dramatist." He made two exceptions. One was *Pygmalion*, which he offered to the producer G.B. Samuelson, knowing full well the impossibility of creating a story centering on a matter of correct speech in a silent medium. And when Eisenstein, whom he greatly admired, visited London in 1929, he offered him the film rights for *Arms and the Man*.

Probably the busiest of all the writers was Eliot Stannard, one of the first to theorize about film writing and to discuss what it takes to be a screenwriter. Stannard started in films in 1915 by acting in and writing *Grip*, based on one of his mother's novels. Journalist Nerina Shute described him as "a gentleman with excitable eyebrows, an elastic tongue, and a remarkable brain." In his autobiography, Michael Powell recalled "a dark, wildly handsome, untidy man, with Fleet Street Genius written all over him."

A rare example of a university graduate entering films, he put his ideas into a series of articles headed "The Art of Kinematography" and the pamphlet "Writing Screen Plays." Unlike most screenwriters, he knew his way around films, having worked variously as actor, set manager, art expert, film cutter, script editor and producer. He had already written 80 screenplays before writing eight for Hitchcock, and co-writing two others, and was obviously an important influence on the young director as he learned his craft. He also wrote four films in which my father starred: *The Mistletoe Bough*, *The School for Scandal*, *Curfew Shall Not Ring Tonight* and *Sailors Don't Care*.

By far the majority of his screenplays were adaptations of novels, plays, historical or biographical subjects, even poems, and in one instance the celebrated painting "The Laughing Cavalier." He adapted works by Fielding, Dickens, Emily Brontë and Shakespeare, as well as plays by popular writers of the day such as Galsworthy, Coward and Novello. Sidney Gilliat, then writing titles, recalled: "If something went wrong on a picture, Stannard was called up—like Shakespeare would have been—and asked to come in and pep up the scenes a bit." Ivor Montagu recalled:

"His method, which caused me wonderment, was to sit down and tap the scenario straight on to the typewriter as he thought of it, without change or erasure."

Whatever the material, Stannard was clear that film needed a particular method of communicating stories and emotions, that there should be a clear theme, and that every scene should relate to it. He was critical of the screenplays that had come his way when he was a script editor: "They were nearly all composed of a series of exciting incidents and nothing else; melodramatic, improbable, and often impossible situations followed each other in bewildering rapidity, but I sought in vain for any central motive or theme upon which the stories should have been constructed."

Stannard is now seen as the patron saint of screenwriters. It's fortunate that he worked so often with Hitchcock, most of whose films have been preserved. The majority of the 116 films for which he is credited as writer have, like so many others of the period, vanished.

There was a considerable debate in these years about the use and value of titles, sometimes known as intertitles. For both directors and actors, the matter was a vexing one. Directors relied on them to explain elements of the action or to fill in the background to the story, which inevitably restricted the way they could shape the film. Some films had no dialogue titles at all, but merely explanatory ones. They were often clumsily used, with individual scenes being preceded by plot summaries that inevitably held up the action. "When is a motion picture not a picture?" asked a *Bioscope* writer. "The answer is when it's a collection of sub-titles."

Michael Balcon wrote, "Dialogue scenes were carefully photographed to enable the editor to cut away from the actor to his 'spoken title' at the moment he opened his mouth to speak, cutting back to his image just as he finished. Good editors could obtain the illusion of actual speech by this device." But many of the titles were naïve or over-simplified, or just plain silly, occasionally causing mirth among the audience. Sometimes the meaning was lost in translation, as in the celebrated case of an American Western. A gunman walked into a saloon and said: "Gimme a shot of red-eye." When the film was shown in France, the title came out as "Donnez-moi un Dubonnet, s'il vous plaît."

Bioscope warned: "Too many companies are using superfluous sub-titles. Their primary purpose should be to cover the necessary breaks, and explain that which is incapable of being shown in action. Every sub-title halts the action even when it does not confuse the mind…. Directors and scenario editors need to develop a greater sense of visual narrative."

Maurice Elvey remembered how the use of titles affected a director's reputation. "You didn't use the sub-title if you could help it, as it was the sign of being a very poor director." Ivor Montagu, who was hired by Hitchcock to re-write the art deco–style titles for *The Lodger*, which had been designed by Edward McKnight Kauffer, criticized one film for the verbosity of its titles, and its patronizing attitude to its audience. "Moods, emotional reactions, moral judgements which are clearly implied in the action and acting, are none the less iterated by written words, presumably in the belief that cinema-goers are below the normal level of intelligence, and will otherwise miss them."

Some directors and writers heeded this advice: They began to explore new conventions, and find ways of telling the story with the minimum of titles, as was the fashion in the Russian cinema. They used them in novel ways, such as splitting them into several shots, adding decorative illustrations, or superimposing them on the pictures. Some films had no titles at all; the camera told the story. One example was director Henry Edwards' *Lily of the Alley*; another was Murnau's *The Last Laugh*, which had just one title. But Montagu cautioned against this practice, suggesting: "The eye-strain of looking at moving visual images on a large screen is so considerable that one must have titles, if only to give the spectator the relief and interruption of the static breaks they form."

9

The Film Press
and the Film Society

"The Society is a communist front organisation, bent on introducing riot and revolution."—George Atkinson, *Daily Express*

Several fan magazines, some of which started as house magazines of the production companies, existed to encourage the star worship that gradually developed during the 1920s. The first fan magazine, "an illustrated weekly for lovers of moving pictures" called *The Pictures*, had been published in 1911. Lavishly illustrated with shots from the latest films, it promised to be "brimful of interest, all thrilling" and to offer its readers "the quintessence of sensationalism."

The Pictures was later absorbed into *Picturegoer*, just one of the many publications that flourished in the 1920s. Others were *Picture Show, Girls' Cinema, Cinema World Illustrated, Film Flashes, Photo Bits and Cinema Star* and *Eve's and Everybody's Film Review*, advertised as "a weekly survey of modes and manners." The magazines' pages were filled with gossip, plot summaries, readers' letters, life stories and glamorous photos of the stars, with tales of their hobbies, likes and dislikes. They also contained the stories on which current films were based.

The early issues of *Picturegoer* ran striking full-color paintings of the stars on the cover, until it became the norm to use photographs. Since the majority of readers were known to be women, there were also fashion notes, homemaking tips, beauty hints and dress patterns, alongside advertisements for perms, lingerie, silk stockings, makeup, vanishing cream, soap powder and household appliances. A sachet of Gladys Cooper's "own" shampoo was given away with one issue.

Other stars contributed articles: Edna Best wrote on beauty aids, Mabel Poulton offered readers tennis tips. Many of the early interviews with the stars were bland, cozy and excruciatingly deferential, effectively little more than promotional puffs for their subjects. But later, more spice was added, and some stars, including Mabel Poulton and my father, used the interview as a platform for airing criticisms of directors or of the film companies. Sometimes a journalist was allowed inside the studio to watch a film being made.

During its early years, *Picturegoer* gave a lot of space to Hollywood stars and fashions, but it also published interviews with British stars and articles on British films, and organized readers' polls and talent competitions designed to identify the most popular stars. It gradually widened its view to look at the European cinema, and to discuss film technique. Once the editor's role fell to the acerbic critic P.L. Mannock, the reviews became more critical, and discussion of foreign films more common.

Catering to a more precisely targeted audience was *Girls' Cinema*, which launched in 1920 as a "New Paper for Girls!" with a feature on "Twelve Famous Love Scenes." It published a commemorative issue devoted to Rudolph Valentino a year after the screen idol's death. *Picture Show* concentrated more on Hollywood, with features such as "Fashions and Fancies in Filmland," a regular "Letter from Hollywood" by the British-born writer Elinor Glyn, readers' questions and answers, and pictures of the stars in their latest films. A pull-out Art Supplement provided coverage of British stars and their films, running chatty articles such as "Pleasing the Modern Man" by Fay Compton, regular features on "Gossip About British Players," and "New British Productions," and short stories and serials by popular writers such as Edgar Wallace.

Like other magazines, *Picture Show* printed letters from readers debating topical issues and the rival merits of the stars. It even published the occasional poem, such as this patriotic verse penned by one of Betty Balfour's fans:

> "Betty Balfour, the Cockney Queen
> Is Britain's hope on the movie screen
> The Yanks may copy St. Paul's great dome
> But only Betty can show us our home."

Between 1914 and 1930, there were some 20 trade papers in existence. Of these, the most important were *Bioscope*, *Kinematograph Weekly* (later known as *Kine Weekly*) and *Cinema* (later *Today's Cinema*), all founded before the First World War. These papers offered news about the industry, but also gossip about the stars and their directors, film fashion news, interviews and reviews, and reports on the latest developments in the British studios. The gossip was relatively harmless, the interviews with the stars generally bland, although the tone became sharper and less reverential as the decade progressed.

Although they published the occasional serious article on film, these papers generally treated it purely as entertainment. At first they were more concerned with publicizing films than offering objective criticism, tending to praise British films in blatantly patriotic and wildly exaggerated terms. Later *Bioscope* became more objective and independent-minded. *Kine Weekly* also adopted a more critical attitude: Its studio correspondent P.L. Mannock, who also wrote screenplays, was especially stringent in his weekly column about the quality of the scripts. A more recent trade paper was *Film Weekly*, aimed at a slightly more sophisticated and knowledgeable readership. It ran solid reviews of the new releases, and even offered readers the chance to win a £500 acting scholarship, bringing them six months' training at Elstree Studios.

Its policy was to adopt a more critical stance toward the stars. One of *Film Weekly*'s sharper writers was the young Nerina Shute, later a biographer and novelist, and a colorful film critic with the *Sunday Referee*. In 1928, at age 20, she became the magazine's studio correspondent, which in practice meant its gossip columnist.

Born in Wales and brought up in her teenage years in Hollywood, she was openly lesbian, moved in bohemian circles, and was a passionate advocate of free love.

Her brilliant pen-portraits of the stars made her both feared and respected, and she became famous for her "impertinent pen" and withering put-downs. She once compared the face of the character actress Marie Ault to "an unappetising loaf of bread"; another time she described Madeleine Carroll as a "ruthless Madonna." Director E.A. Dupont was so enraged by critical comments that Cedric Belfrage had written about him in *Film Weekly* that he banned Shute from the studio, simply because she was from the same paper; she later crept back in disguise. Hitchcock took the same action against her, only for her to disguise herself as an extra on the set, where she continued to report the gossip.

As films became more popular, so the mainstream papers and weekly and monthly periodicals started to review films and appoint specialist critics. A contributor to *Bioscope* in 1924 complained about the lack of coverage of film compared to that given to art and the theater: "New films are dismissed in half a dozen inches of space, containing merely the barest details, not always accurate, of the week's releases." Looking back at the mid–1920s, Ivor Montagu, one of the first real intellectuals of the cinema, recalled in his autobiography *Youngest Son*, "It was a grievance amongst us enthusiasts for film art that the quality press in general ignored the cinema," he complained. "There was no counterweight to the cheap gossip and rehashed publicity material that so often masqueraded as film journalism."

Several papers had already appointed film critics before the 1920s, including in 1919 the *Daily News*, the *Evening News* and the *Westminster Gazette*. From 1921, the critic of the *Evening News* was Jympson Harman, who also acted as script consultant for director Herbert Wilcox. *The Daily News*, later the *News Chronicle*, appointed E.A. Baughan, who was satirized by Shaw as the critic Vaughan in *Fanny's First Play*. *The Times* began coverage in 1920, and by 1925 was running a regular feature, "Film World." The *Daily Express* had George Atkinson, and the *Illustrated London News* Michael Orme, the pseudonym for the actress-writer Alice Augusta Greeven.

One especially critical reviewer was Walter Mycroft, from 1922 the *Evening Standard*'s man. Later a director and prolific producer, in 1928 he was appointed head of the scenario department, and then director of production, at British International Pictures. He provided the story for Hitchcock's *Champagne* and co-wrote the 1930 film anthology *Elstree Calling*. As a critic he had a distinctly international outlook, championing in particular the German cinema. A stern critic of American films, he accused them of frivolity, vulgarity and "a false outlook on life."

Ivor Montagu also had strong views on foreign cinema. The critic Penelope Houston later referred to him as "an inspired odd-job man," but he was considerably more than that. The son of a banker, thickset and sturdy, he was a socialist and then a Communist—and allegedly an agent for Stalin. In 1925, he became the *Observer*'s film critic, but was quickly disillusioned when he was restricted to two or three paragraphs per piece. When the paper cut heavily his article about the controversial American film *The Big Parade*, he resigned in frustration and suggested Angus MacPhail as his successor. He moved on to the *Sunday Times*, and later wrote for the *New Statesman*.

Montagu and Adrian Brunel were working in a Soho side street in what he described as "a sort of film knackers business—repairing and re-beautifying ravaged pictures," and doing post-production work on completed films. He provided this service for *The Lodger*, and then acted as editor on two of Hitchcock's other silent films, *Downhill* and *Easy Virtue*. In 1929, his translation of the book *On Film Technique*, by the Russian director Vsevolod Pudovkin, helped promote ideas about editing and screenplay construction, which had a strong influence on Hitchcock. His career also included writing screenplays, film criticism and directing, notably three short comedy films for actress Elsa Lanchester.

C.A. Lejeune began on the *Manchester Guardian* as a music critic writing about opera, but then switched to cinema, and from 1922 wrote a weekly column, "The Week on the Screen." A witty writer, she tended to look down on popular films, preferring to champion the more literary kind. In 1927, she decided that "the injury which the British studios have drawn to themselves by praise of bad and inefficient workmanship is almost incalculable. In the name of patriotism they have misled the public over so many trivial British pictures that the few good ones have been sceptically received."

A friend of Hitchcock, she cited his *The Ring* and *The Lodger* as rare examples of good British films. Keen to introduce the British public to the work of foreign directors, she wrote extensively about Swedish, German and French films. She compared the British industry unfavorably with the European cinema: "It simply has nothing, neither character nor courage, neither commercial success, skill, nor artistic sense. It has no big men and no ideas." One of the first female film critics worldwide, she moved in 1928 to the *Observer*, where she remained for over 30 years.

Another early female critic, and one of the most prolific and influential, was Iris Barry. She was film editor on the *Daily Mail*, which in 1925 had the highest circulation of all the newspapers. She also contributed to *Vogue* and wrote in a rather different manner for the weekly highbrow *Spectator*; its editor, the writer John St. Loe Strachey, had hired her "to do something about cinema." Her taste was catholic, her discrimination sharp. She asked pointedly: "Why must all American movie mothers be white-haired and tottery, even though their children are mere tots? Does the menopause not operate in the US?" But she also stated, "We owe the present vitality of the cinema as a whole to the Americans … their best films are the best in the world." She claimed wild horses would not drag her to a British picture if an American one was on offer.

Other critics, hired to write about theater, branched out from their original brief to cover film. Sydney Carroll, formerly theater critic of the *Sunday Times*, began to review films for the paper in 1925. His successor James Agate, at first skeptical about cinema, nevertheless wrote about it occasionally, and eventually became film critic of the *Tatler*. But the low status of film criticism at the time was reflected in the Critics' Circle set-up, when the entry into its ranks of film critics in the late 1920s provoked a great deal of snobbery among the theater and music critics.

The problem with many of the film critics was their tendency to oversell British films and directors, especially in relation to the American output. Typically, and absurdly, the *Pall Mall Gazette* critic suggested that George Pearson's *Love, Life and*

Laughter "surpasses even the genius of D.W. Griffith." According to Montagu, there was often pressure on critics to praise films for which renters were taking advertising space in their papers, with money or hampers at Christmas being provided to ease their way. "The opportunities for corruption and venality were not only rife but hard to resist," he reflected later. "With experience, quite a lot of critics begin to learn which side their bread is buttered on." When Montagu became a critic himself, he realized "how difficult it was, be you ever so honest in desire, to treat equally the films shown in Theatre A, where you would be provided afterwards with champagne and a caviar sandwich buffet, and those at Theatre B, whence I had been thrown out for complaining about having been invited on a press ticket and then made to stand at the back."

Literary magazines also gradually got into the cinema act, the genteel monthly *London Mercury* being one of the first to publish a film column. Of the weeklies, *Bystander* ran a column from 1923 headed "Picture Plays as Seen from the Stalls." One great film enthusiast was the young Graham Greene, who as a student appointed himself film critic of the magazine *Oxford Outlook* (of which he happened to be the editor). Later in the decade, when he was a sub-editor on *The Times*, he wrote several pieces on cinema for the paper.

Greene later described himself as a passionate reader of *Close Up*, a polemical monthly published between 1927 and 1933 from a chateau in Switzerland. It had a small circulation but considerable influence in Britain and elsewhere, catering to the growing intellectual audience for film, to those filmgoers who were hostile to the mainstream output, and who saw cinema as an art form rather than just entertainment. The magazine had a notably international outlook, reporting on developments in Europe, France, Germany and Russia. Major literary and cinematic figures— including Eisenstein—contributed articles on the latest film theory.

Close Up was vigorously opposed to the standard commercial films, its editor Kenneth Macpherson arguing that British films were timid and over-praised. In his first editorial, he wrote, "There is a minority of several million people to whom these films are tiresome, a minority that loves the film, but has too much perception, too much intelligence, to swallow the often dismal and paltry stories and acting set up week by week before it on the screen. This minority has got to have films it can enjoy, films with psychology, soundness, intelligence."

The magazine attacked the optimistic view of the quality of British films. One critic, Oswell Blakeston, was especially hard on British directors, writing that they "have no more pretensions to be called film directors than they have to be called plumbers or clothes dealers." The magazine was skeptical about the chances of a revival in the industry after the passing of the 1927 Cinematograph Act. It mounted a crusade against film censorship, and was loftily dismissive of the average filmgoer's taste: "Really the Englishman can only be roused to enthusiasm on the football field," it announced. "One doesn't mind that, but in the face of it one does ask, why attempt art?"

Like Graham Greene, many of the film enthusiasts who subscribed to *Close Up* were young, university-educated, and from a middle- or upper-middle-class background. They were also likely to be members of the Film Society, a pioneering body set up in 1925 to cater to the growing interest in the European film scene among the more intellectually inclined filmgoers.

Its origins lay in a chance meeting between Ivor Montagu and actor Hugh Miller. Montagu had been in Berlin with a commission to write about the German cinema for *The Times*, while Miller had been filming *Venetian Lovers* alongside my father in Munich. The two men met in the corridor of the Dover-to-London train, and by the time they reached Charing Cross they had agreed on a plan to form a film society, to screen worthwhile films which could not get a commercial showing in Britain. They took as their model the Stage Society, established in London in 1899, which had staged unknown and often controversial works by Shaw, Ibsen, Strindberg, Cocteau and Pirandello, plays that were thought unlikely to get a commercial production.

At the time, a group of like-minded film people were holding regular social evenings, which they called "hate parties." After viewing a film, they would congregate in Adrian Brunel's London flat and discuss people and situations, who they were actually making films for, and what aspects of the British film industry they hated most. The participants included Montagu, Balcon, Wilcox and Saville, actors such as Miles Mander, and others on the fringes of the film world. They favored the idea of a film society and agreed to give it their backing.

The society's first prospectus stated that it had been founded "in the belief that there are in this country large numbers of people who regard the cinema with the liveliest of interest, and who would welcome an opportunity seldom afforded to the general public of witnessing films of intrinsic merit, whether old or new." It aimed to show films "which represent the work which has been done, or is being done experimentally, in various parts of the world. It is in the nature of such films that they are (it is said) commercially unsuitable for this country."

The society was set up with the help of the calm and capable Iris Barry, who together with Walter Mycroft was a member of its first council, and championed the society in print. A collection of artists, scientists and writers became founder members and subscribed a £1 share guarantee to help launch it: Augustus John, John Maynard Keynes, Roger Fry, J.B.S. Haldane, Julian Huxley, H.G. Wells (who insisted on being described as "a man of letters" rather than a "writer") and Bernard Shaw. There was also crucial support from within the film world, from Balcon, Asquith, Saville, Brunel and Pearson, from the designer McKnight Kauffer, and from several theater people, notably Ellen Terry, Edith Craig, Ben Webster, Ivor Novello and the young John Gielgud. One surprising opponent was C.A. Lejeune, who argued that the society could be of no use unless it was open to the public.

The society's first private screening took place one afternoon in October 1925. The founding group was determined to secure the best West End cinema, the best orchestra and the best music. With the help of Sidney Bernstein, owner of a small chain of cinemas, they were able to use the recently renovated New Gallery Kinema in Regent Street. The screening attracted 900 members and their guests, mainly from the bohemian world, including many young men from Chelsea and Bloomsbury who, according to one report, "sported beards, while the young women wore homespun cloaks."

The main feature was *Waxworks*, a German expressionist film directed by Paul Leni and starring the leading German actors Emil Jannings, Conrad Veidt and Werner Krauss. Thereafter the programs were screened once a month on Sunday afternoons. They usually included four or five films, a mixture of experimental works, revivals of old favorites and new foreign art films which had no other means of distribution. Visiting Paris and Berlin, Montagu and Mycroft obtained prints of the best of the European feature films, then re-titled and edited them for the home audience.

As a membership society, the Film Society was allowed to show films not yet classified by the British Board of Film Censors (BBFC). This was a very authoritarian body: it banned the German film *The Cabinet of Dr. Caligari* because of its frightening content, and also the works of Eisenstein and Pudovkin, including *Battleship Potemkin*, *Mother* and *October*, which were seen as subversive propaganda. While audiences included Virginia Woolf and Clive Bell from the Bloomsbury Group, according to Iris Barry the programs did not appeal exclusively to bohemians and left-wing intellectuals: They could, she said, attract "as many Daimlers to the square yard as any opera or play."

In its early period, the society was especially interested in showing German films, then considered especially admirable for their expressionist qualities: their decor, imaginative use of lighting and stylized performances. There was also interest in the French avant-garde cinema. Later in the decade, attention turned to the Russian cinema, which ten years after the 1917 revolution was flourishing. Before 1926, few people in Britain knew of its existence, since widespread opposition to the Bolshevik regime kept its films out of the cinemas. Certain sections of the press claimed the society had been formed "to communise the country." But when Sergei Eisenstein's *Battleship Potemkin* caused a sensation in Germany, it prompted the celebrated producer Max Reinhardt to state: "I am willing to admit the stage will have to give way to the cinema."

This event in turn created an interest in Britain, especially in the editing and the technique of montage employed so boldly by Eisenstein, Pudovkin and Dovzhenko. Eisenstein cited D.W. Griffith as an influence, but also Charles Dickens, whom he credited as the true inventor of film montage. Here Montagu was one of the prime movers. In 1929, after a visit to the Soviet Union, he was instrumental in bringing Pudovkin and Eisenstein to London, to give a series of lectures on film as guests of the Film Society. Eisenstein spoke excellent English and his lectures, held in Foyle's bookshop, were a huge success. They proved to be a significant influence on the later British documentary movement.

During his time in London, Eisenstein attended a screening of *Battleship Potemkin*, which still could not be shown to the general public. The film had been banned by the fiercely anti–Semitic home secretary William Joynson-Hicks, who disliked films, and especially those of a radical nature. It was refused a certificate by the BBFC, which feared it would stir up revolutionary fervor. Remarkably, it was to remain banned until 1954.

This censorship provoked the scorn of Bernard Shaw, who observed: "The film's suppression is an undisguised stroke of class censorship, and utterly indefensible."

But perhaps the ban was not quite as absurd as it seems. Some months before, at a showing of Pudovkin's *The End of St. Petersburg*, a section of the audience was so roused by the caption "All Power to the Soviet" that they broke into "The Red Marching Song," and continued singing it during the national anthem. The Soviet films were considered controversial, and provoked protests and questions in the House of Commons. *Daily Express* critic George Atkinson even suggested the society was a Communist front organization, bent on introducing "riot and revolution." It was an absurd accusation; the paper had to print a retraction and pay costs.

The Film Society was responsible for the first screenings in Britain of films now regarded as classics, including *Battleship Potemkin*, *Greed*, *Nosferatu*, *Mother* and *La Passion de Jeanne d'Arc*, as well as early films by Jean Renoir, Ernest Lubitsch and Fritz Lang. It continued its monthly screenings until the Second World War, when it was decided to close it down. By then, there were film institutes and libraries, film archives, film festivals and serious press criticism of film. The society had laid the foundation for the gradual programming of art films in commercial cinemas, and for the film society movement, which began in 1929 in several British cities.

The Publicity Machine

"England is the land where publicity is apparently considered vulgar, unnecessary, and not worth the expense."—Nerina Shute in *Film Weekly*, 1929

An article in *Film Weekly* under the heading "Personalities Going to Waste" asked: "Is bad salesmanship the root cause of the British film industry's position of inferiority in regard to America? Why is it that British artists and British films receive such poor publicity, and the former have to go to America to become world famous?"

British efforts compared poorly with the highly organized publicity machine favored by the Hollywood studios. During the 1920s, there was growing criticism in both the trade and national press about the failure of British film companies to exploit and promote the talent of their homegrown stars. Comparisons were made with the infinitely better treatment actors received in Hollywood, where "Tell the world!" was the ringing slogan. The salaries there were much larger, the working day shorter, the conditions infinitely better, and the publicity operated in a much higher gear. The studios even employed letter-writing staff members to deal with the torrent of fan mail.

As it became clear that the British public went to the cinema primarily to see their favorite stars, the film companies slowly woke up to the commercial value of promoting them, and a new role of publicist or publicity agent began to assume importance. The critics were scornful of their efforts. One complained that the papers and magazines could never get hold of good pictures of the new stars because none were ever taken. He argued that they should be more heavily promoted, paraded before the press, and displayed in films tailored to their talents. "The British studio, broadly speaking, does none of these things," he wrote. "It sometimes makes a brave announcement that this or that artist has been signed on contract for a period. Thereupon, it lies down and goes to sleep."

Nerina Shute also highlighted the film companies' failure to publicize their stars, especially in contrast to American practice. Writing in *Film Weekly* in 1929 as the talkies were taking off, she described England as "the land where publicity is apparently considered vulgar, unnecessary, not worth the expense. With the utmost gentility we allow America to push us off the pavement—smiling grandly from a sitting posture in the gutter."

In fact, certain stars had been busy throughout the decade promoting their films and themselves. Many of them undertook a hectic program, speaking at civic luncheons, opening new cinemas, judging beauty contests and much else. Violet Hopson's duties included presenting military medals, touring factories and escorting schoolchildren on visits to the cinema. According to *Pictures and Picturegoer,* when promoting *Her Son* in Dundee she had to "open a bazaar, visit several factories, launch a ship, and make appearances at kinemas."

In the summer, the stars appeared in public at the annual Kinematograph Garden Party in the Botanic Gardens in Regent's Park, and later the Theatrical Garden Party in the gardens of the Royal Hospital in Chelsea, where in 1927 it was announced that "famous stars are willing to act, dance and gamble" for the benefit of their public. They also did the rounds of dances and fancy-dress balls—including the annual Kinema Club Carnival, "the British film stars' own revel," organized by Billie Bristow. There they dressed in costumes worn in their recent films.

The production and sale of memorabilia was another way companies promoted their films. But after C.A. Lejeune attended the *Loves of Mary, Queen of Scots* premiere, she suggested the merchandise and other paraphernalia on show was in danger of eclipsing the film itself: "There are programme girls and commissionaires in fancy costume, exhibits from the film, copies of songs or books from which the films have been adapted, souvenirs, photographs." She had also seen "a monkey ... a hooded falcon ... white roses ... red roses ... and a handkerchief stall—for the tears shed when watching." But this was small beer compared to the Hollywood craze for memorabilia; for instance, Valentino's fans could buy *Sheik* perfume, soap, Vaseline and chewing gum.

Fan magazines fed the growing hunger for news and gossip about the stars, their lives, their hobbies and their homes. Several fan clubs were set up, to bring filmgoers closer to their screen idols and publicize their films. The stars began to endorse commercial products such as soap, shampoo, cigarettes, toothpaste, face cream and chocolate, while actresses offered makeup tips for their fans.

Many of the most popular stars were also featured on London Underground posters and on sets of cigarette cards, the collection of which became a popular hobby. My father was included in the first series of the cards, printed toward the end of the silent era. Known as "The Working Man's Encyclopedia," because the information on the back could be readily absorbed by those with little education, the cards often included slogans such as (for the glamorous Benita Hume) "There's none that's sweeter than Benita" or simple rhymes like "A girl who's not a might-have-been / She's made her mark on stage and screen."

Sometimes enthusiastic fans interrupted the stars at work. While Owen Nares was on location making the horse-racing picture *All the Winners*, production was stopped by regular invasions of "pretty girls with cameras," who were searching for him. Ivor Novello's fans were able to board special excursion trains laid on to Scotland, so they could watch him at work on Culloden Moor in *Bonnie Prince Charlie.* During scenes being shot on the Isle of Arran, he was besieged by the fans. But he clearly enjoyed being the center of attention, mixing happily with the locals while still wearing his highland kilt off set.

Thousands of fans wrote to their favorite stars, many seeing the film life as the last word in glamour. Dorothy Boyd aimed to bring film-struck girls back to reality: "There still exists a pathetic illusion that once you get into a studio, real life will turn into a sort of dream," she wrote in *Picturegoer*. She outlined the seven components of the typical dream:

> 1. The instant you arrive at the studio the producer will gaze at you in rapture and exclaim: "Boys! This is the star we've been looking for. Come right in, cutie!" 2. You will sign a five-figure contract in a palatial office with a gold pen and a bored expression. 3. You will cease to regard water as a drink. Champagne alone will touch your Clara Bow–like lips. 4. You will either have a car, or the sons of noblemen will drive you about in theirs. 5. You will never go to bed before 3 a.m. 6. Invitations to cocktail parties will be strewn about your luxurious apartment. 7. All eyes will turn in your direction when you enter a room. All the Most Important People will whisper to each other: "You know who *that* is?"

One of the themes of Anthony Asquith's 1928 film *Shooting Stars* was the uneasy relationship between a rising star actress who wants to protect her complicated personal life, and a fan magazine journalist seeking to uncover the intimate details for her readers. This was less of a problem for stars at the start of the 1920s, when journalists were rarely inclined to probe in any depth. When interviewing the stars, they treated them with deference, often seeming more like their publicists than objective reporters. But this situation gradually changed as film companies came to understand the desire of the fans to know about the stars' off-screen lives.

Many stars did their best to protect their private lives and fend off the journalists. Some were just shy or poor communicators, or chose to give that impression. "Clive Brook is one of the most reticent of screen actors," wrote a *Pictures and Picturegoer* reporter. "Of himself he will talk little, or not at all." In the same magazine, Josie Lederer wrote: "Betty Balfour is demure and charming, but monosyllabic—on first acquaintance. You have to break the ice of her shyness before you can discover the fascinating little bundle of mischief and high spirits that the film public knows as Squibs of London Town."

Nerina Shute, one of the sharpest of the film journalists, defended her approach with characteristic sarcasm: "Stars write me outraged letters because I have an old-fashioned habit of telling the truth. They would like the public to believe they came down from Heaven the day before yesterday—with a harp in one hand and a recipe for omelettes in the other. Actually the public is far more attracted when told they have failings, just as ordinary mortals do."

Beauty and sex are two of the most powerful ingredients in cinema of any period. But whereas in the 1920s beauty was held in great esteem and heavily promoted in the female stars, the question of sex was handled much more circumspectly. In part this was due to censorship, but also to the fact that it was, as Chili Bouchier recalled, still very much a taboo subject in public life. But later in the 1920s, spurred on by Hollywood, the concept of "sex appeal" began to appear in the film magazines and papers.

11

The Coming of Sound

"Talkies are ruining the oldest art in the world, the art of pantomime, and ruining the great beauty of silence. They won't last a year."—Charlie Chaplin, 1929

It was the showing of the film *The Jazz Singer* in New York in October 1927 that set the cinematic revolution in motion. It was not essentially a talking picture, although it contained some ad-libbing by Al Jolson (including the celebrated line "You ain't heard nothin' yet!"), and it had a musical accompaniment. But the real sensation for the audience was hearing Jolson sing.

The film opened in London in September 1928. According to film historian Kevin Brownlow: "In Britain the film was released first of all as a silent. (The industry could never resist cheating its customers.) People flocked to see it, because of all the publicity from the U.S., but then couldn't work out what all the fuss was about. Having squeezed that lemon, the distributors brought it out at the Piccadilly Theatre in sound—making another fortune."

After seeing the film, George Pearson said to his wife: "We have been present at the death of the silent picture." He was right. The other American film companies thought this Warner Brothers experiment with the Vitaphone system, shot on the only sound stage in Hollywood, was a colossal blunder. But when the public came by the thousands to see and hear the result, they rushed into producing pictures with sound. In July 1928, the first all-talking feature film, *Lights of New York*, was released in America. The movies had become the talkies.

In the first two decades of the century, there had been many experiments with sound on both sides of the Atlantic. Primitive forms of apparatus aiming to introduce synchronized sound were introduced in cinemas and music halls, but none proved satisfactory. A 1920 editorial in *Pictures and Picturegoer* offered a typical view of the time: "There have been many attempts at synchronising the voice with the film, but so far all of them have detracted from rather than added to the pleasure of theatregoing. Directly there is added a mechanical-sounding gramophone, the illusion vanishes.... We emphatically do not want speaking pictures."

Following the success of *The Jazz Singer,* one obstacle to the introduction of sound was the lack of a suitable amplification system to suit the larger cinemas. There was also reluctance on the part of producers and theater owners to pay the extensive costs that re-equipping studios and cinemas would entail. The film world was split between those who considered sound as a passing novelty, and those who saw it as a great advance. Many people were initially skeptical. One company executive rashly suggested: "Talkies are merely a temporary craze, like broadcasting and greyhound racing." Others dismissed it as "an American fad like roller skating." Michael Balcon recalled: "Many of us were snooty about the talkies. We took a purist view that the silent film was the great universal medium, that it could never be surpassed. It was the visual image that counted, and nothing else. But the talkies killed the silents stone dead."

Miles Mander, then in the middle of filming *The First Born*, doubted the idea would catch on, stating in *Bioscope*: "No one is going to persuade me that our public is going to tolerate for long an entertainment which tends to eliminate any artistic merit which the silent medium may possess." Some people felt sound would only be of value for supporting or novelty films, or for those of a political, educational or advertising nature. Others suggested it might be useful for music, songs and sound effects, but that dialogue could not enhance a film. Silence, it was argued, was a universal language.

Ernest Betts, later a *Daily Mail* film critic, asserted: "The spoken word, mechanically introduced, is not proper to the film medium, and tends to destroy the illusion which the film is trying to build up." Paul Rotha, whose influential book *The Film Till Now* was soon to be published, concurred: "A film in which the speech and sound effects are perfectly synchronised and coincide with their visual images on the screen is absolutely contrary to the aim of cinema. It is a degenerate and misguided attempt to destroy the real use of the film, and cannot be accepted within the true boundaries of the cinema." He suggested that the talking film would "pass as soon as its showmanship possibilities became exhausted." Ivor Montagu confessed that he was "among those who cannot bear the idea of the introduction of the human voice, however pleasant it sounds, into one's quiet, smooth watching of visual images on the screen."

H.G. Wells stated firmly: "There's no future in talkies, no future in talkies at all!" Evelyn Waugh felt they "had set back by twenty years the one valid art of the century." In the article "Famous Authors Discuss Talkies," the popular novelist Ethel Mannin spelled out her objections: "A talking film is a contradiction in terms. I see no future at all for the talking film, which must always destroy itself and defeat its own ends by its essential unreality. Why should anyone go to see photos of people talking when they can go to the theatre and see real people doing the same thing, only better?"

Such views now seem astonishingly blinkered, but they were widely held at the time. George Pearson was, in his own words, "a stubborn renegade" when he defended sound passionately in *Bioscope*:

> With this new thing, those who know their mother tongue, who realise its fluidity and clarity, who love music, who feel the power of poetry, who have dramatic instinct, will come into their own…. The screen play will be freed from the shackles that have confined its advance…. It will open its arms to the English-speaking people who have a thousand-year-old history, and a literature and a tradition and a mental background without parallel…. The "talkies" give us a new vision, a new opportunity, a new and clean page in world history. It is a British Daybreak. How many of us will be waking early?

Other directors were skeptical, prefiguring the fictitious Hollywood star Norma Desmond in *Sunset Blvd.* who, looking back at the silent era, says: "We didn't need dialogue, we had faces then." Denison Clift observed: "I do not believe there is a future for talking pictures, because the spectator can never forget the fact that he is watching photographs of people, not real people." Adrian Brunel, who had directed Ivor Novello in *The Constant Nymph* and *The Vortex*, resented the talkies for "smashing the art of the silent film…. The restful silent drama was stabbed in the back." Anthony Asquith also spoke in defense of the silent film, stating that "he did not think the talking picture had much to do with films proper, which expressed themselves in terms of pictures." In his innovative *Cottage on Dartmoor*, he mocked the sound idea, showing a cinema audience straining desperately to catch the words of what was clearly intended to be a poor-quality soundtrack.

There were widespread fears, especially in Europe, that the human voice would kill the art of film, and many anguished articles were devoted to the subject. In Italy, playwright Luigi Pirandello, whose plays, novels and short stories had been given the screen treatment, defended the silent film: "The screen play should remain a wordless art because it is essentially a medium for the expression of the Unconscious." In France, the celebrated director René Clair saw the silent film as an art form like music and sculpture, but felt that with sound added it would be just a copy of life. "Can the talking picture be poetic?" he asked. "There is reason to fear that the precision of the verbal expression will drive poetry off the screen just as it drives off the atmosphere of daydream." He described sound as a "savage invention," as a "redoubtable monster, an unnatural creation," and spoke of "the deplorable use our industrialists will not fail to make of it." Its arrival was for him the end of a dream, the disappearance of a universal film language.

In America, Mary Pickford memorably observed that "adding sound to movies would be like putting lipstick on the Venus de Milo." Chaplin was also fervently hostile to the change. "I don't believe in talkies for myself, because I'm a pantomimist," he said. "And talkies won't last a year." Conscious of his international audience, he announced plans to continue to make silent films, which he called "non-talkies." Al Jolson suggested that Chaplin disliked the talkies because his voice was too gentlemanly for his Little Tramp character.

Hitchcock too was unhappy about the development, reflecting later: "The silent pictures were the purest form of cinema, the only thing they lacked was the sound of people talking, and the noises. But this slight imperfection did not warrant the major change that sound brought in." This essentially remained his philosophy: "When we tell a story in cinema," he observed, "we should resort to dialogue only when it's impossible to do otherwise." He liked to describe the talkies as "photographs of people talking."

Certain theater stars were also resistant to the change. Sybil Thorndike confessed to adoring silent films, arguing that they gave more scope to the spectator's imagination. "The silent films are so restful, and one can exercise one's imagination throughout in a fascinating way," she said. "Take the love scenes. I always let my imagination fill in all kinds of little gaps and extras in a way which to me is entirely satisfying, but the talkie tears away the last shreds of fantasy and only leaves me cut-and-dried facts."

Articles appeared in the press with apocalyptic headlines such as "Are Talkies the Birth or the Death of British Films?" and "Have the Talkies Killed Screen Romance?" Those critics who saw film as an art form felt the addition of dialogue spoiled its purity. In *Heraclitus, or The Future of Film,* Ernest Betts called it a "most spectacular act of self-destruction," and wrote despairingly: "The soul of the film—its eloquent and vital silence—is destroyed. The film now returns to the circus whence it came, among the freaks and the fat ladies."

In the *Tatler,* James Agate referred to "these wretched and preposterous things known as talkies." *Picturegoer*'s editor deplored the supposed loss of film's universal appeal. "The film, the only real conqueror of the Tower of Babel, is throwing away the greatest of its victories—the establishment of a world brotherhood based on the human eye, which is independent of language barriers."

C.A. Lejeune supported the new system, arguing in the *Observer,* "The millions of picturegoers who are willing to pay for personality have discovered a new way of getting value for money." In a similar vein, Ronald Colman saw the benefit to a wider audience: "The talkies are bringing drama—good drama, created by people who know how to do it—to everyone in the world at a price that is within everyone's reach. Heretofore, the best in the theatre was available only to people in metropolitan centres—and consistently available there at prices which were out of the reach of the majority. Now there is no place so remote that its inhabitants may not enjoy the performances of the most distinguished luminaries of the theatrical world."

"Silent pictures are finished, and a good thing too," announced Dublin-born director Rex Ingram.

In Russia, Eisenstein and his fellow directors Pudovkin and Alexandrov published a joint manifesto, welcoming the advent of sound. Hitchcock summed up the consequences of the radical change that it brought:

> The most important factor in the making of a talkie is silence. I am no longer able to give instructions to my artists while the camera is turning; no longer can the cameraman call instructions to the electricians; and no longer can the noise of the crank be heard. Carpenters on adjoining sets who, in spite of the studio whistle to cease hammering, still managed to break noisily into a dramatic scene by the banging of nails, are dumb, and all the myriad noises of the old silent studio have been stilled.

When musical director Louis Levy returned from America to report on the Jolson phenomenon, his enthusiasm was greeted with scorn and derision. Meanwhile, *Bioscope* noted, "The continued silence was beginning to impose a strain, and as we waited for news of the first British feature-length 'talkie,' the atmosphere grew sick with ugly signs. Fleet Street believed the bottom had fallen out of the British film business, and almost said so in as many words."

Actors' careers stalled as they waited for the studios to be equipped for sound. Directors were also caught on the hop. Denison Clift, just completing his last silent film *High Seas* late in 1928, reflected the widespread uncertainty. "Whether they will be a far-reaching success, and bring a higher literary art to the screen, or whether they are going to be a calamitous failure and lose money in bushels for their promoters, depends on the quality of the first year's talkies." Despite his initial optimism, George Pearson, with two silent films still in production, became thoroughly downcast. "I became a recluse; my old silent world lay in ruins about me," he remembered. "I saw no door opening into the new world."

Eventually the companies realized that the change was not a passing fad, that it was now, as one American put it, "sound or sink." Balcon recalled, "Our stock of films was, to all intents and purposes, unsalable. The public demanded films which talked and sang, preferably like Al Jolson." There followed a frantic scramble to redesign and soundproof the studios. The changeover happened at an astonishing speed, creating uncertainty about what equipment to buy; one studio found that theirs had become obsolete just three weeks after they had bought it.

When in April 1929 studios such as British Talking Pictures and British and Foreign Films announced they would make no more silent films, it caused a sensation. Films that had just been completed were suddenly withdrawn, reappearing soon afterward with sound added, though only to certain scenes. "They were half mute, with the last reel or two suddenly becoming voluble," Balcon recalled. "Peculiar hybrids they were, but they were saved from the scrapheap, and didn't fare badly with audiences."

Yet the creation of these part-talkies was soon on the wane. As the flood of talking films turned into a torrent, the cinemas responded: huge banners were draped outside the main ones, announcing "ALL-TALKING FILMS." By December 1929, a silent cinema was the exception in the London area, and 685 cinemas were equipped for sound nationwide. In America, where the crude early talkies had been dubbed the "shouties," Warner Brothers declared triumphantly: "At Last, Pictures That Talk Like Living People!"

There were some attempts to stem the tide. A skeptical article in the usually progressive *Manchester Guardian* poured scorn on the whole idea. "We have had a silent *Chu Chin Chow* film, now we are going to have a talking one. Where is the difference?" it asked. "A bad film will not be any less bad or old-fashioned because it can be appalling noisily as well as visually, and, unless everybody is most careful, a number of these new pictures will reproduce the case of a well-known star, whom many people find pleasant to look at but disconcerting to listen to."

Yet by 1930, silent films were for the first time in the minority, and by 1931 some 75 percent of cinemas were equipped for sound. Many companies who tried to ignore the new situation were swept away. The effect on cinema was worldwide, as Michael Powell recalled in *Life in the Movies*: "All over Europe sound-synchronised films were sweeping the board. Some of them were semi-talkies, some of them had only one sound scene, others had synchronised sound effects and music. Studios were going dark all over Europe. Technicians were out of work. The American market had vanished overnight. People were demanding talkies in their own language." The French were slower than the British to adjust. As no French studio had the necessary sound equipment in place, the first French talkie was made at Elstree.

In November 1929, all the films on release in London were either synchronized with sound recordings or full talking, but only ten percent of the cinemas were equipped for sound. Some of them could not afford the equipment and were forced to close. Many of the early sound films were clumsy and crude, as directors and technicians struggled to master the new technology. The equipment that was used was necessarily primitive, and there were problems of amplification. Sometimes there was a mismatch between sound and picture: When Clive Brook's first talkie *Interference* was screened in London, the needle stuck in the groove, and he went on repeating a phrase over and over while the scene continued.

There were many critical voices about the new set-up. When *The Return of the Rat* was re-released as a talkie, the *Kine Weekly* critic wrote: "The picture has no ascertainable advantage over the original silent version. The dialogue in the various scenes to which sound has been added would be more effective if it were more in keeping with the characterisation, while the speech of the actors, although perfectly clear, is a trifle too deliberate and sometimes altogether too loud." For a brief moment it was thought that voice doubles would be acceptable. But the process of synchronizing outside voices with the lips of silent stars proved unsatisfactory, and was soon discontinued.

On behalf of the stage players, Sybil Thorndike, who had just made her first talkie *To What Red Hell*—billed as "The Greatest British Drama Yet Produced"—asserted, "The talkies still have a long way to go before there is perfect reproduction of the voice. However clearly one enunciates, there are many sounds which get slurred or distorted." There were also concerns about a particular aspect of love scenes: "Is Screen Kissing Indecent?" asked *Film Weekly*. One contributor to *Picturegoer* suggested there was "too much squish and squash noises" in scenes that involved kissing.

The use of sound initially meant the cameras could barely move, an obstacle which encouraged directors to make films full of lengthy dialogue scenes. Because of the fear of intrusive sounds, it also briefly reduced the amount of location work. Scenes became longer, often four or five minutes in length, instead of a previous average of between 30 seconds and a minute. Rehearsals needed to take place before filming began, with actors expected to be word-perfect by the time they arrived on the studio floor.

The actual shooting was now the joint work of the recorder—or the "mixer" as he was known in America—and the cameraman, who worked in close conjunction. Because the camera still made a whirring noise, it had to be put into a soundproof box and remain immobile. So the cameraman was stuck in a glass-fronted booth, and sometimes nearly suffocated. Ronald Neame, then just a junior camera assistant, remembered: "We were locked in by the sound department so that we didn't make a nasty noise and spoil their beautiful dialogue." It was difficult for the actors too, as John Longden recalled: "The sound department insisted on the microphone being placed within eighteen inches above your head, which made acting very difficult." Sometimes shooting had to be halted for several hours while an intrusive hum or whistle was located.

There were problems of another kind in the studios. Jack Cardiff was involved in the shooting of *The Informer*, the last big-budget silent film made in England. "It was decided there should be one sequence in sound," he remembered. "But our stage had no soundproofing, and because we could hear the traffic and other daytime noises, it was decided to shoot the sequence at night. At night however we had birds singing away in the gantry, so we had to fire revolvers with blanks to keep them quiet for a couple of minutes while we hurriedly shot the scene." Herbert Wilcox experienced the same problem: "The walls had to be padded with glass-fibre wool to soundproof the studios. But the sparrows decided this was a very good place for nesting, and came into the studio in their hundreds. So we had to shoot a gun to frighten them out."

The actors did not immediately benefit financially from the changeover to sound. In 1930, Nerina Shute wrote in *Film Weekly*:

> Few people realise that since the talkies arrived, the stars have suffered so much that camera-men, directors, dialogue writers, and even the young men who bang things with hammers, are in many ways far better off than the stars.... These actors are quite often paid by the day, like workers in the crowd. And five or ten or fifteen pounds a day is not very much when you work about fifty days in a year.... Behind the scenes they are all complaining.

Pointing out that Madeleine Carroll, Donald Calthrop, Dodo Watts and my father were currently the only British stars under contract, she added: "Madeleine Carroll gets £200 a week whether she is working or not, but the average arrangement of this sort provides a retaining fee of £15 or £20 a week (sometimes only £10), with an understanding that only while actually working does the artist receive a proper wage."

With stage actors and plays being used more frequently, there were justifiable fears that the change would see a return to more static films. With their ready-made stories and dialogue, and an existing audience, stage plays were inevitably the first to attract producers looking to exploit the arrival of sound. In the early months, several were transferred virtually unchanged, a camera simply being set up on the stage. The practice gradually gave way to proper adaptations.

There was also concern about the effect on stage actors and their audiences, and whether the new kind of film would supplant the theater. Asquith wondered if talkies "might be a menace to the theatre." Hitchcock expressed a similar fear: "Talkies are the most dramatic form of entertainment yet discovered, and it seems to me that the stage is bound to suffer badly." Balcon begged to differ: "All that is being said about the talkies killing the theatre is so much stuff and nonsense." Sybil Thorndike agreed. "The talkies will rather tend to bring the public back to the play," she argued. "At present there is a boom, but it will be a short-lived one, the main reason being that people will very soon tire of looking at photographs talking, and want once again to see actors and actresses in the flesh." American critic George Jean Nathan said in characteristically waspish style: "The day that sees men waiting at the stage door for an electric phonograph to come out will see the day that the talkies will triumph over the theatre."

The race to become the first full talking picture was between Hitchcock's *Blackmail* and Elvey's *High Treason*. Hitchcock won: like Saville, he had been quick off the mark, getting his hands on the first sound apparatus to reach Britain. Over the decades he told different versions of how he had incorporated sound into the film. In 1936, he wrote:

> I was bitterly disappointed when I was told it was to be a silent picture. I was convinced that the talkies were no mere flash in the pan, and that the day of silent films had passed. I felt certain in my own mind that, when the picture was finished, I should be asked to add dialogue

to it, or to make it entirely as a full-length talkie. Therefore, when producing the film in silent form, I was imagining all the time that it was a talkie. I was using talkie technique, but without sound.

His foresight paid off: after British International Pictures suggested adding dialogue to a few reels, he persuaded them to let him make a full-blown talkie instead. A comparison of the silent and sound versions makes it clear that he re-shot a few scenes with dialogue, and added music and sound effects. The second version was held up as a good example of the imaginative use of sound, but some critics now argue that the silent version is superior. Certainly Hitchcock was already demonstrating his preference for "pure cinema" rather than "photographs of people talking," observing later: "I've always believed you can tell as much visually as you can with words. That's what I learned from the Germans."

By the end of the decade, the talkies were starting to improve. As Hitchcock put it: "We are reaching the point where the new form of entertainment will contain the best of the old silent film and the best of the stage, moulded into something which is neither one nor the other, but which will be a completely distinct medium of expression." By 1930, the last commercial silent film was being made. That year, around three-quarters of the films to receive a trade showing were talkies; of those, almost 90 percent were full-talking films. But George Pearson observed: "No matter the heights to which the sound film might grow, the silent film would still remain its living and sustaining root."

The director Norman Walker stated: "Voices are the only things that count nowadays. We shall have to get busy and find some really capable stars. Youth doesn't matter so much. A beautiful voice is the main essential." Such a voice was required to combat the primitive quality of the first sound systems. Yet only a few stars were felt to have the kind of voices that would prove an asset. Among the established stars, they included John Longden, Jameson Thomas, Miles Mander, Estelle Brody and my father. Newcomers Madeleine Carroll and Eve Gray were also thought likely to succeed.

Many people felt that stage actors, with their training and ability to project, would have a distinct advantage over those who knew only films. But others thought they would be at a disadvantage, since so many of them spoke in markedly upper-class tones. Balcon recalled: "With the coming of sound, there was resistance to anyone who did not speak 'stage English.' Accents, dialect, regional or class intonations meant that you were restricted to character parts. The lamentable preference was for the English of the drama schools and of South Kensington." The director Graham Cutts pinpointed another drawback of a theater background: "The voice of stage people is always a little affected," he argued. "They roll their r's and play on their words in a way that annoys the sensitive microphone. The result is seldom as good as the untrained voice." Such problems seriously limited the stars' appeal to a mass British audience, especially outside London and the Home Counties.

In America, British actors, with their clear, often stage-trained voices, found themselves much in demand. They were helped by their obvious advantage over those European players with whom they had previously had to compete. Until then, as Jack Cardiff observed, "the titles spoke perfect English." Now that had all changed.

Yet here again, accent was crucial. While home from Hollywood to make his first British talkie, Clive Brook warned, "America has no use for the affected British accent—which of course is held in deserved contempt here too, among sensible people." With an accent that Nerina Shute described as "subdued Rolls-Royce," he admitted that at first he faced a problem: "When Ruth Chatterton and I made our first talkie, the great Middle West could not understand a word we said."

The changeover to sound proved problematic in *The City of Play*, whose cast included Chili Bouchier in her first leading role. She stated in *Shooting Star*,

> Nobody had considered the rather odd assortment of sounds which would issue from the mouths of the leading players. There was the stage-trained, dark-brown voice of Lawson Butt, the regional accent of Pat Aherne, and my Minnie Mouse squeak. I arrived on the set to find the camera confined in a padded cell, swathed in layers of thick blankets which muffled the gentle and comforting whirr of the motor. The microphone, which restricted our movements, hung a few inches above our heads like the Sword of Damocles. A new arrival, the sound man, was incarcerated in a glass booth at the other end of the studio. His voice was relayed through a loudspeaker attached to the studio roof. I had rather a squeaky voice, and I had no stage experience. At too-regular intervals "Speak up, Miss Bouchier" boomed out like the voice of God. It sounded so terrible, it was taken down after just a couple of days. So I took elocution lessons, and my voice got stronger and stronger.

A further problem was the presence in Britain of foreign players in films already in progress. The cast of *The Informer* included the Italian-Hungarian star Lya de Putti, whose accent did not sit easily in the mouth of her character, a working-class Dubliner—but then neither did the aristocratic English voice of Joan Barry, the actress who spoke the lines instead of her. Others playing in the film, such as the Swede Lars Hanson and the Dutchman Carl Harbord, also had to be dubbed by native English speakers. Hitchcock had a similar problem with *Blackmail* and Anny Ondra's Czech accent. His solution was to place Joan Barry just out of camera shot with a microphone, and for her to speak the words—though her Mayfair accent jarred in the mouth of a shopgirl character.

The requirements of a good voice, a suitable acting style, and an ability to remember lines proved too much for certain stars on both sides of the Atlantic. Many of them failed to make the transition to the talkies, and saw their careers dwindle, or in some cases simply collapse.

12

Winners and Losers

"Before the talkies, I used to play everything, alley cats, ladies' daughters,
and this and that. Now I was just alley cats."—Mabel Poulton, reminiscing
in 1971

Picturegoer described the impact of the arrival of sound in Hollywood: "The
studios realised that actors and actresses with well-trained, vibrant voices were
essential to the success of the talkies. So trainloads of Broadway celebrities were
brought to the movie capital. The day of the beautiful but dumb had passed. The
talkies demanded actors who could not only screen acceptably, but speak without
murdering the English language."

At that moment, 80 percent of full-time Hollywood actors had little or no training. "Hollywood is completely out of control," Herbert Wilcox reported, after producing one of the first talkies there. "Stars, on whom thousands have been spent on
publicity, are finding themselves out of work, and in their places are actors, hitherto
unknown, who can demand almost any sum for their services."

Among the Hollywood casualties was Emil Jannings, who spoke with such a
strong, guttural German accent that American audiences could not understand
him, and he returned to his native country. His regular co-star Vilma Banky, who
had played opposite Valentino in *Son of the Sheik*, was similarly unlucky: after making the part-talkie *This Is Heaven* and two more films, her career collapsed because
of her thick Hungarian accent.

There was a considerable flight of European stars making the return trip
across the Atlantic. The elfin-like Lya de Putti, who had gone to Hollywood after
her successes in *Varieté* and *Manon Lescaut*, chose to come to England to make
The Informer. Her accent was parodied in an interview she gave to *Picturegoer*, in
which she stated: "I do not sink ze talkies will last. How can zey make talkies zat
will be popular in every country? Zey would have to make copies in every language,
and zat is not possible. Zat is why most of the continental artists are coming here.
Zey make one or two pictures in Europe while zey wait and see how ze talkie craze
lasts."

Apart from Pola Negri, who spent the 1930s in Germany as one of Hitler's
favorites, and Conrad Veidt, who emigrated to Britain in 1933 and eventually became
a British citizen, almost all the Hollywood stars with Continental accents disappeared from view within a couple of years of the birth of the talkies. MGM feared
that Greta Garbo would suffer a similar fate, as did the star herself: She insisted that

in case her English pronunciation proved fatal, an "export" version in German (her second language after Swedish) should also be made.

Herbert Wilcox saw little future for her in the talkies: "She speaks too brokenly for reproduction." But from the moment in *Anna Christie* that she uttered her famous first line ("Gimme a whisky—ginger ale on the side—and don't be stingy, baby"), her career was safe, and she continued as MGM's top attraction. Her low, husky voice and Swedish accent became part of her allure, one writer declaring, "Garbo talking was an even more magical figure than Garbo mute."

Garbo's appeal was also down to her mesmerizing beauty and instinctively realistic acting. Her leading man in the silent era, John Gilbert, was not so lucky. His dark good looks and piercing eyes had cast him as a Latin Lover, a type then much in vogue. His career was not helped by a dissolute, alcohol-fueled private life. But even before the talkies arrived, his histrionic style of acting was being derided by both fans and the critics, especially after *A Woman of Affairs*, his last silent picture with Garbo. Like other actors, he thought the talkies required a more theatrical delivery and what voice teachers called "pear-shaped tones." When, in his first talkie, the inappropriately titled Ruritanian potboiler *His Glorious Night*, he declared his love for his leading lady, it prompted gales of laughter from audiences across the country. It was widely rumored at the time that a sound technician had deliberately distorted his voice. But other male stars playing romantic leads, such as Charles Farrell, had similar difficulties. They were not helped by the often unrealistic, overblown dialogue of their films.

There was another problem, as one critic noted: "It isn't that Mr. Gilbert's voice is insufficient, it's that his use of it robs him of magnetism, individuality and, strangest of all, skill." The new system exposed his limitations as an actor. He made few further films, and eventually drank himself to death at the age of 36.

Other stars took a little time to adapt. Lillian Gish heartily disliked her first experience of sound, feeling she was treated like a novice while making *One Romantic Night*. "I don't want to make another talkie," she said. "I shall become a little old maid, looking after my invalid mother, going through the linen and counting the glass." Yet she quickly took to sound, and was soon billed as "The Miracle Girl with the Miracle Voice."

Many of the Hollywood stars had to take new screen tests so that the studios could assess their voices. Among other actresses, Clara Bow, the quintessential 1920s "jazz baby," famously dubbed the "It Girl," briefly made the transition despite her nasal tones and slight Brooklyn accent, but soon retired to her ranch in Nevada. Norma Talmadge was handicapped because her Brooklyn accent failed to match her public image. Dorothy Cumming was another star whose career ended when the talkies arrived; she became a designer of wallpaper patterns.

Louise Brooks, who had caused a sensation as the star of *Pandora's Box*, but left Hollywood when sound arrived, was skeptical of the notion that voice quality was the main reason for stars dropping out of the business. "That's the official story," she told critic Kenneth Tynan years later. "The truth is that the coming of sound meant the end of the all-night parties. With the talkies you couldn't stay out until sunrise any more. You had to rush back from the studios and start learning your lines, ready for the next day's shooting at 8 a.m."

British actors experienced mixed fortunes with the advent of sound. The archetypal Englishman Ronald Colman, who made his talkie debut in *Bulldog Drummond*, not only survived but thrived. He was blessed with an attractive voice, and his natural, unforced and understated acting style complemented his easy charm. Basil Rathbone possessed a fine voice, creating a sensation when he talked in *The Last of Mrs. Cheyney.*

Clive Brook had several successful years in Hollywood before returning to Britain and appearing in the occasional film, focusing meanwhile on his stage work. John Loder played in Paramount's first talkie, *The Doctor's Secret*, but never made much headway in Hollywood, and soon returned home to a string of roles in the 1930s as the decent, dependable upper-class Englishman. Stewart Rome made a smooth transition to sound, continuing to play leading parts in the 1930s before dwindling into character roles. But during the war, his reputation was severely damaged when he appeared in "A Sunday Thought for the Coming Week," a series of three-minute religious homilies which provoked jeers from audiences. In one cinema, tomatoes were thrown at the screen.

Jameson Thomas went to America because his wife had tuberculosis and needed a warm, dry climate. His voice was not good, and he was limited to playing small roles. He never achieved anything like the level of fame he had managed in Britain, perhaps because, as one film magazine put it, "he was too shy, too gentle, and unassuming in the pushful world of celluloid." But Miles Mander had a long and successful career in British and American films, notably in *The Private Life of Henry VIII*, and in Hollywood in *Wuthering Heights* and the 1935 *The Three Musketeers.* He also continued directing and writing screenplays.

Ivor Novello found the talkies a less sympathetic field than the silent films, and retired from the screen in 1934. His clipped West End accent grated on the ears of filmgoers, who now needed leading men to have more than just a beautiful profile. "Someone said I was too English," he told the *News of the World* in 1933. "It seemed such an absurd remark to make, until it was explained that there were at least five thousand picture houses in America whose audiences had never heard an Englishman speak. English was like a foreign language to them."

John Longden had a drink problem, and ended up playing police inspectors and other small roles. Gerald Ames gave up acting at the end of the silent era, and died young in 1933 of a heart attack after falling down the steps at Knightsbridge tube station. Basil Dean was convinced the talkie era was "going to hand the screen back to stage artistes."

Among actresses, there were several notable casualties, one of them being Mabel Poulton. Balcon recalled the moment she and Ivor Novello first met to work on *The Constant Nymph*: "Mabel grinned in her friendly way and said, ''Allo, 'ow are ya?' Ivor thought it was a joke, and replied in equally broad cockney, only to discover this was Mabel's natural accent." This proved her downfall, making her no longer suitable for many of the roles she had previously played. As she recalled later:

The Constant Nymph was a tremendous success. I had offers from America, and my studio, for whom I was working for tuppence halfpenny, were about to give me a marvellous contract, worth £5,000 a year instead of £20 a week. So I was excited. The contract was coming along in a few days, but then suddenly overnight came Al Jolson. There was no word then about keeping me on, because I had this slight cockney accent. The talkies came in, and everybody wanted stage people, those with good diction without any accent.

At the time, when it was clear the talkies were here to stay, Poulton's anxiety was evident. "I'm rather frightened of talkies," she confessed to Nerina Shute in June 1929. "They're so—so *different*. I'm taking a step in the dark, and no one knows it better. For the present I must content myself with just synchronising my silent pictures. In that way one gains experience. But in the future I am hoping to make a proper talkie." The following month, *Picture Show* reported: "Mabel Poulton is having some tests made of her voice, and I'm told the results are delightful."

But she was far from delighted. In her autobiography, she wrote: "When sound was to be added to *The Return of the Rat*, we had a voice test at Wembley. The reaction of all of us, including Ivor, was dismay. Our voices didn't sound like our own. When the film was shown, the dialogue was so abrupt and stilted it caused a laugh." According to Gainsborough's publicity manager Bill O'Brien, who was present in the studio projection room when she heard herself talk for the first time, she said: "Surely that's not how I *really* sound," then burst into tears.

Later it was reported in *Bioscope* that she had "packed up and put in a year's hard study on elocution, singing, dancing, and the hundred and one things that go to the successful talkie artist." Even then she was unable to lose her accent completely. After appearing opposite my father in the silent and sound versions of *Taxi for Two*, she was reduced to playing small supporting roles. "Before the talkies I used to play everything, alley cats, ladies' daughters, and this and that," she said later. "Now I was just alley cats." She struggled with a drink problem, while a well-publicized comeback in the mid–1930s was a failure. She died at 93, ending her life in a retirement home for impoverished actors and actresses, in a house which had previously belonged to Ivor Novello, whom she had worshipped for decades.

Although Estelle Brody got away with her minimal dialogue in *Kitty*, her voice too was considered unsuitable by British producers, and within a year she was working as a typist. When Maurice Elvey was planning a sound version of *Hindle Wakes*, her slight American accent spoiled her chance of playing the Lancashire heroine again, and the part was given to Belle Chrystal. With no work forthcoming, she tried her luck in Hollywood. This move alienated many of her British fans, who felt she had betrayed them. She soon discovered that her fame in Britain cut little ice in Hollywood. Disillusioned, she returned to England, married, and was not seen on screen again for another 20 years, after which she made sporadic appearances in character roles.

Lya de Putti never recovered from having her voice dubbed for the added sound sequence in *The Informer*. It proved to be her last picture, as Nerina Shute reported in *Film Weekly*: "She pretends she doesn't care. She fights to keep smiling when she tells you that the decision is her own, that she doesn't want to make pictures. It doesn't ring true, I'm afraid. Talkies have ended her public life. And whatever she says, however she laughs, she can't quite disguise the tragedy of it."

Another victim of the change was Betty Balfour. Since she was not a real cockney, her voice was potentially suitable for various roles in the talkies. But she soon fell out of favor, and was away from the screen for four years. Even another Squibs film, a musical in 1935, failed to revive her career, and her appearances became fewer and fewer. After a failed attempt to return to the stage and a broken marriage, the star once dubbed "The Queen of Happiness" attempted suicide, and eventually became a recluse.

The most tragic case was that of Lilian Hall-Davis, wife of the stage actor Walter Pemberton. Her film career never recovered once sound was introduced. Hitchcock noted of her work in *The Farmer's Wife*: "On the set she suffered from self-consciousness. She had an acute inferiority complex in regard to her ability to play certain parts." After her fame in the silent era, she made only four talkies, one of them in Germany. Suffering from neurasthenia and severe depression, she felt she could no longer work as an actress. According to her friend Joan Morgan, her decline was partly to do with "not sleeping with the right people." In 1933, an *Evening News* journalist observed her watching a film being shot. "To my suggestion that she return to the screen she returned the same evasive answer as she gave to those who offered her work. 'No thank you. My nerves are gone.'" In October 1933, she told a friend: "At 35 I'm too old for films. The trouble with living is that death will follow." She then went home, turned on the gas oven and cut her throat.

Some actresses just quietly faded away; others moved into related careers. Violet Hopson had walk-on roles in just two sound films, then turned to designing uniforms for usherettes. Joan Morgan, after losing the chance of a Hollywood contract, decided that her looks were now old-fashioned, and she didn't want to change. "I thought if my career was simply going to consist of little bits of fluff, then I'd better quit while I was ahead." After making a single sound picture, she went on to write screenplays, novels and plays under the name Joan Wentworth Wood, and also *Camera!*, a book about the early British cinema.

Moya Nugent left the screen after only three films and built up a successful West End stage career, becoming Noël Coward's favorite character actress. Edith Evans, who rose to the top of the theatrical profession, was reputed to have upstaged everyone in the second of her three silent films, *East Is East*, but she made no more. She actually deleted them from her entry in *Who's Who in the Theatre* and avoided the screen for the next 30 years.

But many actresses did well in the brave new world of sound, especially those with a solid grounding in the theater. Fay Compton had no problem making the transition, although she devoted more time to the stage than to the screen. Chili Bouchier's career, which included a substantial amount of theater work, lasted 60 years. When she started in films, she felt her voice was "mean and mingy," but soon afterwards, while filming *Dawn*, she heard Sybil Thorndike's resonant voice during an off-set moment. "From then on I watched my vowels," she recalled. "I took elocution lessons and went into the theatre to learn how to project. That stood me in good stead with the advent of talkies." She went briefly to Hollywood in the 1930s; finding it "rough, tough, and heartless," she broke her contract with Warner Brothers, and was blacklisted.

Madeleine Carroll, despite appearing to have a slight lisp in her first talkie, had a charming voice to match her icy, limpid beauty and well-bred manner. She married and temporarily retired, then returned to the screen to star in two of Hitchcock's best-known British films, *The 39 Steps* and *Secret Agent*. Apparently frustrated by the inefficiency of the British studios, she launched her Hollywood career in 1935 at a salary of $350,000, rose to prominence opposite Ronald Colman in *The Prisoner of Zenda* and became an international star.

And what happened to the directors when the silent era ended? Hitchcock of course became a household name, both in Britain during the 1930s, and subsequently in Hollywood. Anthony Asquith too had a distinguished career, directing half a dozen plays or screenplays by Terence Rattigan and three by Bernard Shaw, notably *Pygmalion*. He also made a string of wartime films, including the outstanding *The Way to the Stars*. Herbert Wilcox was another key figure in the early sound days, specializing in commercially successful costume dramas, musicals and romances, many of them featuring his wife Anna Neagle.

Maurice Elvey continued tirelessly on into the sound era, directing both quota quickies and more substantial works, including three of Gracie Fields' films. He carried on through and after the Second World War, directing dramas and later comedies, until the loss of an eye forced him to retire at age 70. Another who came into his own was Victor Saville, who proved equally adept at directing comedies, musicals and serious dramas. His lighter films included *The Good Companions* and *Evergreen*, which made Jessie Matthews a star, while his more serious works were typified by the excellent *South Riding* and the first sound version of *Hindle Wakes*. In the 1930s, he also directed films for Alexander Korda, who during the war was responsible for employing him, in conjunction with Greta Garbo, to help root out Nazi sympathizers in Europe. Eventually he turned back to his favorite career, that of producer.

Others fared less well after the silent days. A.V. Bramble made only a couple of talkies before fading from sight; a landmine explosion during the Second World War left him completely deaf. The transition to sound finished off Fred Paul's career as an actor, while as a director he made just two low-budget musicals. Fred Rains directed only one further silent film after *Land of My Fathers*, although he acted in half a dozen talkies. Manning Haynes remained busy in the 1930s, but failed to live up to his early promise, directing a series of run-of-the-mill thrillers, comedies and romances.

Some directors took different paths. George Pearson produced the 1930 Hollywood film of the stage hit *Journey's End*, directed by James Whale, then worked mainly in quota quickies. He later joined the GPO Film Unit to make documentaries. Denison Clift directed only one more film, *The Mystery of the Marie Celeste*, based on his own story and starring Bela Lugosi. But he continued to write screenplays for low-budget films, and had considerable success in the theater, with plays staged on Broadway and in the West End.

The foreign directors also had mixed fortunes. The Australian George Beranger made only two further films after directing *Sinister Street*, both silent, but continued his prolific acting career, notching up over 140 films. The Frenchman Louis Mercanton made 20 talkies in three years before dying relatively young in Paris. E.A. Dupont, after *Atlantic* and two more British talkies, returned to work in his native Germany. In 1933, this Jewish refugee moved to Hollywood, but worked only on formulaic B-pictures. He was dismissed for slapping one of the Dead End Kids who was mocking his foreign accent, and subsequently became a film publicist and talent agent.

Many contracts of actors and technicians were dropped. It was a harsh time too for musicians playing in cinemas: Almost overnight, some 20,000 found themselves out of work. One man was seen playing his violin in the street, a placard around his neck announcing, "Ruined by the Talkies." Another victim was Eliot Stannard, who had long been opposed to the use of sound in films, having stated many years before it was introduced commercially: "The whole theory of kinematography is against this innovation." After his contract ended, he made just four quota quickies in the early 1930s, then disappeared from view.

With his fine voice and realistic style of acting, my father was one of the fortunate actors who moved smoothly into the talkie era. Because of his stage experience, he also had no trouble learning his lines. Looking back at the end of his decade in silent films, he spoke of his good fortune:

> I get a thrill out of my work that is denied to those who spend their lives behind office doors. Pictures bring me money, happiness, and the kind of adventure one does not get drafting policies in an insurance office. Though the road to stardom has cost me lean days, hard times, and the pangs of turning deaf ears to the appeals of others, I'm glad I answered the call of the moving shadows. I've made money, had my mead of applause, and had the thrill of being really alive.

His next film was to bring him into further prominence, giving him a small but significant place in British cinema history at this moment of seismic change.

PART THREE

Into the Talkies

13

Kitty

"I used to think that seeing oneself on the screen was bad enough, but hearing one's own voice is much worse. Frankly I don't recognise it; I didn't know I sounded like that."—John Stuart, after the first showing of *Kitty*, 1929

In 1929, a film was made to celebrate the opening of the Empire Cinema in Leicester Square, which had previously been a music hall, and was now fully equipped for sound. Those appearing in it included actresses Cicely Courtneidge and Dorothy Boyd, critic Hannen Swaffer, writer-producer Ivor Montagu and my father.

In his brief appearance in RAF uniform, my father salutes, removes his cap and speaks:

> Good evening, ladies and gentlemen. I must apologise for appearing this evening in uniform, but I'm sure you will excuse me, as I have not had time to change into evening dress. I have just finished work and come off the set, where I have been working on Victor Saville's production of *Kitty*. I would be very proud indeed if one day my work is shown in such a magnificent cinema as the new Empire. My congratulations to MGM, the founders of this colossal house. Good night, everybody.

He puts his cap back on, salutes again and leaves. It may have been the first time he had appeared and spoken on screen as himself, and he delivers his brief speech in a stiff and nervous manner.

Kitty (1929), billed as a "weepie," was an adaptation of Warwick Deeping's popular sentimental novel about class divisions and the consequences of the First World War. First made as a silent film, the story centers on a romance between a shopgirl and an airman, the last of the line in a noble family. After receiving a letter which falsely says his fiancée has been unfaithful, the airman is so traumatized that he crashes his plane. Paralyzed, he is confined to a wheelchair. It's a potent melodrama and a classic Oedipal struggle, in which his possessive mother attempts to prevent his marriage to the shopgirl.

My father starred as the airman Alex St. George—Gaumont had "sub-let" him to Victor Saville—and Estelle Brody played the shopgirl. This was the seventh time they had acted together; one fan wrote to ask him, "Why not marry the girl?" The role required him to convey a wide range of emotions—suffering, rage, depression, ardent love and the agony of his paralysis—which he managed with considerable success.

This was Saville's second film as a director. Wanting a realistic background of boats and water, he had a fake cottage and tea garden built on Green Isle in the Thames at Henley. The *Evening Standard* critic watched the stars at work there:

> Mr. Stuart spent the day in a wheel-chair, looking pale and sad. After the female extras plunged into the river, he sat on the bank, watching them, until the consciousness of his affliction made him draw down the rim of his panama and avert his face. Estelle Brody, who stood behind him, patted his cheek and kissed the back of his head. The setting sun cast long shadows on the lawn. The portable gramophone played sentimental melodies. The scene was shot three or four times, but so simply and so naturally did Miss Brody and Mr. Stuart play it that we felt the pathos every time, and there was a brief silence after the camera stopped.

But there were also bad moments. While filming a scene in the studio, my father was temporary blinded in one eye after his pupil was scorched by a powerful arc lamp. Klieg Eye, a form of conjunctivitis, was extremely painful. Despite the injury, he gallantly kept his promise to open the Rialto cinema at Upper Norwood, but had to be led onto the stage by actress Anna May Wong.

Saville was one of the first in Britain to realize that sound was no passing novelty. Visiting Hollywood, he had discovered that the film companies were lining up to buy equipment and soundproof their stages, and that the main question was whether films should be fully or only partly talking. He therefore decided to add sound to the last three reels of *Kitty*. "I was convinced that, in a very short time, if anybody opened their mouth on the screen and no words came out, audiences would be completely baffled."

Adding sound to *Kitty* (1929) in a New York studio, with (left to right) Estelle Brody, the American star Dorothy Gish, Dorothy Cumming and director Victor Saville.

PICTURE SHOW, July 27th, 1929.

REGISTERED AT THE G.P.O. AS A NEWSPAPER.

"Broadway"—Richard Dix—Betty Compson. Art Plates Inside.

Vol. 21.
No. 534.

JULY 27th, 1929.

every Saturday

2ᴰ

Picture Show

JOHN STUART
and
ESTELLE BRODY
talk in "Kitty"

See page 10.

British Talkie Stars!

John Stuart

JOHN STUART is back in England again. He had a marvellous time in America and he got on splendidly with everybody. Have you heard about John Stuart's flat? The interior is like a country cottage and it is extremely artistic. It will be very interesting to hear and see John Stuart and Estelle Brody, when "Kitty" is shown, all the more so because they have been screen "sweethearts" on many occasions. It is in "Kitty" that for the first time they live "happy ever after!"

"Hear Estelle Brody and John Stuart, Britain's premier film stars, speaking the Mother Tongue!" ran the publicity for *Kitty* (1929).

He commissioned the playwright Benn Levy to write pieces of dialogue for the last couple of reels of *Kitty,* and asked Hubert Bath to create a complete musical score. Since British studios had no sound equipment yet, he decided to re-shoot the scenes in New York. In March, my father sailed on the *Aquitania* to join him and Estelle Brody there.

The actors worked for two weeks in the RCA studios on Seventh Avenue, where the sets were reconstructed on an experimental sound stage. The conditions were primitive, with the cameras encased in large, immobile glass booths. "All the lighting in the studio is incandescent, which makes the sets unbearably hot," my father reported. "Everyone here is making a new kind of liquid make-up, which goes on so smoothly that it gives perfect photographic results."

This was his first trip to America, and he took full advantage of it. "Miss Brody and Mr. Stuart have had a fine time, seeing the shows and being feted," the *Evening News* reported. "Mr. Stuart was made a member of the Lambs' Club, the famous association of theatrical folk." He also visited a Harlem nightclub and took in Coney Island, Broadway and Fifth Avenue.

A report in *Bioscope* revealed him to be a convert to the talkies. "From America he has brought back confidence and enthusiasm—though that was probably a fairly easy load for a man with a voice like his. He says British producers should realize that silent pictures are fading out, that talkies are no 'here today' novelty, but will be the stuff of film life in the days ahead."

Soon after arriving back in England, he wrote an article for *Picturegoer,* describing in detail the lead-up to the moment he first heard his voice on screen:

The first thing I did on my arrival at the studio in New York was to have a voice test for the "mike," combined with a make-up test for the cameraman. It was a terrifying moment, calculated to give even the world's most experienced actor stage-fright.

The recorder, or microphone expert, placed the microphone a little in front and above my head, and asked me to say something when he gave me a signal. Meanwhile he disappeared behind the camera into a square padded box containing the recording machines, and I was then told to speak. When I had finished he came out of the box and told me next time to speak louder and a little slower. So I tried once again, and this time he was satisfied.

Next the cameraman had all the lights turned on me, to see at which angles I would be turning my head. When he was satisfied, all was ready for the great moment—the voice test. A vital moment for the artist, as now, with the advent of the talkies, one's voice means as much as one's looks and acting abilities in the silent films. I was naturally anxious and nervous, as no one had heard my talkie voice, and all wondered, particularly myself, how it was going to register.

My final instructions were: "When you see a red light appear under the camera, start talking." The director, recorder, and cameraman all being satisfied, the test was ready to be shot, and the lights were put on. Immediately the set was bathed in a beautiful soft light from the many incandescent lamps. The great value of these lamps is that they do not flutter or take time to warm up, or make any noise.

The assistant director then shouted "One bell" and a huge bell was rung for silence. It is similar to a burglar-alarm bell used in big shops over here, and it rings for half a minute. Immediately everyone stopped working and stood still, no matter what they were doing. Simultaneously a red light appeared in all departments throughout the building, to warn others that a scene was being shot, and all the doors communicating with the studio were closed. There was complete silence for one minute in order that the recorders should have time to detect the slightest sound which might spoil the "take."

In the part-talkie *Kitty*, he and Estelle Brody were the first actors to talk on screen in Britain, a fortnight before Hitchcock's full talkie *Blackmail* was released.

The assistant director then said "Start your recorders," and the engineers in the padded box set the recording machines in motion. When these were going properly he signalled to the cameraman with a white light, and the cameraman started turning the handle. When the camera was well started he signalled to me by means of a red light, and I started speaking my lines as instructed. When I had finished, the order was given for "Two bells," the signal that the "take" was over.

My first worry was—what did my voice sound like? To which the recorder replied "OK." On the following morning I was invited to come and hear for myself. I sat in a chair in the projecting room, as if I was in a dentist's chair waiting for him to pull out all my teeth. I held my breath, and then it happened. There I was on the screen, and I was hearing myself too. It seemed quite uncanny: I could hardly believe that it was my voice talking; but it was true enough. "Fine, John," said Victor Saville. And I breathed again.

The silent version of *Kitty* had been released in January, the new version with some sound scenes came out in December. So *Kitty* became the first British part-talkie to be screened in Britain. Its world premiere was held in mid–Atlantic, when it was shown to 500 passengers on the liner S.S. *Majestic* on which Saville, my father and Estelle Brody were returning home.

Afterward my father commented: "I used to think that seeing oneself on the screen was bad enough, but hearing one's own voice is much worse. Frankly I don't recognise it; I didn't know I sounded like that." But his pleasant, unforced tenor voice was universally praised. The use of sound in *Kitty* was widely welcomed after the trade show. The *Bioscope* critic wrote: "The introduction of dialogue towards the close

Kitty **brought him his best reviews yet, his voice being considered ideal for the talkies.**

acts like a tonic." According to *Picture Show,* "All this moving story has been made to the accompaniment of sound, but suddenly, at the most poignant moment, John Stuart talks!"

The *Cinema Times* described his voice as "screen perfect," and it was said to resemble Ronald Colman's. *Picture Show* reported: "It is said that John Stuart's voice has proved ideal for recording purposes, and that tests of it have been inquired for by numerous well-known American producing companies." The *American Moving Picture Review* published a particularly striking portrait, above this caption: "John Stuart, regarded as one of the handsomest men on the British screen, is a likely candidate for honours in American films."

After he made a test for Paramount at their Long Island studios, it was screened in Hollywood and he was offered a five-year contract. A friend estimated it was worth around £25,000 a year, or as much in a month as he was earning in a year. Yet he turned it down, apparently on patriotic grounds. "I am a British actor," he said, "and if I am any use to the screen I want to give my services to British pictures." One report suggested he may have asked too high a price. Another suggested he stayed in Britain because British International Pictures got in first with a talkie contract. The *Evening Standard* critic pointed out:

Mr. Stuart's engagement by a British firm at a time when the Goldwyns and the Laskys had their eye on him is not only a commendable piece of enterprise. It is significant of the change that the talking film has made in the assessment of acting values. John Stuart, still only thirty, has for so long been one of the best-known British film actors that one cannot term his talkie success a comeback, but it is likely to increase his prestige immensely.

During his time in New York, he had gone each evening to a "talkie theater," where the long queues convinced him that silent pictures were dying. He had watched scenes being shot at Paramount, Fox and Warner Brothers, where all the productions were now talkies. "Those talkies! They are far in advance of anything we have yet seen in this country," he observed on his return to Britain, telling *Film Weekly*: "In New York they can't understand why England has been so slow to take up the talkies. They admit that we have every advantage—good voices, good actors, and brilliant authors. Then why didn't we jump in, as they express it, while the time is ripe? Naturally I couldn't give the answer."

British International Pictures' extensive publicity for the first British screening of *Kitty* emphasized its romantic elements. "You'll love this plucky girl who fought the world for her man!" ran the publicity ads. The nature of the cast's background was also emphasized in this proud boast: "The cast were all trained on the speaking stage and have excellent recording voices."

Kitty gave my father the best reviews of his career so far. "He quite definitely proves himself to be one of the finest picture actors in the world," wrote the *Sunday Dispatch*. The *Evening Standard* stated, "Mr. Saville has put Mr. Stuart in the front rank of screen actors." "He scores a great acting and vocal success in Britain's first 'talkie,'" was the view of the *Daily Express*. The *Bioscope* critic observed: "The scenes between husband and wife are finely acted. The ovation bestowed on Estelle Brody and John Stuart when they appeared on stage in person after the trade showing was well deserved."

My father recalled the astonishment at the trade show at the Hippodrome when Kitty kidnaps him, and they suddenly talk. "It caused quite a sensation in the cinema. It hit them like a bomb. When these voices came out of the screen, everyone was amazed. They thought it all so real, so marvellous." The critics were especially struck by a later scene in which Kitty pretends to be drowning in the river, to get him to use his legs to rescue her. "I put my all into it, and walked very slowly, making a lot of grunts and groans. The critics burst into applause, which was unusual for such a normally critical audience, who were not easily moved." This moment was reflected in their reviews. "His efforts to walk, his gasps and groans are wonderfully done," stated the *Star*, while *Film Review* praised "one of the finest and most stirring examples of acting ever seen."

The new version was reviewed in the national as well as the trade press. The *Bioscope* critic concluded: "Even as a silent film, *Kitty* was a fine example of British production. The talking version is more successful than any American part-talkie I have seen, and so far as intelligence in introducing dialogue is concerned, it certainly shows a very marked improvement."

I viewed the two versions on the same day to see if this was the case, and found interesting differences. In the second version, the sudden arrival of dialogue three-quarters of the way through is certainly striking. The painted sets for the new riverside scenes shot in New York are not well matched with other scenes. The second film also gains a lift from the introduction of sound effects—taxi horns, planes, cars, rain and so on—and a new and attractive musical score played throughout. There's even an added song for Estelle Brody, who has a sweet voice.

Yet much of the new dialogue is banal, resulting in certain scenes having less emotional impact than they did in the silent version, and tending to hold up the story. The reconciliation at the close between mother and son has considerable power in the original, but the simplistic explanation of their previous conflict given by the mother in the sound version—"It was the way you were brought up"—lessens the force of the story. Brody gives a sympathetic performance as the loyal heroine, determined to stand by her man and bring about his recovery, but her slight American accent is mildly distracting. Dorothy Cumming gives a convincing portrait of the snobbish, aristocratic mother, while Marie Ault plays Kitty's kind, reliable mother with convincing naturalism.

The critics were particularly impressed by my father's natural, light and unaffected voice. Their reviews were unanimous on this point:

- John Stuart, who acts with considerable expression, has a clear and cultured voice, which is in my opinion better than any man's yet recorded.—*Film Weekly*
- His voice records so remarkably well that talkie enthusiasts will be sure to want more of him.—*Daily Sketch*
- John Stuart shows the enormous possibilities of the English voice.—*Sunday Chronicle*
- He has a wonderful speaking voice which records naturally and as simply as we like to think our typical English speak.—*Morning Advertiser*

The *Daily Express* film critic suggested: "His voice will strengthen his screen personality as it has done for many film artists in America. What is more, it may establish that personality in the United States as silent films may never have done. Mr. Stuart is one of the few British film actors whose name means anything at the box-office." Significantly, *Kitty* was shown in America, and also Australia where, according to the *Australasian*, it became "the first long British talkie to be shown in Melbourne."

In America, a *Film Daily* critic wrote:

> This reviewer found its spoken sequences a delight, and to listen to John Stuart's remarkable voice and beautiful diction was a treat. Out in Hollywood they think they have a few dialoguers who know the English language, but they haven't heard this baby yet. If some American producer doesn't hop this bird fast, it just proves another of those inexplicable oversights.

The *New York Evening Journal* was equally approving: "The most distinct talking sequences we have yet heard are those in which John Stuart has a part. This young English actor's characterization is one of the outstanding performances of the season. He combines an easy naturalness with a perfect and serious understanding of his role."

On the other hand, the review in *Variety*—which routinely rubbished British and European films—was totally dismissive:

Kitty with or without its dialogue is useless. This entire picture is an entire waste of time, from producer to public. In this latter day of picture-making *Kitty* is almost as primitive in its making as occurred in the British first days. What was said then, that England doesn't know the first thing about picture-making for world distribution, remains true.

This vicious attack on British films, which also had *The Constant Nymph* in its sights, provoked an angry retort from the editor of *Film Weekly*. In a piece headlined "American Press out to Kill British Films—Scandalous Attack on Two Excellent Pictures," he accused *Variety* of publishing unnecessarily abusive reviews of two films much praised in Britain. The motive, he suggested, was to prevent British films from breaking into the American market.

14

From Dupont's *Atlantic*
to Pabst's *L'Atlantide*

"In *Men of Steel* a new John Stuart comes into being. Now at last he has a part in which he must portray character rather than sex appeal."—Cecilie Leslie in *Film Weekly*, 1932

Most of the early talkies were adapted from stage plays, and my father's first all-talking picture was one such. *Atlantic* (1929) was based on a recent West End play by Ernest Raymond, *The Berg*, which drew on the real-life sinking of the *Titanic*. *Atlantic* was filmed at Elstree and on a large liner berthed in Tilbury Docks where, according to *Kine Weekly*, "all-night work in acute and sometimes perilous discomfort has been something of a nightmarish ordeal to most of those concerned." My father, and no doubt others, had to sleep during the day to stay awake during the filming at night.

In an attempt to emulate Hollywood, several directors were brought in from Europe to work in the expanding British cinema. For *Atlantic*, it was E.A. Dupont, a German expressionist director, famous for his virtuoso film *Varieté* starring Emil Jannings, and praised for his visual sense in the stylish *Piccadilly*. The first multi-lingual talkie, *Atlantic* was made in three versions so that it would be acceptable in French- and German-speaking countries. The English cast played a scene first, then the other two casts repeated it.

The British cast was said to be the strongest yet for a British film. But although *Atlantic* received excellent notices at the time, it now seems unbearably slow and ponderous, as if tragedy requires people to act at a quarter of their natural speed. Apparently Dupont's English was none too good, and the actors spoke slowly so that he could understand the dialogue. Yet this still doesn't account for the lengthy pauses, especially John Longden's famous, seemingly endless one before he tells passenger Valentine Dyall: "The—ship—has—three—hours—to live." On the television documentary series *Yesterday's Witness*, Longden commented: "Dupont was a bit Teutonic, and made it very heavy. I dragged the speech out to such an extent that even he was satisfied. But it now seems absurd."

My father played Lawrence, newly married to Madeleine Carroll (still a relative newcomer to the screen). Carroll's background was unusual for a film star: she had a degree from Birmingham University, and had given up a teaching career to become an actress. "She was rather ill at ease, wondering what it was all about," my father remembered. Her squeaky voice and hesitant manner in the film confirmed his memory.

At Dupont's request, my father grew a mustache for the part. In the early scenes, he acts in an easy, debonair way. But with the news of the ship's imminent sinking, he slows down his delivery like the other actors, and is less convincing. Portraying terror is clearly not his strong suit. But the critics liked what they saw. "John Stuart reveals hitherto unexpected abilities," claimed *Cinema*; the *Daily Chronicle* felt that he "improves out of all recognition on any of his former work"; *Bioscope* thought he was "very successful in a very difficult part."

Yet despite his obvious popularity, he was then out of work for eight months. According to the *Daily Film Renter,* "Every time he got a good notice his chances of getting work seemed more remote than ever." Not surprisingly, he was reported to be seriously considering several offers from America. But eventually he was back in the studios, playing parts opposite four actresses at different stages of their careers.

In *Taxi for Two* (1929), his co-star was Mabel Poulton. Small in stature, with a wistful, child-like expression, she had achieved stardom despite her impoverished working-class background. She was born into a poor London East End family: her mother ran a stall in Dalston selling jewelry, her father made overshoes for boots and shoes. At 16, Mabel was working as a secretary at the Alhambra Theatre in Leicester Square, where the London premiere of D.W. Griffith's classic film *Broken Blossoms* was to be held. Griffith had asked for a theatrical stage setting, a *tableau vivant* of one of its scenes set in a Buddhist temple, to act as a prologue to the film. The Alhambra's manager noticed Mabel's resemblance to the film's star Lillian Gish and offered her the job, which involved reclining in a kimono on a divan in front of the screen three times a day.

There she was spotted by director George Pearson, who gave her a small part in *Nothing Else Matters*, a sentimental melodrama about an old

In *Atlantic* (1929), a story based on the sinking of the *Titanic.* He and Madeleine Carroll played newlyweds aboard the liner (courtesy the Cinema Museum, London).

music hall comic. Petite, blonde and mercurial, she went on to play a range of characters from Victorian heroines to prostitutes, but specialized in feisty or mischievous working-class characters, roles which she approached with great intensity.

Balcon thought she had "that inner something which enabled a few silent-screen actresses to convey emotion without the power of speech." The poet John Betjeman remembered her affectionately as the archetypal working girl, "a girl with a pathetic face, pathetically beautiful, who seems to stand for all the thousands of people who only come out of their offices during the rush hour to go back to their little furnished rooms."

The role that made her truly famous was Tess, the young girl in *The Constant Nymph*, based on Margaret Kennedy's best-selling novel. Some 50 actresses, including the young Daphne du Maurier, were tested for the role before Poulton was chosen to play opposite Ivor Novello. In her poignant portrayal, her spirit positively glows on screen. It no doubt helped that she fell in love with Novello: She considered him her "absolute ideal," and was mortified that he treated her merely as a young sister.

More than one critic felt her performance meant her status was approaching that of the leading American stars. She was now compared to Mary Pickford rather than Lillian Gish, her performance prompting the film's producer Basil Dean to state: "She possessed a quality of emotion that I have not seen surpassed on the British screen before or since." Her broad appeal to filmgoers was summed up by John Quill in *Film Weekly*: "Through her veins runs the blood of the English people; her pulse beats in accord with the pulse of London; her life, until the films claimed her, was as the life of her audience; and for this they love her."

In *Taxi for Two*, she plays a shopgirl, whom *Picture Show* found "brimming over with personality and vivacity." My father is Jack Devenish, son of a titled woman. He falls in love with the shopgirl and poses as a taxi driver in order to win her hand. Some scenes were shot in Harrods, where "twenty of the prettiest staff girls were utilised," and where my father "made love to Mabel Poulton over a cash register at the hosiery counter." It was a slight, Cinderella-type comedy, in which his performance received only cool notices. The film was co-directed by Denison Clift and the Hungarian-born Alexander Esway.

In 1930's *The Brat* (also known as *The Nipper*), the title role was played by Betty Balfour. She was the public's most popular actress and Britain's only female international star of the time. She made her name playing valiant, put-upon, working-class girls in simple, sentimental stories.

She was discovered by George Pearson, who nurtured her career in the 1920s, making 11 films with her, including the Squibs comedy series that made her a star. Squibs was a spirited cockney flower-seller with a heart of gold, working in Piccadilly and involved in a series of low-life intrigues, romances and adventures. She proved a rare exception to the stereotyped working-class characters then appearing on British screens.

Small and gamine-like, lively and endearing, with huge blue eyes and curly blonde hair, she was also a skilled comedienne with a delicate touch, known especially for her mischievous sense of humor and sunny disposition. She topped the

With Mabel Poulton in *Taxi for Two* (1929), a silent picture hastily converted to a talkie (courtesy the Cinema Museum, London).

polls as the most popular British star from 1924 to 1927; at the height of her fame, she was said to be receiving 5000 fan letters a year. "She has joie de vivre," *Film Weekly* noted. "She is English, but somehow she has escaped the stiff-necked formality that typifies most of our race."

In *The Brat,* she returned to the kind of cockney waif role that had made her name, playing a singer in an East End pub, while my father appeared as the producer and musician Max Nicholson. This was her first independent "talk and song" picture: When no financier would back it, she raised the money herself. A *Picture Show* reporter, visiting the set during the filming of a cabaret scene, found my father "looking particularly attractive in scarlet Chilean clothes, which suited his dark hair to perfection." The film was helmed by Swiss director Louis Mercanton, best known for handling the celebrated Sarah Bernhardt in *La Reine Elisabeth.*

My father's co-star in the melodrama *Children of Chance* (1930) was Elissa Landi, a young actress noted for her beauty, aristocratic bearing, grace and intelligence. Her mother was an Austrian countess, her father an Italian count. Born in Venice, she was raised in Bavaria and Austria and educated in London. A trained pianist and dancer, she studied for three years for the Russian ballet. Her early ambition was to be a playwright, so to increase her understanding of theater she joined the Oxford Repertory Players, where she discovered she had acting ability.

In between her film appearances in the 1920s, Landi was regularly on the West

Attending a screening of _Taxi for Two_ with Mabel Poulton (in fur) and members of the John Stuart Fan Club.

End stage, her roles including Tessa in _The Constant Nymph_ and Desdemona. She was fluent in four languages, and had several novels published. Writer Elinor Glyn called her "the most beautiful creature in England" and "that extravagant freak of nature—a film star with a brain!" Labeled "The Empress of Emotion," she was hailed by the American critics as being as great an actress as Garbo.

There is no sign of this in _Children of Chance_. In this story of mistaken identity, she plays two parts, the chorus girl Millie and her double Lia, a model involved in crime. While moderately convincing as innocent Millie, Landi is unable to cope with portraying the tough, fast-talking Lia. My father plays Gordon, a cheerful, charming but none-too-bright young man unable to tell the two women apart. Initially drawn to Lia, he ends up falling in love with Millie. Mabel Poulton gives a perky performance as Millie's impish friend, while John Longden merely offers a pantomime villain. Director Alexander Esway clumsily crams several scenes with up to a dozen characters on the set. A separate German version was also made; dual-language films were common during the early years of sound, before dubbing became more established.

In _Kissing Cup's Race_ (1930), my father co-starred again with Madeleine Carroll. Since their appearance together in _Atlantic_ she had risen rapidly, and was now considered the British female star of the moment. Moore Marriott, Chili Bouchier and Stewart Rome also featured in the film. My father plays the impoverished Lord Jimmy Hilhoxton, who has to sell his horses to clear his debts. The filming took him to stables at Epsom, Windsor racecourse, and a polo park in Hertfordshire. The film was advertised as "the first British racing talkie."

"John Stuart and Miss Carroll are both horse lovers," *Kine Weekly* explained, "and a happy feature of the production is the speed with which these two clever artists got on to intimate terms with the beautiful animal whose performance would mean so much to them in the famous race." But my father suffered an accident, as he recalled in *Caught in the Act:* "While we were shooting in the polo park, the director Castleton Knight wanted me to gallop my pony right up to the camera, then swerve away to the side. The pony had other ideas. It charged straight at the camera, stopped dead in its tracks, and deposited me underneath the camera's legs. I was stunned for a while, but fortunately no damage was done."

In an article headed "Talk has Saved Old England," my father is one of four stars—Madeleine Carroll, John Longden and Betty Balfour are the others—who are said to have

Children of Chance (1930), an early crime talkie starring Elissa Landi, was a bi-lingual film, of which only the English version has survived.

"made good in British talkies." In a ballot to find the best voice for the talkies, he received the highest number of any artist in British films. Herbert Thompson, writing in *Film Weekly,* observed: "The ideal talkie voice is pure English without exaggeration or affectation of any kind. The artists on the screen whom I think have the ideal voices include George Arliss, Ruth Chatterton, Norma Shearer, Ronald Colman, Clive Brook, Herbert Marshall, and John Stuart."

During a break from filming my father had a chance to take a holiday. Now the owner of his first car, a Chrysler, he told *Film Weekly:* "When I take my holiday I shed my work-a-day self like a worn-out garment and make for the Norfolk Broads. Here, in a wherry, I wander at will, lazing in backwaters, defying time, weather and convention. It is time to indulge one's hobbies, in my case boating and fishing."

He was out of work for several months. The press were baffled by the failure of the film companies to find further roles for such a popular actor. He was clearly not happy with his stalled career. "If you make a success in this country the producers get scared," he complained. "They think you want too much money. It's a heart-breaking business. I hate to leave England, but a few more months more of this and I'm off to Hollywood."

Film producers were now busy recruiting West End stage stars, prompting him to observe: "The best way to enter a talkie studio is via the stage door. The fact that I have had three years' stage experience seems to have been lost sight of, and as I believe it is better to show what you can do rather than grumble, I am turning to the stage once more, in the hope that I shall have a chance to prove my ability as an actor."

He next dipped his toe into Cine-Variety, a new idea which involved variety turns or sketches being staged in cinemas between feature films. *The Bachelor Husband* (1930) was a 25-minute three-hander comedy sketch based on *Eve's Fall*, with Sonia Bellamy and Gerald Rawlinson also featured, and my father both acting and directing. According to the publicity, it was "A Laugh-a-Second Love Romance with a Piquant Plot and Intriguing Situations" offering "Ten Year's Laughter in Twenty Minutes."

It played three times a day for a week at the Granada Super-Cinema in Walthamstow, and for another week at the Metropole in Victoria, where there was standing room only. *Film Weekly* noted, "John Stuart had an excellent presence, a gift for humour as well as for romance, and a delightful speaking voice." It then played in other cinemas and on music hall variety bills in Didsbury and at the Eastbourne Royal Hippodrome, with Muriel Angelus and Kenneth Buckley taking over the other two parts. My father told a reporter: "I chose a farce because I prefer to make people laugh than cry."

With time to kill in their dressing room, he and Gerald Rawlinson wrote a "fox-trot song" called "Out of My Depth in Love," my father providing the lyrics and Rawlinson the music. One night during the interval, the words were put on the screen, the organ played and the audience sang the song. It was said to have created something of a stir—"Film Star as Poet" ran one headline—and resulted in an offer of publication from a leading music publisher. Soon afterwards, my father sang the song at the Bristol Film Club Ball and signed copies of the sheet music.

He also took part in a mixed evening of music and sketches at the Palladium organized by *Film Weekly,* in which "Miss Dorothy Seacombe & Mr. John Stuart present a comedietta, *A Perfect Little Fool.*" Also on the bill were the comic duo Charlie Naughton and Jimmy Gold (before they joined the Crazy Gang troupe), the contralto Carrie Herwin singing a song from *The Belle of the Ball*, and the American stage and screen actress Tallulah Bankhead acting in a one-act sketch, *The Snob.*

As a result of these Cine-Variety appearances, he received two film offers. He opted for *Midnight* (1930), a crime comedy drama helmed by George King, Britain's youngest film director, who was making a point of employing actors he felt were being neglected. The film featured Eve Gray and introduced Ellen Pollock, with my father playing Larry Byrne, a secret-service agent disguised as a burglar. Obviously relieved to be working again, he described it as his finest talkie part yet, giving him a chance to appear for the first time as more than a "decorative hero."

His reviews were good without being brilliant: "John Stuart reveals an unsuspected but thoroughly welcome lightness of touch" (*Cinema*), "An easy, intelligent portrayal" (*Kine Weekly*), "A pleasing rendering" (*Bioscope*)—these are typical examples. *Picturegoer* wrote: "He seems to improve in every film I have seen him in lately, and one begins to be fearful lest America should step in and take another of our male leads to Hollywood." Another critic was more effusive: "We have seen John Stuart act in many British films, and not once has he given a disappointing performance. His acting is always smooth and accomplished: he's the typical London clubman. In *Midnight* he plays a familiar role with a freshness and vigour that give this brief film a certain sparkle and style."

At the beginning of 1931, no doubt to his relief, he signed a new joint contract with Gaumont-Gainsborough. His first film for them that year was *The Hound of the Baskervilles,* in which he played Sir Henry Baskerville. The film was produced by Michael Balcon and directed by Gareth Gundrey, with a screenplay for Arthur Conan Doyle's famous story by the popular writer Edgar Wallace.

The assignment presented him with yet more physical challenges. The exteriors were shot in Fogintor, a vast, disused stone quarry on the edge of Dartmoor, two miles from the famous prison. In one scene, he had to fight with Lou Langford, playing the escaped convict. "I was supposed to hit him on the jaw," he recalled, "but Lou felt I didn't do it realistically enough, so he made me hit him as hard as I could. He didn't bat an eyelid, whereas I went out with an injured wrist." A startling photo from another scene shows him pinned to the ground by an enormous hound, with a paw fastened on his neck. But in his memoir, he remembered: "The bloodhound was so unferocious it was difficult to make him otherwise. I think he thought I was playing with him."

Hoping to track down a copy of the finished film, I discovered that for years only the visual elements had survived. Later the soundtrack turned up, and the integrated print was shown at the Sherlock Holmes Society in London. It was never made available commercially, but it turned out that the British Film Institute had a copy, so I was able to watch it in full in their viewing room.

Dressed in a series of well-cut suits, my father brings out Sir Henry's more humorous side and gives another polished, laid-back performance. He received good notices: *Kine Weekly* noted "a powerful characterisation," while *Picturegoer* thought he made "a personable and likeable hero." But it's a clumsy, mediocre version of the famous story, with many of the exterior scenes on the moor shot in almost total darkness, so that it is sometimes impossible to decide who is fighting with whom, or whether a hound or a human is involved.

Robert Rendell is dull and uncharismatic as Holmes, but Frederick Lloyd is lively as Dr. Watson. A reporter from *Cinema* visiting the Gainsborough studios remarked, "John Stuart was on the set in a dinner jacket, which is his recognised screen uniform." A *Film Weekly* reporter provided a snapshot of him in action: "Sir Henry Baskerville spends the morning falling off a sofa to register fright when his butler's wife throws a pair of boots at him. I commiserate with John Stuart on his unbecoming bruises. 'That's nothing,' he says. 'I've had sunstroke on the set before now, besides being temporarily blinded in one eye, and having a camera fall on me and knock me unconscious. What are a few bruises more or less?'"

In June 1931, *Picturegoer* returned to a familiar theme:

In the sound version of *Hinde Wakes* (1931), he again played the mill-owner's son, with Muriel Angelus, soon to be his second wife, playing his fiancée.

The part of Sir Henry Baskerville was played with spirit by John Stuart, that capable young actor who has remained faithful to British films for so long. What has his patriotic fidelity gained him? Nothing save fame in his own country. I am sure that he would soon become notable all over the world if he were to venture Hollywoodwards. Why one of our film companies doesn't sign Mr. Stuart up on a long-term contract and boost him for all he is worth passes my comprehension.

He was next cast in the sound version of *Hindle Wakes* (1931), adapted and directed by Victor Saville. He again plays the mill owner's son Alan Jeffcote because, as Saville later explained, "he had done so well in *Kitty*." Newcomer Belle Chrystal proves to be a tougher mill-girl than Estelle Brody. Her henpecked father was played by Edmund Gwenn, her mother by Sybil Thorndike, who had played Beatrice in a 1912 London stage production. My father reminded her of his walk-on part at the Old Vic in *The Trojan Women*: "I, the extra of yesterday, met her now on an equal footing. Dame Sybil still remembered the young man who supported her over the flames of Troy in the Waterloo Road just after the war."

Although some scenes were again shot in Blackpool and Llandudno, and also in the Royal Exchange in Manchester, the dance hall was a replica built in the Lime Grove studios. With a swifter narrative, the film was a half-hour shorter than the silent version. One critic pinpointed the recent improvement in film technique, suggesting that if the two versions were played one after the other, "the silent would merely arouse laughter." Having watched them myself on successive evenings, I agree.

The talkie version has the advantage of Stanley Houghton's strong, earthy dialogue, with its no-nonsense northern moralizing, and continual talk of "brass" and how to make it. This gives more power to certain scenes, including my father's confrontation with Norman McKinnel, cast again as his father. In his early scenes in

In the adventure drama *Verdict of the Sea* (1932) he foils a group of diamond robbers.

Blackpool, dressed in dashing style in a light suit and trilby hat, he shows himself to be an accomplished dancer, and his pleasing, unforced voice is an obvious asset in a part that is somewhat bland. One critic observed: "A polished player, John Stuart does wonders with a thoroughly ungrateful part." Another wrote: "There is increasing strength in this popular film player. I think if he had received half the opportunities of some of the other young men in pictures, he would by this time have been of star rank."

In director Maurice Elvey's *In a Monastery Garden* (1932), he plays Michael Ferrier, a composer accused of murder who turns monk to atone for his sins. The film was described by one critic as "so bad it is actually entertaining." The subplot, involving a feisty ballet dancer flirting with my father and Hugh Williams, was marked by stilted dialogue and dreadful acting.

Verdict of the Sea (1932) was filmed on location in Polperro in Cornwall, which stood in for a South Seas island. "A raging sea! A fight for love! A fortune in diamonds!" exclaimed the publicity. My father plays Gentleman Burton, a former doctor fallen on hard times. He helps foil a mutiny after joining the crew of a tramp steamer, and uncovers a secret diamond plot. Moira Lynd, the captain's pretty daughter, wanders around the ship, making it clear she is attracted to him and not tough guy Cyril McLaglen. Directed by Frank Miller, it's an untidy film, with a great deal of chaotic and unconvincing fight scenes.

At this moment, Hitchcock entered my father's story again. *Number Seventeen* (1932) was based on a play by J. Jefferson Farjeon, described as "a joyous melodrama." Hitchcock took a different view, and didn't want to direct it. He was compelled to do so contractually; to get revenge, he and the playwright Rodney Ackland, who wrote the screenplay, pulled the play apart and made it ludicrously complicated in the hope that no one would take it seriously. Some modern critics, especially French ones, do just that. "A disaster!" is how Hitchcock later described it to François Truffaut.

You can see what he means. The story, set in a deserted house, is totally confusing. It begins effectively enough, as my father, playing Detective Barton, walks along the street, into the house, and up the stairs, followed by a hand-held camera. But Hitchcock is clearly more interested in creating light and shadow than a plausible story. He creates his first "MacGuffin" (his trademark red herring, in this case a diamond necklace) and ends the film with a ridiculous race between a bus and a train, clearly a model, which finally crashes into the sea at the channel port. My father dives into the sea to save the heroine (Anne Grey) from a watery grave.

In contrast to the weird acting of Leon M. Lion and the horrendous artificiality of Donald Calthrop's performance, there's a quiet and easy authority about my father's playing. There's also a pleasingly sparky one from Ann Casson, Sybil Thorndike's daughter, playing the girl next door, whose fate is literally tied up with my father's: In one scene, they swing precariously together over a stairwell on a rope attached to a broken banister.

He had a very different role in *Men of Steel* (1932): James "Iron" Hag, the ambitious and unscrupulous foreman of a steel works. "A new John Stuart comes into being," wrote Cecilie Leslie in *Film Weekly*. "It has always amazed me that he has made such a considerable reputation for himself in view of the anaemic parts he has been called upon to fill. Now at last he has a part in which he must portray character rather than sex appeal." She described his playing of one scene: "Dressed in filthy overalls, his face shining with dirty grease, he seems to be an entirely different person. 'I don't like women,' snaps the new John Stuart; the first time, I feel sure, that he has ever had such a line to say."

Director George King shot several scenes among the mammoth cranes and giant cauldrons of the Dorman Long steelworks on Teesside in northeast England. Instead of the usual well-groomed and noble romantic hero, my father plays a nasty, aggressive steelworks foreman who, in his working-class accent, shouts and sneers at the boss. And when he reaches the top of the company, he becomes overbearing and tyrannical, falling for the boss' seductive daughter (Benita Hume), at the expense of his pretty secretary and sweetheart (Heather Angel).

This was a real departure, and the "new John Stuart" was rewarded with decent notices. *Picturegoer* thought he gave

A desperate moment for his detective hero and Ann Casson, in the thriller *Number Seventeen* **(1932), his second film under Hitchcock's direction.**

"an excellent performance"; another critic stated, "The part provides him with solid material to prove that he is a great artiste"; a third called it "his first really great part," and added, "It will open up a new era for him."

Both of his female co-stars were shortly to sign Hollywood contracts. My father also received an offer, and applied for a quota number to allow him to work in Hollywood. *Bioscope* reported: "John Stuart, probably the most popular juvenile lead of the past four or five years, after being idle—more or less—is to try his luck in Hollywood, which should bring him greater renown and more abundant credit than any of the quota pictures in which he has played during the past year."

In the *Evening Standard,* he delivered an uncharacteristically bitter attack on the British film industry:

As the tough foreman of the steelworks in *Men of Steel* (1932), he confronts the company's boss, played by Franklin Dyall (courtesy the Cinema Museum, London).

I am so tired of hearing my friends say "Why don't you go to Hollywood" that I have decided to go in September—unless anything turns up. It is better to be out of work in Hollywood than in London—heaps better. If Americans take you up, they do not drop you if you become successful. They continue to build up an actor, help him, encourage him, write a story around him, and do not overwork him. The result is that American actors give of their best and the industry flourishes.

Money is not spent in the right way in British film production. British executives will not pay £1000 a year to let the public know that they have a good actor. They are afraid of making those big strides which England will have to make in order to compete in the world market of films. I would like to see the production side of the British film industry better organised, and particularly would I welcome some of the drive, courage, and enthusiasm which have placed Americans where they are.

Then came a big break. One of those who visited the set of *Atlantic* was the eminent Austrian director G.W. Pabst. He had entered films as a director in Europe in 1923. Widely considered a master of his craft and praised for his visual inventiveness, he was best known for making *Pandora's Box* with the magnetic actress Louise Brooks. He had recently finished directing *The Threepenny Opera* with singer Lotte Lenya.

He was now preparing to film no less than three versions—in German, English and French—of Pierre Benoît's best-selling novel *L'Atlantide* (1932), a story of the discovery of the lost city of Atlantis. Its star Brigitte Helm, who spoke all three languages, played the seductive queen of the city in all three versions, shot simultaneously scene by scene. My father was cast in the English version, *The Mistress of Atlantis*, as the French soldier hero Lieutenant St. Avit, who succumbs to the potent charms of the queen and narrowly escapes death.

He spent six weeks filming in the Sahara while based in the town of Tougourt, then another month in Berlin shooting the underground interiors for the scenes in the lost city. (While in Berlin, he was reported "to have used up some of his spare hours visiting the [city's] night haunts.") Later he wrote in praise of Pabst's personality and his methods: "He was absolutely charming and made one feel quite at ease—he had a grand sense of humour and was most amusing. He referred to me as 'The Englander.' He interfered little with the actors. We had one or two rehearsals and then we shot the scene.

A poster for the English version of the tri-lingual film *L'Atlantide* (1932).

He would always say: 'Now we try.' He was very meticulous, but he never lost his temper."

My father is on screen virtually throughout, giving a strong, restrained performance. It's another physically challenging role, requiring him to leap on and off a camel, engage in a gunfight, run endlessly round the maze of underground tunnels, get hooked on a drug and kill his best friend while under the influence. He also has a strong scene playing chess with Helm, where he faces death if he loses. After they finished playing the scene, Helm apparently said: "You English are so cold, you do not know how to make love." His response was to bite her ear and tell her: "Ah, but I'm Scottish!"

On February 27, 1932, a news item appeared in *Film Weekly*: "We are informed by John Stuart and Muriel Angelus that there is no truth in the suggestion that they are engaged to be married." It was followed a week later by another report: "So John Stuart and Muriel Angelus are to be married. Though it was a 'secret,' everybody in the film world knew about it."

As the French soldier-hero in *L'Atlantide* he was cast opposite the *Metropolis* star Brigitte Helm.

Born Muriel Angelus Findlay into a medical family from Ayrshire in Scotland, she had worked as a child model. She made her singing debut at 12, eventually dropping her surname and becoming a popular music hall performer. She was on the Drury Lane stage at 15 as a fairy in Basil Dean's production of *A Midsummer Night's Dream*, then joined *The Midnight Follies* and danced in a West End production of *The Vagabond King*. She entered films toward the end of the silent era with *The Ringer* (1928), the first of three movie versions of the popular Edgar Wallace play. She was described as "a sweet-natured actress who played ingénue and 'other woman' roles."

She had met my father briefly in 1928, on the set of *Sailors Don't Care*. She had only a tiny part, and her scene was eventually deleted. During the filming, he noticed "a very pretty young girl selling chocolates, who asked me for a signed photo, which I duly sent her." Later she claimed that "it was love at first sight."

Was it mutual? In his memoir, my father states without explanation: "In 1928 my marriage to Jeanne started to break up. Very soon afterwards we separated, and a year later we were divorced." According to his brother Eric Croall, the two events were linked. Eric's wife Julie told me: "Eric liked Jeanne very much, because she encouraged John and helped him with his career. So he was very cross with him for losing her. He said they split up because of Muriel, who made a play for John, and that went a little bit to his head."

They were shown together in the press at various functions, including the Bristol Film Club Ball, the Brighton Carnival Ball and the Midland Dancing Championships in Birmingham, where they acted as judges. At a variety concert in the Borehamwood village hall, on the bill with other stars, they took part in a sketch in which, *Film Weekly* reported, "John Stuart was a gr-r-raceless villain, with snarls and ha-has, while Muriel Angelus, bubbling with laughter, played a disrobing scene, with plenty of dainty lingerie."

Together with Estelle Brody, John Longden and Leslie Howard, the pair signed copies of the *Film Weekly Stars of the Screen* annual in the Selfridges store in Oxford Street. More surprisingly, they were seen together in a London restaurant in the party of Oliver Locker-Lampson, who had just founded the Sentinels of Empire. Also known as the Blue Shirts, this was a quasi-paramilitary organization established "to peacefully fight Bolshevism and clear out the Reds!" I very much doubt that my father, who never seemed interested in politics, took an active role in this dubious set-up.

He and Muriel had co-starred in two films. The first, *Eve's Fall* (1930), a cheerful comic quota quickie short, was about a girl who loses her memory after a fall in a block of flats and is convinced she is married to the bachelor living there, Jack Tremaine, played by my father. Directed by Monty Banks, the film was, according to *Talking Picture News*, "delightfully saucy but always refined." Muriel's performance was described by another critic as "pouting, wayward, and persuasive." The second film was *No Exit* (1930), a lightweight romantic comedy, also a quota quickie. My father played Bill Alden, a penniless novelist, Muriel his publisher's daughter Ann Ansell, who mistakes him for a famous writer.

Just before news of their engagement broke, my father remarked in an interview: "Love is so disturbing that a man should not meddle with it till he's old enough to stand shocks." Having now meddled with it, he said of his fiancée: "She has a wonderful voice for talking pictures, and she is a fine singer. She is the youngest star in the country, only nineteen." In fact she was 22; it's not clear whether he knew this, or whether she misled him as well as the public. With her "fair hair, wide grey eyes, and a charming mezzo-soprano voice," she was said to be "climbing the ladder"; she was considering stage offers from both the West End and Broadway, and might at the end of the year go to Hollywood "accompanied" by my father.

"In Love with Photograph—Now She's Married the Original" ran a headline in one paper, after the couple tied the knot at Kensington Register Office on February 1, 1933. "I think I must have been in love with John ever since he sent me that photograph," said the bride. Because of their busy schedules—he was filming *The Lost Chord*, she was rehearsing with George Robey for the comic opera *Jolly Roger*—they arrived at the Register Office at 8:30 in the morning.

My father was wearing a light tweed overcoat and black trilby hat, while Muriel "is dressed in a n[-----] brown velvet suit with a heavy fox fur round her shoulders, and a close-fitting brown hat over her flaxen curls." The hour was so early that their friends arrived just as they were leaving. Only two people were present as witnesses: Irvine Asher, production chief at Warner Brothers, and actress Thérèse Vincent, then starring in *Wild Violets* at Drury Lane. There was no best man. "No time even for breakfast, but we may snatch a cup of coffee," my father told reporters. In fact, they had a wedding breakfast at the Grosvenor Hotel.

A week later, while Muriel was on tour in Manchester, my father took time off for a "one-day honeymoon." Muriel remarked coyly: "We are so amazed at having a day to ourselves that we don't really know what to do." My father talked of her future: "Muriel is not giving up her stage career. She has only just started to make a name for herself, and she means to go on."

They moved into a new flat in Kensington. Muriel designed the white-wood furniture, made for them by a film studio carpenter who referred to their rooms as "sets." My father had his portrait painted by a Mr. Christie. He bought a very distinctive Humber car, "a rather flashy affair, picked out in red and silver enamel, and flashing with gleaming plate," according to one report. He announced that he and Muriel hoped to travel and honeymoon on the Continent, and maybe buy a country cottage. But by August they had only managed to snatch a couple of weekends off.

My father complained about their Box and Cox existence: "I get back from the studio and Muriel has left for the theatre. I fetch her at the end of the show, we go home, and at 7.30 I'm off again to the studio. For six months we've hardly seen one another." He claimed that he had not had a holiday for three years. It was a situation that must have put a strain on their marriage.

Other Films

He appeared as a bank manager in the comedy short *The Wrong Mr. Perkins* (1931), a tale of mistaken identity directed by Arthur Varney. In the comedy *Little Fella* (1932), he played a major who leaves his fiancée to marry an orphan who has a baby. "Much of the comedy material is crude," wrote one critic. "However it will make a good second feature, and should appeal to women."

Women Are That Way (1932), another comedy short, was about a psychoanalyst who falls in love. Hal Walters, Joan Marion and Sunday Wilshin appeared alongside my father.

With Gracie Fields
and Conrad Veidt

"John Stuart's performance is a very good one indeed, and his simplicity and sincerity atone for the histrionics of Cedric Hardwicke and Conrad Veidt."—*Era* on *Bella Donna* (1934)

My father was now a freelance actor, his contract with Gaumont-Gainsborough having ended. During 1933, he was busier than ever, notching up no less than a dozen films. But many were no challenge for someone with his ambition and past record.

He appeared first in *The Wandering Jew* (1933), based on E. Temple Thurston's stage melodrama. The director again was Elvey, who had directed a silent version ten years earlier. It tells the story of the eponymous figure, who demands the release of Barabbas at the crucifixion. Because he has insulted Christ, he is doomed to wander the earth, adopting different occupations—a crusading knight, a merchant, a doctor—during subsequent centuries.

The title role was played by Conrad Veidt, the German actor who fled the Nazis, proclaiming himself a Jew, which he was not. He had caused a sensation when he appeared as the murderous somnambulist in the celebrated silent film *The Cabinet of Dr. Caligari*. In his review of that film in his book *"Have You Seen…,"* film historian David Thomson pinpointed his persona: "Veidt was a creature from Poe's nightmares—tall, gaunt, glowing with a mixture of illness and ecstatic anxiety…. He was an attenuated, hyper-sensitive figure, the aesthete or artist tormented by dark forces and driven to violence."

Veidt's performance in *The Wandering Jew* is ponderous in the extreme. It's marked by slow-motion acting: long pauses, and a great deal of staring, as if he were still inhabiting his *Caligari* character. Also featured are Marie Ney, Anne Grey and a young Peggy Ashcroft, making her screen debut: she gives a convincingly passionate performance as the prostitute who unwittingly betrays Veidt to the Spanish Inquisition. She actually disliked filming, thought the film was "terrible," and rarely appeared on screen in the next 30 years. My father played Pietro Morelli, a monk in the service of Veidt, and appeared in two short scenes with the German star. It must have been a blow to his ambition.

The film is filled with chaotic crowd scenes and has a confusingly episodic storyline, with characters often appearing without any indication as to who they are. Understandably it bewildered the public and divided the critics, drawing comments

Conrad Veidt and Peggy Ashcroft were among the stars in *The Wandering Jew* (1933), in which he played a monk (courtesy the Cinema Museum, London).

that ranged from "wonderful" to "boring." The *Observer* described it as "just a series of orthodox pageants, with wigs by Clarkson and a vast crowd of extras running about in fancy dress."

Throughout the 1930s, variety-based entertainment films—mixing music, slap-stick and stand-up comedy—were immensely popular, most notably those that starred George Formby and Gracie Fields, the much-loved "lass from Lancashire." My father had a moderately interesting role in *This Week of Grace* (1933), her third film.

Fields was affectionately known as "Our Gracie"; her cheeky personality on screen, her warmth as a comedienne and her astonishing singing voice—described as a cross between a chirp and an operatic trill—made her England's highest-earning star and the top box office draw during the years of depression in 1930s Britain. Yet she later made it clear in her autobiography *Sing as We Go* that she was not happy with the experience of filming, and was critical of all her films except her first, *Sally in Our Alley.*

Her films were unashamedly vehicles for her very distinctive talent. In the *Spectator,* Basil Wright pinpointed the secret of her success: "She really does represent a common denominator for those millions of English folk who like humour and sentiment of the type known as homely. Her personality is not merely powerful; it represents an intimacy with each audience which can arise only out of the true traditions of English music hall."

The story, as described by *Picturegoer,* was "just another variation on the old Cinderella theme, with Gracie as a factory girl who, through the whim of a duchess, finds herself in temporary possession of an ancestral castle and estate.... Most of the detail is extraneous, and introduced to give Gracie's versatility a chance of exploitation." Directed by Maurice Elvey, it co-stars Henry Kendall and Nina Boucicault, and features a good deal of creaky acting.

As the castle's resident librarian Henry Baring, my father acts as Gracie's mentor, supposedly "educating" her in a few months, teaching her the King's English, and transforming her accent, dress and knowledge of poetry. He remembered a snatch of the dialogue: "When I said I was satisfied with her progress, she said, 'Well, if you're satisfied, blimey I am!'" His hair dyed gray, and with an unexplained limp, my father is a model of calm, both charming and natural, and establishes a genuine and dignified rapport with Gracie. But the film was seen as her poorest; one critic described it as a "cheapjack quickie."

Despite his starring role in *L'Atlantide,* he was clearly not satisfied with his screen career. "I want to be a star," he declared in August to a surprised Philip Slessor of *Film Pictorial,* who thought he was one already. "I want to reach a point where, instead of being subsidiary to the stories in which I play, the stories will be subsidiary to me. I'd like to be a star rather than a featured player, which is what the lot of most British actors amounts to." He cited Madeleine Carroll, Herbert Marshall and Evelyn Laye as rare examples of the star breed, and continued: "How I envy the Hollywood stars! If they're under long-term contract, they know that they will have to make four or five pictures each year. They can reckon on having so much holiday each year. They can go away occasionally and forget about films, as I'd like to do."

Director Maurice Elvey's *The Lost Chord* (1933) was inspired by Arthur Sullivan's song of that name. My father plays David Graham, a musician who becomes embroiled in the domestic rows of an aristocratic family, and kills the father in a duel. Twenty years later, he falls in love with the daughter of the dead man, who becomes engaged to him in gratitude for his helping her with her acting career, but ends up marrying the young doctor whom she really loves.

My father aged convincingly, not just due to his makeup and graying hair, but also to his more mature demeanor. But I notice a flaw in his acting technique which had started to become apparent: a tendency when hearing some revelation to stare into space or look downwards, rather than engage directly with and react to the person talking.

During the early talkies he had his portrait painted by Mabel Greenberg.

The daughter is played very sensitively by Elizabeth Allan. There is also a pleasingly fresh and romantic performance by Jack Hawkins, cast as the young doctor; in later years, he was to become Britain's top box office star, specializing in authority figures and doughty war-time heroes. The momentum of the plot is lost in the middle of the film, as a result of an overlong and gratuitous party scene, clearly inserted to allow the pianist Billy Mayerl and the singer Tudor Davies to display their talents.

My father's next film was the romantic family drama *The House of Trent* (1933), directed by Norman Walker, who was mainly known for making morally earnest films. He played both John Trent and Dr. Trent and, according to one critic, provided "a sound and realistic study in the dual role of father and son"; another wrote, "John Stuart acquits himself well, investing his roles with conviction throughout." Anne Grey—another actress soon to escape to Hollywood—played his wife and then his mother.

Also in the cast was Norah Baring, who had attracted attention in Hitchcock's *Murder!* She recalled the impact of his personality in the studio: "Filming with John is always a pleasant experience, and the intervals between laughs are very rare. He kept everybody from the electricians to the artists in a state of mirth. On days when he was not working, a kind of gloom descended on everyone in the studio."

My father had another double role in *The Pointing Finger* (1933), the story of a family struggle for a peerage and an inheritance, in which he plays his own half-brother, Lord Rollestone. With their very different personalities—one basically cheerful, the other serious—the two parts allow him to display his acting range, which he does with impressive effect. This is despite an absurd plot featuring a portrait of a monk linked to a curse on the family, and scenes supposedly set in the African bush which give more than a hint of Shepherd's Bush.

Leslie Perrins is moderately convincing as the villain, and Viola Keats has some lively banter with my father in his cheerful role, but the rest of the acting is poor. The film was directed by the normally well-respected George Pearson, a leading director and the most forward-looking in the silent era (he had a thorough knowledge of foreign films). During the 1930s, Pearson mostly turned to directing quota quickies, and this clumsy effort belies his earlier reputation.

Crime films and thrillers were made in abundance during the 1930s, and my father featured in several, of varying quality. *The Four Masked Men* (1934), also directed by Pearson, was a heavy-handed thriller in which a gang of four commit a series of robberies before being unmasked. A large number of dinner jackets and dressing gowns are featured in this sluggish story. The Australian-born Judy Kelly, a relative newcomer to the screen, is stiff and self-conscious as the woman in love with my father. He by contrast is very much at ease as the barrister hero Trevor Phillips; *Picturegoer* thought him "dignified and natural." There's also a subtle, very real performance from Miles Mander as a distressed victim of blackmail by the gang; but Richard Cooper's upper-class buffoon is pure caricature. A reporter watched my father and Judy Kelly working in the studio and noted director Pearson's performance: "George was dancing about all over the place, standing on a chair and waving a handkerchief at his artists."

My father then played a young architect who helps to solve a kidnapping in *The Black Abbot* (1934). A dire thriller directed by George A. Cooper, it's marked by disreputable acting, notably by two "lovable" working-class cockneys, and by

Playing a musician in *The Lost Chord* (1933), he falls in love with Elizabeth Allan. Like many of his co-stars, she soon embarked for Hollywood.

Richard Cooper, repeating his upper-class buffoon from *The Four Masked Men*. My father, co-starring again with Judy Kelly, rises above this nonsense with a relaxed performance as the hero Frank Brooks.

The thriller *Blind Justice* (1934), directed by Bernard Vorhaus and based on Arnold Ridley's play *Recipe for Murder*, had a promising cast, featuring the popular stage stars Frank Vosper and Eva Moore, and John Mills and Roger Livesey at the start of their distinguished film careers. My father co-stars as John Summers, the brother of the beautiful Irish redhead Geraldine Fitzgerald, making her film debut before moving to Hollywood. *Kinematograph* noted "a sound piece of acting from John Stuart."

Literary adaptations were another popular genre of the period. His next film, *Bella Donna*, was based on the novel of that name by Robert Hitchens. The third screen version of the story, it was directed by Russian-born Robert Milton. Not for the first time, critics described this as "the part of his life," *Picture Show* commenting: "Never has John Stuart had a role which gives him so much scope to show off his versatile powers."

He plays Nigel Armine, an idealistic, cheerful, and naive engineer, who marries an upper-class, ambitious, and self-centered English woman (Mary Ellis). They move to Egypt, where she develops a sudden passion for a blatant womanizer (Conrad Veidt), whom she describes unambiguously as "someone who knows the woman in me." She tries to poison her husband to gain her freedom, but is foiled by his long-time friend and doctor (Cedric Hardwicke). Interestingly, my father has more screen time than Veidt. The beautiful American stage star Mary Ellis, making her screen debut, mixes sensuality with a distracting self-consciousness. She was yet another of my father's leading ladies who was to sign a Hollywood contract soon after they worked together.

It's a wordy melodrama, in which the players move almost in slow motion around a cramped set. It divided the critics, with certain performances felt to be more suited to "the German school of acting." But my father avoids this criticism, as the *News Chronicle* noted, observing: "John Stuart does handsomely by the deluded husband." The *Era* critic agreed: "The one player who succeeds in being credible in sheerly impossible circumstances is John Stuart, as the aggrieved husband. His performance is a very good one indeed, and his simplicity and sincerity atone for the histrionics of Cedric Hardwicke and Conrad Veidt."

Histrionics is an odd word here: Hardwicke is steadily low-key, while Veidt makes for a one-dimensional, oily seducer, with his face crudely darkened to make him seem Egyptian. But the qualities of simplicity and sincerity are spot on for my father, who is also convincingly amorous in his early romantic scenes with Mary Ellis. Only at the climax, when he discovers she is poisoning him, does he revert to the long stare he sometimes employs in this kind of situation.

At Easter he took time off from filming to attend the traditional fashion parade in Hyde Park. The journalist Mary Castle caught the excitement of the crowd there, estimated at a quarter of a million. "Then there was a rush. A man with a top hat and morning suit, and two smartly dressed women appeared. The crowd roared: 'There's John Stuart, see him? Who's that with him? The tall one is his wife, Muriel Angelus, and the little one in black and white is Carol Coombe. Look, their skirts are so tight they can only just walk.'"

He was then back in the studio for the quota quickie *The Blue Squadron* (1934), an Anglo-Italian aviation drama based on the Italian film *L'Armata Azzura*, and directed by George King. He and Esmond Knight play boyhood friends who become pilots in the Italian air force, and rivals for the same woman (Greta Hansen). Surprisingly, they played Italians, Colonel Mario Spada (my father) and Captain Carlo Banti (Knight). When Banti crashes, Spada gallantly puts aside their rivalry and rescues him.

He appeared next in another quota quickie, *Grand Prix* (1934), directed by St. John L. Clowes. As Milton Rosmer's son Jack Holford, he invents a new kind of racing car, and has to win a big race in order to win the girl. During the filming at Cricklewood Studios, when a car he was driving was supposed to burst into flames, the studio itself caught fire. One report states that he hadn't realized the flames were real, and that after being rescued from the car by his fellow-actors he remarked coolly: "I thought it was a bit hotter than it used to be." This sounds like studio spin, since another report suggests he had already left the studio, and it was a double in the car.

He appeared next in the romantic melodrama *D'Ye Ken John Peel* (1934), directed by Henry Edwards. Set in the period just after the Napoleonic Wars, it had John Garrick as Peel, Leslie Perrins as the smooth villain Charles Hawksley, and Stanley Holloway as Peel's servant, delivering his celebrated monologue "Sam, Pick Up Tha' Musket." The heroine Lucy Merrall was played by pretty Winifred Shotter, a former singer and dancer who had made her name on stage in leading roles in the Aldwych farces.

My father appeared as Tim Freeman, a soldier of the regiment, who at night disguises himself as the masked, devil-may-care highwayman Captain Moonlight. He is planning a final hold-up before fleeing to Paris with his lover Sally to live on his ill-gotten gains. It was a role that allowed him to show off his horsemanship; "real Dick Turpin stuff, and very enjoyable" is how he described it. As a reporter from *Film Pictorial* visiting the Twickenham Studios wrote: "I watched him leap on a charging steed, all covered in lather (made from soap flakes) resulting from a wild and adventurous ride, and pull it up in the space of some twenty yards. Try it, and you won't find it easy."

He had recently started to take singing lessons, and the role also gave him a chance to display his vocal ability in what *Era* called "good popular entertainment." This was his singing debut on screen: "John Stuart Sings!" ran one headline, echoing in its own modest way the famous "Garbo Laughs!" publicity slogan for *Ninotchka*. Striding into an inn dressed in his regimental outfit, he jumps onto a table and delivers a drinking song with great panache, revealing an attractive tenor voice.

It was Muriel who persuaded him to develop his singing. *Picture Show* gives a brief glimpse of their domestic scene: "She sits down at the piano, and John stands near, listens to her singing for time on end. Suddenly she stops, looks up, and says firmly: 'Your turn, John!'" He then decides—or perhaps is persuaded—to take lessons with her teacher, the celebrated singer Herbert Caesari, a mentor of Gigli, and the man said to have passed the *bel canto* tradition on to a new generation.

Next came *Once a Thief* (1935), a quota quickie of a higher standard than most such films. My father plays Roger Drummond, a pioneering scientist mistakenly accused of stealing a necklace, imprisoned, then released so he can prove his innocence. Dressed for once in casual clothes rather than the trademark dinner jacket, he provides a spirited performance, in a part which allows him to express a wide range of conflicting emotions. He is well supported by Derek Gorst as a scheming rival scientist and Nancy Burne as the owner of the necklace, who gradually becomes convinced of his innocence and, inevitably, falls in love with him.

Directed by Frederick Hayward, *Lend Me Your Husband* (1935) was a light comedy on the theme of marital fidelity, or the lack of it. In the part of Jeff Green, he is married to Nora Swinburne, a specialist in genteel roles, who allows him to spend a weekend in a country cottage with her zany best friend, played by Nancy Burne, knowing that she will quickly drive him mad.

The early scenes feature some smart dialogue, notably between Swinburne, who gives a cool and sophisticated performance, and Annie Esmond, who plays her mother. But in the cottage scenes between my father and Burne, the film descends into knockabout farce and becomes extraordinarily silly. My father is unable to find the right tone, underlining his basic inability to deal with comedy.

In his next picture, *Abdul the Damned* (1935), promoted as "The Life and Intrigues of the Monarch who was the Enigma of Europe," he joins a cast headed by two Hollywood stars. There was the tall, blond and handsome Swedish actor Nils Asther; openly gay, he was known as the "Male Garbo" after appearing in two of her films. Having been blacklisted for an alleged breach of contract, he came to England to continue his career. There was also Adrienne Ames, an American actress who had small roles in the silent era, but became popular in Hollywood in the 1930s for playing society women.

Abdul the Damned tells the story of the cruel monarch Abdul Hamid II, sultan of Turkey, and the rebellion against his repressive regime that led to his banishment. Historical dramas had become a popular genre several years ago. *Abdul the Damned* was influenced by the work of the Hungarian producer Alexander Korda, who had come to Britain in 1931 and established a tradition of lavish productions, the best-known being his recent *The Private Life of Henry VIII* starring Charles Laughton.

Abdul the Damned became one of the most ambitious films ever made in Britain. The exterior scenes were filmed in Constantinople; the huge sultan's palace and Turkish streets were built at Elstree. *The News of the World* approved of this ambition: "British productions are no longer hole-in-the-corner affairs, but line up now with the best that Hollywood can devise."

The film gained an extra resonance for being made against the backdrop of Hitler's rise in Europe. In the title role was the great Austrian actor Fritz Kortner, a leading actor and director in the German theater and cinema, whose Richard III was regarded as a fine performance that students throughout Germany were encouraged to watch. He had recently fled the Nazi regime, and stopped off in Britain, as had another Austrian, the film's director Karl Grune, noted for his groundbreaking silent film *The Street*.

British actors Eric Portman and Esmé Percy were also involved, the latter as a very camp chief eunuch. But according to *Picturegoer*, there was "more than a spot of bother" about finding a juvenile lead to play Captain Talak-Bey, leader of the Young Turks. Charles Farrell, John Loder and Raymond Massey were all cast but came "unglued," but finally in my father "they have a hero who fits the part like a skin and is sticking to it like glue."

It was another dashing role in uniform of the kind he relished, and his revived mustache looks more suitable with a

He played Captain Talak-Bey, leader of the Young Turks, in the lavish and ambitious *Abdul the Damned* (1935).

fez and a smart white uniform and cape than with a trilby and lounge suit. "John Stuart once again shows he is one of the best actors in British films," commented the *Daily Mail*. The *Sunday Pictorial* noted, "For once he gets a part worthy of his talent."

But to me, it's a less than convincing performance. He seems to play on only two notes, severe and charming, the latter in his scenes with Adrienne Ames, who plays a Viennese opera singer, and the former in his role as the rebellion leader. He's quite overshadowed by Asther as the ultra-smooth chief of police, and in particular by Kortner, who gives an arresting performance as Abdul. With the help of Ashley Dukes' literate screenplay, he manages to evoke sympathy for this bloodthirsty tyrant. "As a study in vileness it is immense," observed *The Times*.

The film went down well with the critics. In the *Daily Telegraph*, Campbell Dixon wrote: "It seems to me one of the three or four best pictures ever produced in this country. Altogether one to see, discuss, and remember." *The Times* observed: "*Abdul the Damned* is an intense thriller. It has novelty, a picturesque setting, and is peculiarly interesting. Rarely have fact and fiction been better blended on the screen." Its world premiere at the Regal, Marble Arch, was attended by dukes, lords, ladies, baronets and others of that breed. They gave my father, Grune and Kortner "huge ovations" when they were presented on stage.

Like scores of other actors, my father took part in *Royal Cavalcade* (1935), filmed as a celebration of George V's jubilee. A fatuous historical pageant covering events during his reign, with episodes directed by six different directors under the supervision of Thomas Bentley, it was seen through the eyes of a penny coin, as it changed hands during those years. It has an embarrassingly deferential narrative, interspersed with interesting newsreel footage and completely unrealistic cameo scenes enacted by stars of the day. They included George Robey, Hermione Baddeley, Seymour Hicks, Matheson Lang, Athene Seyler, Esmé Percy, Marie Lohr and John Mills.

My father was involved in a scene showing Scott of the Antarctic and his expedition coming across their rival Amundsen's deserted tent at the South Pole. Frank Vosper was cast as Scott, Austin Trevor as Captain Oates; my father, heavily hooded but just about recognizable, plays another expedition member. He looks anxious, as well he might, as Captain Oates goes outside for a moment and may be a little while, while Scott writes a farewell letter, ending "For God's sake look after my wife!"

My father's fondness for the monarchy is apparent in a letter written to a distant relative in Australia in January 1936. "How dreadful it is to think King George died last Monday night," he says. It's written on notepaper headed Vadis Productions Ltd in Regent Street, of which the sole directors are John Stuart and H.G. Inglis, who later became a film producer. Had he set himself up as a producer, perhaps to produce a Roman epic? Or, more likely, formed a company for tax purposes? I can find no further reference to this body.

He and Heather Angel took part in a television experiment, at a time before any public service set-up had been established. The engineer John Logie Baird asked them to record a scene in his studio in Long Acre in Covent Garden, and it was then beamed onto the screen at the Metropole in Victoria, apparently the first time this had been done. "It was only a test," he observed, "and the quality was a bit flickery."

He and Muriel were now living in northwest London in St. John's Wood, at 6 Spencer Court, 32 Marlborough Place. Muriel had reportedly "gone off films" and was concentrating on her singing, under the tuition of "one of the finest professors in Europe." She had made her pantomime debut as the principal boy in *The Queen of Hearts* at the Lyceum, and was now cast in the lead as a singer-dancer in the hit Russian operetta *Balalaika* at His Majesty's. "Muriel is a sensation," wrote *Film Pictorial*, "and I imagine it will be impossible for her to ignore the lure of films much longer." At some point, her work was interrupted when she had a serious attack of appendicitis. To recuperate, she and my father took a holiday in their cottage near Newquay in Cornwall.

But her musical ambitions clearly rubbed off on my father, who in October made his concert debut in Reading. He was in distinguished company: at the top of the bill on her farewell tour was the celebrated coloratura soprano Luisa Tetrazzini

("The World's Most Famous Prima Donna and the Greatest Personality before the Public Today"), while Harold Fielding ("The Brilliant English Boy Violinist") and Adela Verne ("The Eminent Pianist") also appeared. With Ivor Newton accompanying him on the piano, my father sang two songs in each half of the program. He also sang in a program called *Sunday Non-Stops* at the Prince of Wales in the West End.

I always remember him as immaculately dressed, and a feature in *The Tailor and Cutter* makes clear how his sartorial image mattered to him, how he strived to achieve what he called "that clean appearance so desirable for a man." His interviewer observed: "He possesses the kind of figure tailors dream of. His conservative taste would not cause anyone any heartburn, and he always pays his bills promptly." That day he was wearing "a double-breasted coat, a dark-blue worsted suit, a single-breasted waistcoat, a white shirt, blue silk socks, and a black soft hat. In brief, his dress was smart without being flashy." He revealed that he goes to Kilgour & French for his suits, and wears a top hat and tails for formal evening occasions.

In the following year, he made only two films. In *Reasonable Doubt* (1936), he plays Noel Hampton, a lawyer whose love for a young girl (Nancy Burne) causes him to defend the man he thinks is her lover, only to discover during the trial that the man is his own son. In his memoir, my father recalled: "Director George King took me aside on the set and said: 'One day I will make you a very big star.' But I never worked with him again."

The Elder Brother (1937), a quota quickie also directed by King, was a tale of two brothers and a matter of mistaken identity, resulting in the elder one being wrongly tried for the murder of a tycoon's wife. Basil Langton is impressively suave as the spendthrift younger brother up at Oxford. In the title role, my father is convincing as Ronald Bellairs, the responsible member of the family. Marjorie Taylor as his fiancée matches him for sincerity in their romantic scenes, and Hilary Pritchard provides a suitably nasty villain.

He now made a second film with "Our Gracie," then at the height of her fame. *The Show Goes On* (1937) was based partly on her own life, telling the story of a mill hand who becomes a musical star. It was directed by Basil Dean, known as Bastard Basil for his frequent cruel treatment of actors. Owen Nares plays the ailing composer who helps her become a music hall success; my father is Mack McDonald, her conventional engineer boyfriend, who dislikes her being on the stage and earning more than he does. It was the first time he was able to use a Scots accent on screen, and it sounds thoroughly authentic: "As soon as he began to read the part he found his native accent rolling off his tongue like water down a funnel," one journalist reported.

The Show Goes On is a lackluster film, with mediocre musical numbers, though Fields' sincerity shines through. She and my father clearly got on well in their previous film together, since it was she who asked for him to be cast opposite her for this one. He kept a photo of her, which she signed "My love to thee, dear John." Near the end of her life, after he had suggested they might meet up when she was next in London, she replied from her Capri home: "Next trip home I'll do my best to find you. I

He was Gracie Fields' Scottish boyfriend in *The Show Goes On* (1937).

too would enjoy a get-together, as it's nice to meet faces one has liked specially, and I liked you very special. Well, lad, take good care of yourself, and bestest luv always. Gracie."

His film output remained generally unexciting. *Pearls Bring Tears* (1937), directed by Manning Haynes, was a slight if ingenious comedy with my father as Harry Willshire and Dorothy Boyd as Madge Hart, who borrows a string of pearls without consent and then loses them. Eve Gray and 20-year-old Googie Withers were also featured. One ambiguous notice read: "It is the actors' tireless enthusiasm that keeps the fun at concert pitch."

Talking Feet (1937), directed by John Baxter, was something of an oddity. Faced with the threatened move of their local hospital to another town, a group of worthies stage a fund-raising show featuring child performers. The undoubted star is nine-year-old Hazel Ascot, a kind of British Shirley Temple, who displays astonishing ability as a tap dancer and an impersonator. The show also includes tedious, overlong offerings from the Dagenham Girl Pipers and the Band of the Royal Marines. In the thin non-musical plot, my father gives a genial performance as Dr. Roger Hood, while Enid Stamp-Taylor is agreeably lively as his romantic interest.

In the low-budget *The Claydon Treasure Mystery* (1938), directed by Manning Haynes, my father appears as Peter Kerrigan, a car designer and novelist. Through a misunderstanding, he is summoned by the elderly Lady Caroline Claydon (Annie Esmond) to solve two murders and a kidnapping, and to find the Claydon treasure. It's a part he plays with a deft, light-hearted touch, having both the best lines and the best suits, and along the way charming the daughter of the manor (Evelyn Ankers). His scenes with both women have an easy naturalism within this heavily plotted crime drama, enacted in the grand house by Finlay Currie, John Laurie, Garry Marsh and Joss Ambler.

This marked my father's fiftieth talking picture. It was because of the mediocrity of most of his recent parts that he now made a bold decision. As he recalled later: "I grew so tired of always being given characterless parts that I set up my own stage repertory company, and took it up north to get some experience in character work."

Other Films

Swiss-born John Daumery directed three of his 1933 films: the comedy *Naughty Cinderella*, in which he co-stars with Winna Winfried and Betty Huntley Wright, in a tale of a young Danish girl who masquerades as a tomboy; the drama *Head of the Family*, with a cast that included Roland Culver, Arthur Maude and the eminent stage actress Irene Vanbrugh; and another comedy, *Mr. Quincey of Monte Carlo*, where he plays the title role opposite Rosemary Ames.

George King directed him in the crime film *Mayfair Girl* (1933), which features Sally Blane, James Carew and a young Charles Hawtrey.

In the melodrama *Home, Sweet Home* (1933), directed by George A. Cooper, he appears opposite Marie Ney as an engineer who accidentally kills his wife's lover.

He was a singer's manager who confesses to a crime he didn't commit in the romance *Love's Old Sweet Song* (1933), directed by Manning Haynes. The cast included Joan Wyndham and Moore Marriott.

Director George King's *Enemy of the Police* (1933), co-starring Viola Keats and A. Bromley Davenport, was a very poor quota quickie. My father played the head of a moral reform society who is mistaken for a criminal.

In *The Green Pack* (1934), a routine murder-mystery based on Edgar Wallace's last stage play, he plays a gold prospector in Portuguese West Africa (as created at the Beaconsfield Studios). Directed by T. Hayes Hunter, the film also features

Aileen Marson and Garry Marsh as his fellow prospectors and Hugh Miller as the villain.

He plays a British agent thwarting a foreign power in the thriller *The Secret Voice* (1936), in which a scientist tries to protect his new invention from enemy spies. His director was George Pearson, his co-stars Diana Beaumont and John Kevan.

16

Stage Matters

"John Stuart carried off with great credit the difficult part of the prophet, keeping him as much as might be on the hither side of priggishness."
—W.A. Darlington, *Daily Telegraph*, reviewing the play *Public Saviour No 1*

Following his West End debut in *Our Betters* in 1923, my father undertook no further theater work for the rest of the silent era, concentrating almost exclusively on his blossoming film career. There was, however, a brief brush with the theater in 1928, when the press reported that he had been appointed the manager of a weekly repertory season at the reopening Greyhound theater in Croydon in South London.

The first play was to be *Loyalties* by John Galsworthy, to be followed by *The Second Mrs. Tanqueray* by Arthur Wing Pinero, *Eliza Comes to Stay* by H.V. Esmond, *The Yellow Ticket* by Michael Morton, *Tilly of Bloomsbury* by Ian Hay, *Caste* by T.W. Robertson, *The Witness for the Defence* by A.E.W. Mason and Harold Brighouse's *Hobson's Choice*. Assuming he took up this position—I can find no other mention of it—it was presumably either administrative or, which seems more likely, a sinecure, designed to attract the public by attaching a star name to the season of popular plays.

It was not until 1934 that he resumed his stage career in the West End. He began at the Savoy in *Finished Abroad*, a satirical play by Joliffe Metcalfe about a finishing school. He was cast as a dashing Italian count who taught the girls fencing. It also starred Ellen Pollock and Carol Coombe, and was directed by the Austrian actress and director Leontine Sagan. Ivor Brown in the *Observer* thought him "every inch a Count Curioni," while another critic wrote somewhat archly: "Mr. John Stuart upheld the standard of decency and chivalry as befitted the only male in the cast."

Printed in the program was a questionnaire he completed under the heading "Confessions," which gives some hint of his current lifestyle. Tennis is his favorite sport, Players his favorite cigarette, the Savoy his favorite restaurant, a fishing village on the Cornish coast his ideal holiday venue. Some questions he answers facetiously: "Who is your favourite tailor?—The one who never sends me in his bill." Others reflect a popular contemporary male attitude to women: "What is your favourite hobby?—Playing the one male part in a company of girls," and "What is your favourite motto?—*Cherchez la femme*."

A feature in *Film Pictorial* noted: "John Stuart is one of those quiet, unassuming men, with an easy manner. He and his wife Muriel Angelus lead a quiet home life, free from the ostentation and pretentiousness so often associated with the stars."

Just before *Balalaika* opened at the Adelphi, the couple finally got away for a month's honeymoon, including one week in Vienna and another in the Austrian Tyrol, from where my father sent a postcard home explaining: "We're just relaxing. Don't think we've turned into mountain climbers—we came up here by railway!" *Balalaika* then ran for over a year, and led to Muriel being offered the part of Adriana in the original Broadway production of *The Boys from Syracuse*, Rodgers and Hart's musical adaptation of Shakespeare's *The Comedy of Errors*.

Was it Muriel grasping this great opportunity that caused their marriage to break up? Or was her leaving for New York a sign that it had already fallen apart? Was it a sudden crisis, or a slow-burning one? As early as June 1931, she was talking about going to America to appear on the New York stage, "and hoping eventually to land in Hollywood." I can find no evidence to show what caused their separation. Muriel was clearly ambitious, probably more so than my father, whose career seemed to be faltering. The little I've been able to discover about their married life suggests she was the driving force.

Whatever the story, in November 1938 she opened on Broadway in *The Boys from Syracuse*, delivering the great Rodgers and Hart standard "Falling in Love with Love" with what the *New York Times* critic called "exquisite sweetness." This led to a contract with Paramount and a move to Hollywood, where she played Ronald Colman's girlfriend in a version of Rudyard Kipling's novel *The Light That Failed*. But although she gave an assured, warm and sympathetic performance as Brian Donlevy's secretary in Preston Sturges' biting political satire *The Great McGinty*, offering to become his wife "for the sake of the women's vote," she never became a star. She left films and revived her Broadway career, having a great success in the long-running musical comedy *Early to Bed*, with music by Fats Waller. She also appeared in the Sigmund Romberg-Oscar Hammerstein musical *Sunny River*.

While she and my father were still together, he was making several appearances on the West End stage. In 1935, he starred in three further plays. In *Public Saviour No 1* by John Frushard, a modern morality tale of Chicago's gangland, he took on the unlikely role of a modern-day Jesus. The play was only passed for performance after the Lord Chamberlain spent three weeks consulting with "ecclesiastical and legal authorities" about the portrayal of Jesus on stage.

Critic W.A. Darlington considered the piece "an odd mixture of crudity, mawkishness, sincerity, and melodrama," but added: "John Stuart carried off with great credit the difficult part of the prophet, keeping him as much as might be on the hither side of priggishness." Other papers also praised him: according to the *Sphere*, "He played the part with easy and quite impressive naturalness," while the *Manchester Guardian* thought it "an admirable study." But some critics felt they should praise his courage rather than his judgment in attempting such a poor part. *The Times* observed: "John Stuart brings a certain smooth accomplishment to his impossible task," and the *Sunday Graphic* critic wrote: "Forbes-Robertson could have done nothing with the part."

However, the play seems to have gone down extremely well on its pre–London provincial tour to Birmingham, Manchester and Blackpool. On its first night at the Prince of Wales in Birmingham, it received 22 curtain calls; my father's landlady was allegedly so impressed by it that she went every subsequent night. At the Black-pool Opera House, the manager told him that "not a single cigarette was lit during one act, although smoking is allowed in all parts of the house." By now he seemed to have no problem in switching between films and theater. But, as so often happened, West End audiences were less impressed; the play opened during a heat wave, and closed after just a week at the Piccadilly. One critic wrote: "After this sad experience I expect John Stuart will stick to the films for a long time to come."

But before the year was out, he was back in the West End in *A Butterfly on the Wheel*, a play by Edward G. Hemmerde and Francis Neilson about infidelity and divorce, which had shocked audiences when it was first staged in 1911. He starred as the co-respondent in a divorce case but, according to the *Morning Post*, "he was rather too ferocious as the lover." Franklin Dyall also starred, but the hit of the production was 21-year-old Greer Garson. Playing the young and innocent wife, she was described variously as "the wonder actress of the season" and "about the up-and-comingest of young actresses." Following her success, she was soon off to Hollywood and international stardom. The production opened in the Playhouse, then transferred to the Phoenix, but only ran for a few weeks.

My father next appeared in *The Limping Man* at the Saville. According to one critic, "Miss Grizelda Hervey and Mr. John Stuart were excellent as the young lovers." The play, a mystery thriller by William Matthew Scott, limped along for a while until the death in January 1936 of George V, which killed off this and other West End productions. He then toured for nine months with Dorothy Boyd in *No Exit*, which he described as "a good little thriller," and received uniformly good notices. From Nottingham, the two of them wrote a joint letter to the film director Adrian Brunel, in which he said: "Well, here we are on tour, doing our provincial focus a treat. Marvellous audiences—most appreciative."

He toured again briefly the following year in *What We All Want*, and was in the theater again in the spring of 1938, but this time unexpectedly. A week before the light comedy *Honeymoon for Three* was due to open in Brighton, its leading man Percy Hutchinson was taken ill. At short notice, my father was persuaded to take over the lengthy part of the man with two wives (Mary Glynne and Phyllis Thomas), and was reported to be word-perfect on the first night. He described it the morning after as "an interesting experiment," and a change from all his recent mystery thrillers.

In the autumn, he arrived at the Sunderland Empire. The 16-week season was typical repertory fare: a selection of well-tried, middlebrow plays, with seats "at cinema prices." Yet as the head of the company, he had a unique chance to play a great variety of roles, including Bulldog Drummond, Lewis Dodd in *The Constant Nymph*, the title role in *Mr. Wu*, the lead in Edgar Wallace's *The Ringer*, the Scarlet Pimpernel and Captain Stanhope in *Journey's End*. The local critic "M St C" regularly praised his polish, versatility and outstanding talent.

As leading man, he gave the traditional curtain speech after each first night, to thank all concerned. As a national celebrity, he was much in demand to do his bit locally, opening fetes, judging beauty competitions and giving talks about working in the theater. He told the local Rotary Club that the West End was child's play compared to acting in rep, where in a typical week he had to perform in one play while rehearsing another and reading a third. At one talk, he stated with his customary diplomacy: "I was told Sunderland audiences were the most difficult in the country, but we have found them the best."

He was sufficiently pleased with provincial theater life to sign up for another season in the summer of 1939. "It's like coming home," he said in his curtain speech, after the first night of the opening show, Robert E. Sherwood's *Tovarich*. The planned 20-week season included the old chestnut *Charley's Aunt*, Jerome K. Jerome's *The Passing of the Third Floor Back* and Shaw's *Pygmalion*. The latter brought him one of his best notices as Professor Higgins, which he played "in a style close to Leslie Howard's" (the film version with Howard had recently premiered).

On September 3, he was appearing in Arnold Ridley's popular play *The Ghost Train* when war was declared. All places of entertainment were closed, and like every other actor he was suddenly out of work. Now 41, and keen to join up again with the Seaforth Highlanders, he was medically examined in Edinburgh. To his great disappointment, he was rejected because of his trench fever in the previous war. With theaters now open again, he landed a part in a touring production of *Faithfully Yours* with Mary Glynne. Then in the spring of 1940, he returned to Sunderland for another 20-week season, this time at the King's Theater. The repertoire now featured more work by well-known playwrights. It included Priestley's *Dangerous Corner*, Emlyn Williams' *Night Must Fall* and *The Late Christopher Bean*, Somerset Maugham's *The Circle* and *The Sacred Flame,* Noël Coward's *Hay Fever* and *Tonight at 8.30*, Ivor Novello's *Full House* and Ben Travers' *Rookery Nook*. His roles, usually the lead, were wonderfully diverse, and included a headmaster, two vicars, an army officer, a publisher, a doctor, a cripple, a colonial official, a farmer and an engineer. Once again his performances were much enjoyed by the local press.

But as the threat of invasion by the Nazis became greater during 1940, there were constant air raid alerts, and audience numbers started to drop. The company took a salary cut to try to keep the plays on, with everyone now on just £3 a week, but eventually they had to give up. It was lucky they did so: The King's suffered a direct hit soon after, and had to be demolished.

In September, one member of the company, William Wightman, presented my father with a copy of John Buchan's autobiography *Memory Hold the Door*, inscribing it: "With admiration at the cheerful leadership he showed his company through the historic and difficult days of March–September."

17

Fatherhood and War

"In *Escort* by Patrick Hastings, John Stuart gives an admirably strong, sincere, unshowy performance."—Ivor Brown in the *Observer*, 1942

In July 1940, my father returned to London just as the Battle of Britain was beginning, and spent most nights sheltering in a Baker Street coal cellar. As there was little work available, he occasionally left London for the country, staying with friends away from the fighting, and managing to get some rest. He also joined the freemasons, becoming a member of the Green Room Lodge of Instruction. Several other actors also belonged, including Lyn Harding, Charles Doran, Leslie Henson, Clifford Mollison, Charles Macdona, Robert Flemyng and Kenneth Buckley. Perhaps, at such an unsettling time for the country, he found comradeship in belonging to such a group?

Although they were not yet divorced, his marriage to Muriel Angelus was effectively over. During that final Sunderland season, the company had engaged a new leading lady, Barbara Francis. She had been married to the actor Cyril Chamberlain since 1934, but he had left her in the early weeks of the war. She was to become my father's third wife, and my mother.

Born in Warwick in 1910, she had taken a two-year course in drama and speech training at the Bristol Studio of Dramatic Art. At 19, she received a glowing testimonial from the famous actor-manager Fred Terry: "I seldom encourage anyone to go upon the stage, but frankly, after hearing you read, after hearing you speak, I should not think I was right in discouraging you." Advising her to apply to Liverpool or Birmingham Rep, he continued: "You have most of the attributes that go to make an artiste who will adorn her profession in the future, and by no means disgrace it in the present, for you have talent, and that I am convinced will not allow of you failing. This letter is very sincere, and an expression of praise which I seldom give."

After taking leading parts with the Ben Greet Players as they toured schools, she joined Barry Jackson's company at Birmingham Rep and became its leading lady. She had played a similar role at Coventry Rep, where her parts had included the title role in Shaw's *Candida*. She toured with Jackson in the U.S. and Canada, and with the English Players in Europe and the Near East, playing in Shakespeare, musical comedy, straight plays and variety.

More recently, she had appeared in several West End plays. There was the satirical comedy *Once in a Lifetime* by Moss Hart and George S. Kaufman at the Queen's; the "musical tantivy" *Over She Goes*, with Stanley Lupino and Adele Dixon, at the

Saville; *Out of the Dark*, with Gwen Ffrangcon-Davies, Henry Oscar and Felix Aylmer at the Ambassadors; and the comedy thriller *I Killed the Count*, with Alec Clunes, Meriel Forbes and Kathleen Harrison at the Whitehall.

She also played Helena in *A Midsummer Night's Dream* during the fifth season of the Open Air Theater in Regent's Park. The strong cast directed by Robert Alkins included Ion Swinley, Pamela Browne, Leslie French, Fay Compton and, in a spot of early gender-blind casting, Phyllis Neilson Terry as Oberon and the slimly built Jean Forbes-Robertson as Puck.

In Sunderland, she was soon attracting excellent notices, being described as "a remarkably fine emotional actress" in *Black Limelight*, and praised for "her dignity and pathos" in *The Late Christopher Bean*. She and my father played wife and husband in several plays, and also the frustrated would-be lovers in Coward's *Still Life*, a one-act play which on screen became the celebrated film *Brief Encounter*. The Sunderland critic described their work as "a moving bit of playing."

Barbara Francis, his third wife, was a leading West End actress during the 1930s.

It is uncertain whether their off-stage relationship began in Sunderland or in London. They were certainly together by November 1940, when she became pregnant. On August 19, 1941, in "Shardeloes," a grand country house near Amersham in Buckinghamshire converted into a maternity hospital during the war, she gave birth to their first child, which was me. Although my father claimed in his memoir that they had married just before Christmas 1940, at that stage neither of their divorces had come through, and it was not until June 1943 that they were actually married, in the registry office in Watford in Hertfordshire.

According to my mother's sister Betty Jones, who looked after me on that day, this had to be a hole-in-the-corner affair to avoid unwelcome publicity. "There was a lot of hoo-hah about it," she told me. "It was our mother who insisted they get married. She worried that if anything happened to them, you would not be entitled to any inheritance. John was very noble to agree, because he must have known what Barbara was like by then."

His false claim about the date of their marriage was to cover up the fact that I was born out of wedlock, a situation then considered a moral disgrace, though less so in theatrical circles. Betty also said: "Barbara was 30, and wanted a baby before she got too old. What she wanted, she had to have, so that was that." My other aunt,

Julie, claimed, "Barbara had made a play for John after hearing he had money from the family firm. I've never really forgiven her for taking all his money away. She was completely selfish. His brother Eric warned him, but he was rather weak and hopeless with money."

So at the advanced age of 43, my father had his first child. I wonder if he had wanted one before, or if his wives had. Muriel might well have been more concerned with her career, but what about Jeanne?

Whatever his feelings, he was clearly delighted to be a father. During my first two years, he kept a Baby's Diary, charting in detail every stage of my development,

Outside their home in Sarratt, Hertfordshire, in 1944, with Barbara and their first son Jonathan, and a second child on the way. Inset: Jonathan and baby Stephen.

including details of my weight, my teeth, my first words and much else. It's very coy and sentimental, but there's no doubting his great affection for his bastard son.

My parents led a precarious existence during this time, staying in several temporary homes in the Home Counties. At the time of my birth, they were living in a room above the Tapping House, a café in Great Missenden in Buckinghamshire. They then moved to a shed attached to Ivy Cottage just outside the town, and after six months into the cottage itself. Forced to move on, they shared a house in the same county with friends in Loudwater. There followed a short stay at the White Bear Hotel in Rickmansworth in Hertfordshire, before they rented Green End Farm, a converted farmhouse in the pretty Hertfordshire village of Sarratt, where they remained until the end of the war.

Like thousands of other men too old or unfit to fight, he joined the Home Guard, first in Great Missenden and then in Sarratt. After living in the village for a few months, he and my mother started a boys' club and created the Sarratt Guild, with she as head of the drama section, and he as honorary secretary. It was clearly successful in keeping the villagers busy and providing a diversion from the incessant war news.

The activities on offer included Music, Singing, Crafts, Literature, Poetry, Painting and Drama. It was an ambitious scheme for a village, with dances and concerts being held, and a competitive arts festival staged, for which buses were chartered and adjudicators came down from London. My father devised an entertainment, the program consisting of songs, Spanish dances, a piano solo, a one-act comedy, carols—and a scene from Frank Vosper's thriller *Love from a Stranger*, played by John Stuart and Barbara Francis.

But offstage their marriage was in trouble. My aunt Betty told me about a week she spent at Green End Farm. "Barbara was in bed with a wisdom tooth and I was summoned to look after you. She was unemployed and very jealous of John, and she gave him hell. He would come down in the morning with scratch marks on his face. He told me he had to lie to the makeup people when he had to do close-ups. She was doing everything she could to spoil it for him."

During this difficult time domestically, my father continued to work in the theater, and seemed to be about to re-establish himself as a star in the West End. For *Escort* (1942), a play by Patrick Hastings about the navy, directed by Basil Dean at the Lyric, he gained several excellent notices. "John Stuart in the part of his life as the captain is outstandingly good," said the *Daily Herald*, while Ivor Brown wrote in the *Observer*: "He gives an admirably strong, sincere, unshowy performance." Richard Watts, the eminent visiting critic of the *New York Herald Tribune*, noted, "Mr. John Stuart was particularly in character." Patrick Hastings sent him a postcard: "Sincerest thanks for a magnificent performance from a very grateful author!" But someone in the Admiralty discovered that the play was giving away top-secret naval information, and it was abruptly taken off after just a few performances.

After this blow, he appeared alongside Beatrix Lehmann, Frank Pettingell and Frith Banbury in *Jam Today* (1942), a play by Roger Burford and Denis Waldock at the St. Martin's. He took the lead in *What Every Woman Knows* (1943), which after a short tour came into the West End at the Lyric.

J.M. Barrie's play about John Shand, a poor Scot who becomes a member of Parliament, also starred Barbara Mullen, Irene Vanbrugh and Nicholas Hannen. For this dour, straight-laced character, originally played by Gerald du Maurier, my father was once more able to use his native accent. His notices were positive, without quite matching those he received for *Escort*. The *Daily Herald* thought he played "with much shrewdness and sympathy," while the *Spectator* wrote, "He was just right; he never struck a false note." But the influential critic of the *Sunday Times* James Agate felt he hadn't caught the essence of his character: "Surely John Shand should be as likeable as he is dense? Mr. John Stuart plays him with an intensity like young Calvin and young Knox combined." The play ran at the Lyric for a reputable nine months.

As Julius Caesar in Shaw's *Caesar and Cleopatra* (1945), directed by Christopher Fry at the Oxford Playhouse.

In June 1944, the V1 rockets began to fall on London, followed by the V2 rockets in September. Since they were expecting their second child, my parents went to stay with my mother's relatives in Leamington Spa, and then journeyed to Wookey in Somerset. My brother Stephen was born in a maternity home on September 9.

Like many in the profession, my father was opposed to the idea that theaters should be allowed to open on Sundays, an issue then being debated in Parliament. His friend Nicholas Hannen sent him a postcard inscribed: "As a souvenir of 22 February 1943 and the fight to Save Our Sundays. May the Stuart charrrrm be laced with steel, tonight and always." There were other connections with Parliament. The Scottish members of the day were invited to see the Barrie play and were afterward treated by the actors on the stage to "a little austerity meal of tea and hot potatoes." In return, the company was invited to tea in the House of Commons.

Soon after this, Queen Elizabeth and her daughters Elizabeth and Margaret came to a charity matinee performance in aid of the Greater London Fund for the

Blind. During the interval, my father and Barbara Mullen were "bidden" to the royal box and introduced to the royals by Irene Vanbrugh. He was clearly a great supporter of the Royal Family, as most people then were, and in his memoir he wrote of a "very proud moment which I shall always remember."

He spent most of the last months of the war at the Oxford Playhouse, where he temporarily joined the Oxford Players, taking a good range of parts in five of their week-long productions. He had the plum role of Caesar in Shaw's *Caesar and Cleopatra*, playing opposite the husky-voiced actress Joan Greenwood. The director was Christopher Fry, yet to make his mark as a playwright.

In the other four Oxford productions, he was directed by Peter Ashmore. He played the retired parish clergyman Rosmer in Ibsen's dark tragedy *Rosmersholm*, with Jane Henderson as his wife and Nora Nicholson as their housekeeper; the Reverend Davidson in *Rain*, Somerset Maugham's steamy story about Sadie Thompson; and Canon Ronder in Hugh Walpole's *The Cathedral*. He also played Professor Higgins in *Pygmalion* for a second time, teaching Yvonne Mitchell's Eliza Doolittle how to be a lady.

The Cathedral opened on May 7, 1945. The next day was VE Day, celebrating the end of the war in Europe. With the war over, he and the family had to leave their Hertfordshire village home. For a short while they shared a house with another married couple in Oxford. They then moved to London, where they lived briefly in Barnes, before moving to Prince of Wales Drive overlooking Battersea Park. Here they rented three different flats in succession in Overstrand Mansions. They settled in the third, which became the family home for many years.

18

Propaganda and Escapism

"By common consent the war ushered in a golden age for British cinema, which merited and received national attention."—Charles Barr, *All Our Yesterdays*

"Now I'm going to take films seriously again," my father announced, after his third Sunderland season in 1940 was cut short by the Second World War.

In between forays into the West End, he spent much of the next five years in film studios, doing his bit for the war effort by taking part in propaganda films. At a time when the public increasingly used the cinema as an escape from their stressful lives, he also appeared in a thriller, an industrial story, a historical biopic, a Gainsborough picture and four comedies. Of varying quality, they were all in different ways aimed at sustaining morale and taking people's minds off the war.

At the outbreak of war, the government closed all the cinemas, fearing the terrible consequences if a bomb fell on a crowded auditorium. But it soon became clear that, during the initial "phoney war," morale would be better served if they were re-opened. This helped the cinema to play a vital role in national life, and quickly free it from the previous dominance of the American output.

As film historian Charles Barr argued in his book *All Our Yesterdays: 90 Years of British Cinema*: "British cinema dealt with current realities, it was on the whole intelligently supported by the state, was popular with British audiences, and it earned respect abroad. By common consent the war ushered in a golden age for British cinema, which merited and received national attention."

Some outstanding films reflected the reality of people's lives. Several had stories centered on life in the armed forces, including David Lean's *In Which We Serve* (the Navy), Anthony Asquith's *The Way to the Stars* (the RAF) and Carol Reed's *The Way Ahead* (the Army). Others, such as Lean's *This Happy Breed* and Frank Launder and Sidney Gilliat's *Millions Like Us*, explored the lives of civilians during the war, in the latter case those of men and women working in a munitions factory. There were also films that raised vital questions about attitudes to the war, including Michael Powell and Emeric Pressburger's subversive *The Life and Death of Colonel Blimp* and Alberto Cavalcanti's *Went the Day Well?*, a disturbing film which reflected contemporary fears of a Nazi fifth column.

The documentary movement, which had grown during the 1930s, now moved from the margins into the mainstream. The resulting films—such as *London Can Take It*, *Fires Were Started* and *A Diary for Timothy*—were often as popular as the

169

escapist entertainment typified by the Gainsborough output. Audiences grew, and by the end of the war 30 million people were regular filmgoers. The studios took a while to get back to work after the declaration of war. Seven of the major ones were idle at the start of 1940, but they resumed production soon afterwards.

Early in the war, my father, somewhat surprisingly, made two films with Arthur Lucan and his wife Kitty McShane, directed by John Baxter, with Lance Comfort as assistant director. Lucan and McShane had attracted a large and delighted following to their long-standing music hall act, with Lucan portraying Old Mother Riley, an Irish washerwoman, and McShane his daughter. The popularity of their knock-about farces was underlined by the fact that Lucan made 14 films between 1937 and 1952, with McShane, a strikingly untalented actress, appearing in a dozen of them.

Lucan was thought by some to be a genius. In drag, dressed in a pantomime-dame costume consisting of an apron, a shawl, an old black dress and a poke-bonnet, Old Mother Riley would invariably uncover spies, or fight off intruders or authority figures with her fists. In his book *The Age of the Dream Palace,* Jeffrey Richards paints a vivid picture of "a comic heroine of titanic dimensions ... this inextinguishable life force of the slums, a veritable Brunnhilde of the back streets ... a breast-beating, arm-waving, finger-pointing, hand-flourishing, elbow-stretching, knee-bending, sleeve-rolling, super-animated, rubber-limbed rag-doll. Here is truly a case of body-language gone berserk."

In the first film, *Old Mother Riley in Society* (1940), my father plays Tony Morgan, a "society swell" who marries McShane. When they hire Old Mother Riley as their maid, the consequences are predictably chaotic. "Another bundle of well-worn gags," ran one review, while *Today's Cinema* reckoned, "John Stuart is quietly effective." It's a comment that accurately sums up his performance, playing the straight man to such an anarchic comedian.

In the second film, *Old Mother Riley's Ghosts* (1941), he plays John Cartwright, an inventor living in a haunted house, who is being pursued by spies wanting to steal his work. "John Stuart ably handles a role below his talents," was the crisp opinion of *Picturegoer and Film Weekly.* He acts easily alongside Lucan, notably in a charming scene in which they chat on a park bench after my father has been kicked out of the family home.

He continued in straight parts in two more comedies, appearing in farces starring the team Alfred Drayton and Robertson Hare, whose stage work in the genre was very popular, notably in the series of Aldwych farces. In *Banana Ridge* (1941), based on a play by Ben Travers, he has only two scenes as Staples, a chief police officer in Malaya, but displays considerable authority in this desperately unfunny film. He then had three brief scenes as the genial Major Gaunt, organizing a concert party in the equally poor *Women Aren't Angels* (1942). In the story, Hare and Drayton get up to mischief in the Home Guard while their wives are away serving in the Auxiliary Territorial Service. Lawrence Huntington directed.

He was subsequently involved in several propaganda films. He featured strongly as the naval commander Commodore Hood in *Ships with Wings* (1941), a film made in tribute to the Fleet Air Arm, and directed by the Russian Sergei Nolbandov, one of Michael Balcon's Ealing directors. It had a strong cast that included

Ann Todd, John Clements, Leslie Banks, Michael Rennie and Michael Wilding. However, the fictitious story creaks, the models of the enemy's bases look ludicrously fake, and the gallant British pilots prevail by means of impossible heroics.

The film attracted hostility from the press for its unrealistic and melodramatic tone, the banality of the romantic subplot, and the low quality of the special effects. Prime Minister Winston Churchill, fearing that the film might spread "alarm and despondency" among the audience, threatened to delay or even cancel its release, since the climax was a disaster for the Fleet Air Arm. In the end, he agreed to its release.

The screenplay was written by Diana Morgan, a successful playwright and actress who became one of the few women writers in British cinema. In an interview with film historian Brian McFarlane for his book *British Cinema*, she observed: "It was harder then for women to get established as screenwriters. Ealing was a very male studio; they didn't like actors very much, and they didn't like actresses at all. So many of their films were male-dominated. I think my having been an actress and a playwright helped."

With *Ships with Wings,* my father's film career had lasted 21 years. There's a jolly picture of him being toasted for his coming of age on screen by Michael Balcon and several of the film's stars, including Clements, Banks, Wilding and Rennie.

He next appeared in *The Big Blockade* (1942), a propaganda film about the success of the economic blockade of Germany. It started as a two-reel Ministry of Information documentary, but then grew, and eventually had 80 speaking parts. It was partly backed by the Ministry of Economic Warfare, which was concerned with sabotage, creating and establishing secret armies of resistance, and black propaganda. Also involved were the

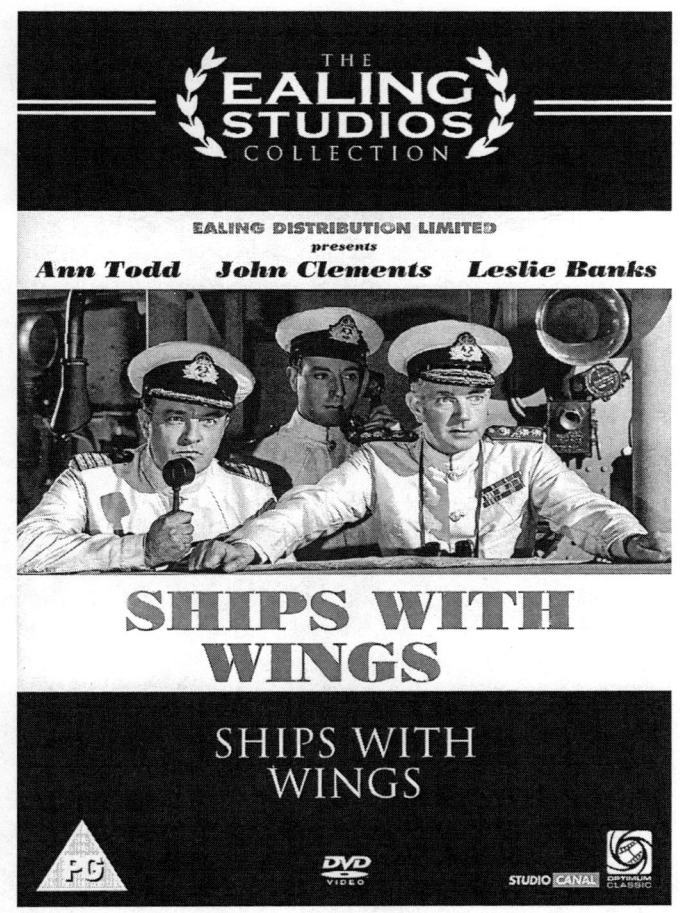

In *Ships with Wings* (1940), a tribute to the Fleet Air Arm, he featured in an all-star cast.

Admiralty, the War Office and the RAF. The film was directed by Charles Frend, another of Balcon's stable of young directors at Ealing; Frend had worked on Hitchcock's films *Secret Agent* and *Sabotage*.

My father appears briefly but effectively as a naval officer, while other stars—including Michael Redgrave, John Mills, Leslie Banks, Michael Wilding and Bernard Miles—also contribute cameos. The film is an uncomfortable mixture of documentary and invented scenes. On the one hand it incorporates facts and figures and politicians' speeches, on the other it has Robert Morley and Marius Goring caricaturing Nazi officers as bullies and cringing cowards, while the British characters remain cool and resourceful, exhibiting the traditional stiff upper lip. *The Times* thought it "woefully unconvincing." Balcon later admitted, "The subject was rather too abstract to be dramatic or exciting."

The propaganda film *Flying Fortress* (1942), made by Warner Brothers with the cooperation of the RAF and the Atlantic Ferry Service, was directed by Walter Forde, a respected director during the 1930s. It deals with the experience of two American airmen (Richard Greene and Donald Stewart) who help fly U.S. planes to Britain, and then take part in the bombing of Berlin. My father plays a ferry pilot, Captain Harvey, and has just one simple scene with his fellow officer Basil Radford and Greene. The film has a strong documentary element and a subplot featuring Betty Stockfeld and the American Carla Lehmann designed to provide the human interest. It ends with a recording of one of Churchill's speeches mingling with a rising crescendo of martial music.

A more conventional film was *The Seventh Survivor* (1941), a spy story about a disparate group stranded on a lighthouse after their ship has been torpedoed. The result is poor; it looks as if it has been filmed in a cupboard. Martita Hunt throws out epigrams, Austin Trevor pretends to be a Nazi, and Frank Pettingell does his bluff Yorkshireman turn. No one is who he or she seems to be. My father plays the unlikely role of international banker Robert Cooper, whom everyone suspects to be a spy. He ambles through his part with his usual relaxed good nature, but struggles with the close-ups where he has to Act Suspicious. The director was Leslie S. Hiscott, the man said to have put the "quickie" into "quota quickies."

Historical subjects were also taken up by the studios, some of them linking the story to the current danger facing Britain; Robert Donat starred in *The Young Mr. Pitt* and John Gielgud played Disraeli in *The Prime Minister*. My father was involved in another in the genre, *Penn of Pennsylvania* (1941; U.S. title *The Courageous Mr. Penn*), a biopic about the founder of the Quakers and the colony of Pennsylvania, William Penn. Directed by Lance Comfort, making his second film as a director, it was clearly designed to bring America into the war. Welsh actor Clifford Evans, with his beautifully modulated voice, gives a fine performance as Penn, catching well his idealism, faith and determination, after the hostility the Quakers face in England, to build a city in America "where people will be free to worship in their own way." The reviews were mixed: the *Guardian* thought it "thoroughly well-documented, earnest and sincere," and the *Birmingham Post* described it as "a wholesome, honest apologia." On the other hand, *Picturegoer* saw "a rather stereotyped parade of historical incidents without much flesh-and-blood vitality."

A large cast includes Henry Oscar as Pepys, Dennis Arundell as Charles II and O.B. Clarence as Lord Cecil. In her third film, Deborah Kerr, aged 20, plays Penn's wife, society beauty Guglielma Springett. She catches skillfully her gaiety, which is subdued by her love of Penn and her idealism; her scenes with Evans are touching and played with quiet assurance. My father turns up as Mr. Bindle, Penn's first convert to Quakerism, and is persuasive in his loyal support and his attempt to persuade Penn to return to America.

He had a much greater part in *Hard Steel* (1941). Set in a steel works, it has Wilfred Lawson giving a typically strong performance as a ruthless and ambitious foreman. My father plays steel worker Alan Saunders, a poet and composer in his spare time. Here he reverts to the kind of role he became known for, the smooth and charming man of integrity, invariably behaving gallantly toward women. It's another opportunity to use the accent of his native Scotland, and he brings his usual warmth and sensitivity to the romantic scenes with Betty Stockfeld; *Today's Cinema* thought, "He registered excellent work." The film was shot at Denham Studios in Buckinghamshire, which meant, as he noted proudly in his memoir, that he had now worked in every British film studio.

He returned to a standard thriller in *The Missing Million* (1942), yet another Edgar Wallace screenplay, directed by Philip Brandon. As Scotland Yard Inspector Dicker, he is hired to find a kidnapped millionaire and, after several murders have occurred, he succeeds. He's quietly effective in the part, and once again gets the girl (Linden Travers) as well as the villain.

He had a much more substantial and demanding role as cynical newspaper editor L.B. Ellington in *Headline* (1943), in which his wife (Anne Crawford) becomes accidentally mixed up in a murder that his star reporter (David Farrar) has to investigate. Ellington is wedded to the newspaper more than to his wife, which caused her to become tangled up in the killing. His performance is suitably angry and forceful, and there's plenty of lively dialogue, much of it humorous. In his interview for Brian McFarlane's *British Cinema*, Farrar observed that it was "a good script, set in the newspaper world which I knew from my own days in journalism."

There was also *Candles at Nine* (1944), an attempt to revive the film career of Jessie Matthews, who during the 1930s had been England's most popular female star. It had exactly the opposite effect, and put an end to her film career for more than a decade.

The plot, about the contested will of a murdered old man, is patently absurd, as is most of the acting: Matthews is incredibly stilted, while Beatrix Lehmann pulls out all the Gothic stops as a murderous housekeeper. Christopher Isherwood called this dire B-feature thriller "the worst and funniest film ever made." My father plays William Gordon, a detective who solves the case and, once again, gets the girl. In doing so, he gives an unfussy, believable performance. It's noticeable that in her scenes with him, Jessie Matthews is clearly much more at ease than she is in the rest of the action.

Madonna of the Seven Moons (1944) was an obvious attempt to exploit the success of other popular wartime melodramas such as *The Wicked Lady*, *The Man in Grey* and *Fanny by Gaslight*. Arthur Crabtree had been the cameraman on the latter two films; now he was making his directorial debut. This was a common situation at the time: because of the war, there was a shortage of directors, so scriptwriters and cameramen were often thrust into the role.

In his memoir, my father recalled the moment he arrived at the studio for the first day's shooting. "I found the building surrounded by fire engines. The studio had had a lucky escape. A bomb had fallen on the marketplace just behind it. Fortunately it happened during the night when few people were about. The stages had to be dried off after the water from the hoses had doused them, and shooting was delayed for two days."

Set in Italy, the film starred Phyllis Calvert in a showy role as a woman suffering from schizophrenia, caused by a traumatic event in her childhood. She leads a respectable married life with her wealthy Italian wine-merchant husband Giuseppe Labardi (my father) and daughter (Patricia Roc), but occasionally runs off to

With Phyllis Calvert as his wife in the popular wartime Gainsborough melodrama *Madonna of the Seven Moons* **(1945).**

Florence to lead a gypsy life as the mistress of vicious and notorious jewel thief Nino Barucci (Stewart Granger).

Three of the cast members spoke of their experience when interviewed for *British Cinema*. According to Dulcie Gray, "There was a revolution going on at Gainsborough at the time—every cameraman wanted to be a director, and quite often was." Phyllis Calvert observed: "It wasn't that Arthur Crabtree was unsatisfactory, just that we found ourselves *very* satisfactory—we did it ourselves." Stewart Granger thought the film was "junk," explaining: "My alibi for doing it was that it was wartime and it provided the escapism that people needed."

Calvert remembered the restrictions on showing sexual behavior: "At that time you couldn't have two people on a bed together unless their feet were on the ground! But Stewart Granger and I got away with it in the gypsy scenes by having a very dark room, with our two heads on the pillow, with just a light on our faces made by the cigarettes we were smoking. You couldn't see the foot of the bed, as it was too dark. Sex wasn't talked about in those days, it was implied."

Patricia Roc played his daughter in *Madonna of the Seven Moons* (1945).

Audiences appreciated the melodrama as a welcome distraction from the war, and it made a fortune at the box office, rivaling top Hollywood films commercially. But it was considered hokum by the critics. "See it to delight your sense of the ridiculous," suggested *Time and Tide*, while William Whitebait decided, "It is notably bad. Everything is treacly: characters, dialogue, situation." Dilys Powell described such Gainsborough productions as "inferior films on trivial, conventional ideas, trivially handled, and undeserving of the popular success they have won." More recently, historians have thought them worthy of re-evaluation.

Interestingly, when I showed the film to a

family group aged from 35 to 85, they were thoroughly gripped. It's a well-crafted film, with effective *chiaroscuro* camerawork by Jack Cox and a high standard of acting from supporting players Dulcie Gray, Peter Glenville and Jean Kent. My father, looking handsome in several sharp suits, displays a subtle range of emotions as his wife's tragedy unfolds, acting with considerable depth and sensitivity. To my mind, this was one of his best screen performances.

Other Films

At the end of the war, he acted as the narrator in *Camera Reflections* (1945), a short compilation of extracts from British silent films.

PART FOUR

Character Actor

19

On the Small Screen

"Clive Brook was having problems with his lines. He got very angry, and threw a glass of sherry over John, who was a sweet, gentle man, and behaved impeccably about it."—Actor John Standing, rehearsing *The Judge's Story*, 1959

In 1939, only 20,000 British households had television sets. Shortly after noon on September 1, the BBC service was shut down without any announcement and remained silent throughout the war. It started again on June 7, 1946, broadcasting to an audience that still remained a tiny minority of the population. In November 1947, my father made the first of many appearances on the small screen.

This was in the small role of the Second Tempter in T.S. Eliot's verse play *Murder in the Cathedral*, the story of the assassination in Canterbury Cathedral of Archbishop Thomas à Becket, played by Robert Speaight. It was filmed live in the studio at Alexandra Palace in London. He then appeared as Alquist in *R.U.R.* (1948), a strange futuristic play by the Czech writer Karel Capek, about robots leading a revolution against their human creators; Patrick Troughton and Joy Adamson were among the robots. He finished the year as Mr. Taylor in an episode of *The Chronicles of Ben*, a series based on the story about a cockney tramp by J. Jefferson Farjeon. In 1949, he appeared as Dr. Armstrong in Agatha Christie's play *Ten Little Niggers*. The thriller also featured John Bentley, Bruce Belfrage and Arthur Wontner.

During the 1950s, his TV career blossomed: He made no less than 58 appearances in a great variety of plays, series and serials. For a start, he appeared in a BBC *Sunday-Night Theatre* production of J.B. Priestley's perennially popular play *Time and the Conways* (1950), which explores the idea of Time in relation to the lives of a wealthy Yorkshire family living between the two world wars. In the same year, he had only one other part, as a police superintendent in the thriller *Mr. Bowling Buys a Newspaper*.

He then featured prominently in several children's programs. He was the Father in an adaptation of E. Nesbit's novel *The Railway Children* (1951), while in a 1957 remake he played Dr. Forrest, with Norman Shelley as the Old Gentleman. Jean Anderson filled the role of the mother in both versions. He appeared as Dr. Lachlan McKinnon in the science fiction serial *The Lost Planet* (1954) and *Return to the Lost Planet* (1955); he played Space Commander Hugh Sterling in *Space School* (1956); and he turned up as the headmaster Dr. Locke in three *Billy Bunter of Greyfriars School* escapades—*The Siege* and *A Piece of Cake* (both 1952) and *Billy Bunter Won't Go*

(1954)—with Gerald Campion as the overweight schoolboy, Kynaston Reeves as Mr. Quelch, David Spenser as Hurree Jamset Ram Singh and an early appearance as a prefect by John Osborne during his brief acting career.

He appeared in two more BBC *Sunday Night Theatre* productions, as Sir Edmund Godfrey in *Ninety Sail* (1954) and as Mr. Fraser in *The Makepeace Story* (1955). He was then back on the beat as a police officer in one of the earliest soaps, *The Grove Family* (1956), which pictured everyday life in a suburban family. Ruth Dunning and Edward Evans starred as the parents. In the same year, he was cast as a blind man in the mini-series *Lucky Silver* and as Mr. Smith in one of the short plays in the series *Nom-de-Plume*.

He featured in a veritable tsunami of crime series during the 1950s: *Saber of London* (no less than 15 episodes), *Mark Saber* (5), *The Vise* (3), *Scotland Yard* (2) and one episode each of *Murder Bag, Boyd Q.C., Shadow Squad, White Hunter, O.S.S., Interpol Calling, The Men from Room 13, White Hunter* and *The New Adventures of Charlie Chan*. He also appeared in one episode of the popular hospital drama series *Emergency Ward 10*.

He took on two roles in the series *The Adventures of Robin Hood* with Richard Greene playing the famous outlaw. In "The Deserted Castle" (1956), which featured Jill Esmond as Queen Eleanor and Ronald Howard as Will Scarlet, he was cast as Pinot, while in "The Byzantine Treasure" (1956) he was Stationarius, with John Longden playing the archbishop. He also played different characters in two episodes of the TV adaptation of Walter Scott's *Ivanhoe*, which had Roger Moore in the title role. In "The Slave Traders" (1958), directed by Lance Comfort, he was Sir Thomas of Highvale, who seeks Ivanhoe's help when his serfs mysteriously disappear; in "The Gentle Jester" (1958), he was cast as Brother Aubrey, with Arthur Crabtree directing.

He appeared as Dr. Firth in two episodes of *Jo's Boys* (1959), an adaptation of Louisa May Alcott's celebrated novel. He was involved in two *Douglas Fairbanks Jr. Presents* productions, which the actor narrated and appeared in. An anthology series of 156 half-hour episodes titled *Rheingold Theater*, it covered a range of subjects, from mystery to farce. He was cast as a police inspector in "Guilt" (1956) and as Prince Schiavoni in "Four Farewells in Venice" (1957).

He also took part in four more plays in the BBC's *Sunday-Night Theater* series. In one of these, an adaptation of Charles Morgan's *The Judge's Story*, he played the brother of Clive Brook, with whom he had worked in the silent era. But this was not a happy encounter, as cast member John Standing remembered: "Clive Brook was over 70. He was very nervous, and having problems with his lines. At one point he got very angry, and threw a glass of sherry over John, who was a sweet, gentle man, and behaved impeccably about it."

During the 1960s, he notched up 40 more TV appearances. He had two unusual parts, first as a butler and then as an anesthetist, in the stories "What Money Can't Buy" (1962) and "Dear Doctor" (1964) in the hit medical series *Dr Finlay's Casebook*, which starred Bill Simpson in the title role, Andrew Cruickshank as Dr. Cameron and Barbara Mullen as Janet MacPherson. He appeared in "The Minister" (1965) in the *Theater 625* series of plays, tackling the role of Androssan alongside a distinguished cast that included Barbara Jefford, Roger Livesey, Mark Dignam and Michael Gough. He was also in two productions in the ITV series *Play of the Week*.

He was involved in yet more episodes of crime series during these years, including *The Man from Interpol* (2), *Spycatcher* (2), *The Sullavan Brothers* (2) and one each in *The Cheaters*, *Sergeant Cork*, *The Pursuers* and *The Human Jungle*. For what must have been a welcome change of both scenery and subject matter, he spent a month in the desert in Morocco, playing the Caid in the family adventure mini-series *Son of the Sahara* (1966). At the end of the decade, he had a small part in the much-praised *The Six Wives of Henry VIII* (1969), starring Keith Michell as the king.

During the 1970s, he continued to make appearances, for example as Dr. Milroy in *Doctors' Lib* (1972), written by Graeme Garden and Bill Oddie; in "Nights" (1975) in the nursing series *Angels*; and as a judge in "The Tattered Anarchist" (1974). The latter was a Season 1 episode of *The Carnford Practice*, a series about a solicitor based in a small Lake District village. He was a clergyman in one of ITV's *Sunday-Night Drama* productions, a judge in the series *Against the Crowd*, a records clerk in "Mr. Calloway Is a Very Cautious Man" in the series *The Adventurer*, with Freddie Jones in the title role (1973), and a committee member in *Members Only* in the *Bowler* series (1973).

He also appeared as Mr. Pettifer in "Countess Ilona" and "The Werewolf Reunion," two episodes of the horror mini-series *Supernatural* (1977), which starred Billie Whitelaw, and in which members of a secret society, including Amanda Boxer, Ian Hendry and Charles Kay, tell horror stories. In 1979, at the age of 80, he made his final television appearance in *Ends and Ways*, in which the lives of ten people involved in a car crash become intertwined. He was cast as a man playing dummy in a game of bridge.

After 32 years of working in British TV, he had appeared 123 times on the small screen.

20

Back to the Theater

In the theater during these immediate postwar years, my father still appeared occasionally in the West End. He took on his second Ibsen role playing Torvald Helmer in Norman Ginsbury's new (1945) English version of *A Doll's House*. The production toured to Birmingham and other major English cities before coming to the Winter Garden theater in London. Playing his wife Nora, who famously walks out on her husband to gain her freedom from a repressive marriage, was Angela Baddeley, a leading West End actress. He also appeared at the Fortune as Warren Wilson in Glanvor Mostyn's play *The Bride Goes West* (1947), a story set in a small township in the American South.

He worked a good deal at the little Q theater in Kew, and directed the occasional production. In fact, he had branched out in this way during the war. In 1943, after the West End run of *What Every Woman Knows*, he directed Barrie's play at Kew with a new cast, while still playing Shand himself. He repeated the exercise at Kew in 1947, with a cast that included Barbara Mullen and Norman MacOwan.

Other plays in which he acted there included Barrie's *A Kiss for Cinderella* (1945), directed by Esmé Percy and starring Nova Pilbeam; *The Faithful Heart* (1946) by the Irish writer Monckton Hoffe; and Aldous Huxley's psychological thriller *The Giaconda Smile* (1949), in which he co-starred with Rosalinde Fuller in the parts recently played in the West End by Clive Brook and Pamela Browne.

While working intensively in both films and television, he appeared in just two West End productions in the 1950s. He was an inspector in *Tomorrow's Too Late* (1952) by Gerald Anstruther at the Comedy, and in the same year he joined Donald Wolfit's company in *Lords of Creation* at the Vaudeville, playing the Earl of Tenplemoran. A comedy by Edward Percy and Lilian Denham, its cast included Wolfit and his wife Rosalind Iden, Richard Bebb, Una Venning and Raymond Huntley.

He toured extensively during these years, with plays that included the controversial *Johnny Belinda* (1950) by Elmer Blaney Harris. A hit on Broadway during the war, it dealt with rape, murder and the abuse of a deaf-mute. In the same year, he was in *Bonaventure* by Charlotte Hastings, in which a nun saves an innocent woman from being executed for murder. He also toured in *Dead Secret* (1953), a comedy by Michael Clayton-Hutton; another comedy, *Book of the Month* by Basil Thomas (1955); and *The Trial of Mary Dugan* (1956), a play by American writer Bayard Veiller. Originally another Broadway hit, it concerned the sensational trial of a showgirl accused of killing her millionaire lover. Such were the kind of plays that were appealing to audiences all around the country.

He was frequently back at the Q theater, where he continued his directing career with *Bonaventure* once again (1951) and *The Man in Grey* (1950), the popular melodrama that had been made into a Gainsborough film during the war. Solely as an actor, he starred there among other productions in the psychological drama *The Governess* (1950), by the author of *Gaslight*, Patrick Hamilton; in *Who Goes Home?* (1950), with Elizabeth Allan and Geoffrey Palmer; *The Heiress* (1951) by the American playwrights Ruth and Augustus Goetz; *The Holly and the Ivy* (1951) by Wynyard Browne, about the problems of a family which emerge at their Christmas gathering; and *After My Fashion* (1952), written by Diana Morgan, for which the cast included Peggy Ramsay, later the powerful theatrical agent.

He took a trip to his native country to act in Christopher Fry's verse play *Venus Observed* (1951) at the Glasgow Citizens theater. He also appeared at two of the little theaters in London. At the New Bolton's in Kensington, he was with Joan Miller in *A Pin to See the Peepshow* (1951) by F. Tennyson Jesse, based on her novel about a real murder trial, and *Rainbow*, a new play by Marguerite Buller. At the New Lindsey in Notting Hill, he appeared in *The Final Ace* (1956), a play by Charles Fenn set in China during the Second World War. He was then invited by the Theatre Royal in Windsor to appear in N.C. Hunter's play *Waters of the Moon* (1953), a recent West End success.

In May 1960 he wrote to Michael Balcon: "At the moment I am rehearsing a new play by Terence Rattigan called *Ross*. Once the play has opened I shall shortly be free to film again, and hope very much to have the pleasure of working in one of your future productions. May I therefore come along and see you some time later in the month?"

Balcon replied promptly: "By all means come and see me if you wish to after the opening of *Ross*, which by the way I hope to see too." But Balcon went on to explain that his schedule for filming Willis Hall's *The Long and the Short and the Tall* was held up because Laurence Harvey was filming *Butterfield 8* in Hollywood and was affected by a strike there, "so I think it will be some months before we are in production again." In September, my father wrote again asking for a meeting, but no reply has survived.

Terence Rattigan's hugely successful new play *Ross* (1960) ran for over a year at the Haymarket. Rattigan sought to explain why T.E. Lawrence (popularly known as Lawrence of Arabia) joined the Royal Air Force under the pseudonym of Ross after his experiences in the Middle East. Under the direction of Glen Byam Shaw, the part was played by Alec Guinness, who bore a striking resemblance to Lawrence. After nine months he left, and was replaced by Michael Bryant.

My father played Group Captain Wood, but also acted as an understudy for the first time: when Anthony Nicholls, cast as the diplomat Ronald Storrs, went to New York to play the role, my father took over the part for several weeks. In his memoir, he reflected on the problems facing an understudy:

> I wonder if many people realize how nerve-wracking understudying can be for an actor. To begin with you have to attend all the rehearsals, which usually last three or four weeks. Then

once the play has opened you have to rehearse twice a week. You have to be on call from ten in the morning until about ten at night, sitting in your dressing-room during the show wondering whether there will be a sudden call. You need to be in the theater half an hour before the curtain goes up, and no later. Should the actor you are understudying be absent through illness or an accident, you have to be ready to go on at any moment, sometimes even during a performance.

He experienced the understudy's worst nightmare during the run at the St. Martin's of Pauline Macaulay's first stage play *The Creeper* (1966), directed by Donald McWhinnie and starring Eric Portman. As he remembered: "Just before the curtain went up Portman fell ill. I quickly got ready, and after keeping the audience waiting for a few minutes I went on. It all went well, but it was quite a moment, happening so suddenly." He also understudied Michael Horden for the production of Alan Ayckbourn's play *Relatively Speaking* (1967), directed by Nigel Patrick at the Duke of York's.

His stage appearances became much fewer in these years. He took part in *The Captain's Hero* (1962), one of the Royal Court's productions without décor, and was in *Difference of Opinion* (1965) at the New Theatre, Bromley, a play by George Ross about skullduggery in the construction world. Finally, having started his stage career at the Theater Royal in Windsor, he returned there in 1972, ending it by playing Sir Henry Angkatell in Agatha Christie's *The Hollow*.

During his 52-year theater career, he had worked in every West End theater, toured extensively to the major cities and towns throughout England, and made 123 stage appearances. A profile in the program of *The Hollow* concluded: "He can look back over a career that has been limitless in its variety, and yet he tackles each new part with a zestful enthusiasm. Why? Because he is still stage-struck. The glitter has not become tarnished. That dashing romantic figure of fifty years ago striding across the silent screen is still encapsulated in a man who looks back over a happy and exciting life."

21

Leading Roles and Cameos

In the postwar years and into the 1950s, the British studios continued to find audiences for a plethora of war films: *The Colditz Story*, *The Wooden Horse*, *Above Us the Waves* and more. There were also the successful Ealing comedies, with *The Man in the White Suit*, *Kind Hearts and Coronets*, *The Ladykillers* and *The Lavender Hill Mob* hitting the mark with audiences still facing austerity after the war. There was also high-quality work from directors such as Carol Reed, David Lean and the team of Powell and Pressburger.

Now moving into his fifties, my father still appeared in the occasional leading role, but smaller parts were becoming more common. With plenty of work in television and the theater to keep him occupied, he seemed content to take on lesser, often cameo roles, creating a steady stream of professional characters in positions of authority.

After playing the understanding husband in *Madonna of the Seven Moons*, there was a gap in his film career of two years. His return to the screen came with the murder mystery *The Phantom Shot* (1947), which also featured Olga Lindo and Howard Marion Crawford. The director was the Italian Mario Zampi, who had come to England in the 1930s, working as an editor throughout the decade before being interned as an enemy alien for the duration of the war. *The Phantom Shot* was his first film after his release from internment. In the 1950s, he earned a reputation in Britain as a director of comedy.

In the leading part of Inspector Webb investigating a killing, my father gives a suave, authoritative performance. The film rises above the ordinary crime story because of an arresting device employed by Zampi, as my father recalled in his memoir: "I took the audience into my confidence, looking straight into the camera, and giving a running commentary on what I was doing and the clues I had unearthed so far. At the end I asked the audience if like me they had solved the mystery." Unusually, Zampi asked him to collaborate on writing the script.

He next appeared as the Duke of Bedford in the humdrum costume drama *Mrs. Fitzherbert* (1947). It's a story from the 1780s, of the eponymous Catholic widow (Joyce Howard) and her secret marriage to the Prince Regent (Peter Graves) and its complicated consequences. An American critic wrote: "It is so rigidly played that the whole thing has the appearance of an animated wax-works on the move." Wearing an unbecoming wig, my father appears fleetingly, and has only a few lines.

During these years, he was frequently cast in the small part of a doctor, for

As the detective inspector investigating a murder in *The Phantom Shot* (1947) (courtesy the Cinema Museum, London).

example as John Hayling in the psychological thriller *Mine Own Executioner* (1947). The film was produced by the influential Alexander Korda, and directed by the actor-playwright-screenwriter Anthony Kimmins, who had directed George Formby films before the war. It starred the distinguished American stage and screen actor Burgess Meredith, one of many figures who worked in Britain after being put on the Hollywood blacklist, following the investigation of the House Committee on Un-American Activities.

The film depicts the tremendous demands made on a lay psychiatrist (Meredith) by his patients, his colleagues and his private life; he assumes the guilt of a suicidal patient, played by Kieron Moore. Dulcie Gray portrays Meredith's wife. It's a tense and powerful thriller made with style. Nigel Balchin wrote the screenplay, based on his novel of the same name.

In *British Cinema,* Dulcie Gray recalled: "Anthony Kimmins was a very positive director. He loved the script, and seemed to like us too." The *New York Times* called *Mine Own Executioner* "a serious, adult and highly interesting film drama, both in point of view and execution.... Although it does not glibly solve problems of psychiatry, it does contribute a sober and edifying view of the complexities of that baffling science." The film was shown at the Cannes Film Festival and, despite fitting into none of the accepted categories, was well-received by both judges and critics.

Escape from Broadmoor (1948) was a short B-feature, the first in an intended series of psychic mysteries. The directing debut of John Gilling, later known for making horror films, it concerns a murderer who escapes from Broadmoor high-security psychiatric prison. Returning to the scene of the crime to rob a safe, he encounters the ghost of the housemaid he killed, and is driven insane.

The film was shot in a furnished house in North London on a shoestring,

The American star Burgess Meredith played a London psychiatrist in the powerful psychological drama *Mine Own Executioner* (1947).

and it shows. My father stars as Inspector Thornton, who tracks down the villain; it's a part which gives him a chance to show the man's humanity, and he turns in a polished, sympathetic performance. His co-star Victoria Hopper, a star of the 1920s, gives the housemaid an amusingly earthbound quality, while in one of his earliest screen appearances John le Mesurier, already an experienced stage actor, is effectively sinister as the murderer.

My father had another decent role in the eerie fantasy film *House of Darkness* (1948), directed by Oswald Mitchell. Laurence Harvey, making his screen debut, stars as an obsessive man who wreaks havoc on his family, and suffers hallucinations after committing a murder. He suggests effectively the character's sinister intentions in his early scenes, and then descends into madness. As the family's solicitor Mr. Crabtree, my father exudes both sensitivity and integrity in his dealings with Harvey and his wife Lesley Osmond.

Man on the Run (1949) was the story of an army deserter wrongly suspected of being involved in a robbery that ended with a policeman being killed. Derek Farr gives a strong, sympathetic performance in the lead role, while Joan Hopkins is quietly convincing as the woman who shields him. Also featured, and not yet a star, is Kenneth More in a small role as a blackmailer. As detective inspector Jim McBane, my father has few lines, and little chance to create a character. The film, written and directed by Lawrence Huntington, provides a vivid picture of the austerity of British life after the war, at a time when desertion was a hot topic. According to *Kinematograph Weekly*, "Smooth acting and direction enable it to put up a good case for the harassed hero, and underline its plot with well-timed thrills," while *Picturegoer* praised the director and the actors "who have made it good and quite thrilling entertainment." Curiously, while Farr's character is court-martialed and given a year's prison sentence at the end of the film, for the version sold to Germany an alternative ending was shot, in which he is tried in a crown court, and then freed and reunited with Hopkins.

My father was given another starring role in *The Man from Yesterday* (1949), a low-budget, semi-occult melodrama directed by Oswald Mitchell. He plays Gerald Amersley, the father in a conventional middle-class family, whose daughter (Gwyneth Vaughan) is engaged to a young man (Laurence Harvey). The calm atmosphere is disturbed by the arrival of a sinister and enigmatic psychic visitor (Henry Oscar), leading to my father turning nasty and being accused of committing a murder. Only at the end is it revealed to have been a dream experienced by his over-anxious daughter.

He was directed again by the prolific Oswald Mitchell in *The Temptress* (1949), a gloomy second feature in which he plays aristocrat Sir Charles Clifford, with Joan Maude cast as his wife. As a much older man than usual, he gives a touching portrayal of an invalid depressed by his wife's blatant infidelities, conveying well his sadness and world-weariness.

He then had a break for a year, during which he was busy in the theater, before landing a part in *The Magic Box* (1951), a commemoration of the innovative photographic pioneer, William Friese-Greene. Obsessed with his dream of creating a moving image, Friese-Greene is played with great spirit and sensitivity by Robert Donat. Directed by John Boulting, with a script by Eric Ambler, this was the British film industry's contribution to the Festival of Britain, and featured cameo performances by 60 actors, including most of the stars of the day: Laurence Olivier plays a dim-witted policeman mystified by Donat's invention, Sybil Thorndike is on screen for 30 seconds as a haughty aristocrat, while Richard Attenborough, Glynis Johns, Bernard Miles and Michael Redgrave were among the many other stars involved.

Like most of the cast members, my father has a non-speaking part. He sits on the platform at a crisis meeting of the film industry in the Connaught Rooms in London, where a clearly ill Friese-Greene makes an impassioned speech before collapsing and dying. The film was based on a misleading biography by Ray Allister, which perpetuated the myth that Friese-Greene was the main inventor of the medium of film, rather than just one of the pioneers. Donat battled courageously with illness during the shooting, and by the time the film was released the Festival of Britain had shut down. The critics were lukewarm, but the film was nevertheless nominated for two BAFTAs, Best Film and Best British Film.

Mr. Denning Drives North (1951) was an engaging murder mystery directed by Anthony Kimmins. A mixture of suspense and black comedy, it has effective lead performances from John Mills and Phyllis Calvert, and good support from Herbert Lom and Sam Wanamaker. According to the *New York Times*: "This little melodrama serves as still another reminder, from a country that jolly well knows how to exercise it, that restraint can work minor wonders. No doubt about it, the British have what it takes." My father plays the small part of Wilson, the butler-manservant of the two principals. It's a notable departure from his usual professional roles, and yet he catches well the man's loyalty and deference to his employers.

During this time, my mother resumed work, now as an adjudicator at drama festivals around the country. She went on to work at the Central School of Speech and Drama in London, then based in the Albert Hall, where she taught students (including Vanessa Redgrave and Julie Christie) and staged their productions. She too entered the film world, teaching a class in film technique at the London Academy of Music and Dramatic Art, and coaching contract artists of the Rank Organisation

With his wife Barbara at the London premiere of Billy Wilder's film *Sunset Blvd.* (1950).

in film technique, movement and voice production.

After my parents separated, my mother moved to Markham Square in Chelsea, and then bought a cottage in Black Lion Lane in Hammersmith, which became her final home. She worked occasionally in the theater, directing *Kathleen* by Michael Sayers for the Repertory Players at Wyndham's, with a cast that included Kate Binchy, Basil Hoskins and Michael Darlow; and also Shaw's *Heartbreak House* for the Tavistock Repertory Company at the Tower Theatre, Canonbury.

My father's next film was the famous Edgar Wallace murder mystery *The Ringer* (1952), of which there had previously been at least half a dozen screen versions. This one was treated as a B-feature, and rehearsed and shot in just three weeks. It was the first film directed

A portrait of the film pioneer William Friese-Greene, played by Robert Donat, *The Magic Box* was made for the 1951 Festival of Britain.

by Guy Hamilton, who was to become one of the most sought-after directors in British films.

The strong cast was headed by Donald Wolfit as Dr. Lomond, alongside Herbert Lom, Mai Zetterling, Greta Gynt and William Hartnell, with Dora Bryan and Denholm Elliott also featuring. My father was surprisingly convincing in an unusual role for him, that of the mysterious gardener. It was not his preferred part. "Being a Scot and having played Dr. Lomond on stage in Sunderland, I would have given anything to play him in the film version. Instead I was just required to coach Donald Wolfit to find a Scottish accent."

The whodunit *Mantrap* (1953; U.S. title *Man in Hiding*), directed by Terence Fisher, offered him another cameo role as a doctor. The plot involves an attempt by Kieron Moore, wrongly imprisoned for murder, to clear his name, with the help of Paul Henreid's private detective. The cast also includes Kay Kendall, Bill Travers and Hugh Sinclair.

The exceedingly dull and ludicrous science fiction film *Four-Sided Triangle* (1953) was again directed by Fisher. After previously focusing on crime dramas, this was Hammer Films' first venture into science fiction, a genre for which they would become celebrated. The plot concerns a scientist who creates a clone of the woman both he and his childhood friend love. The film starred James Hayter, Stephen Murray and Minnesota-born Barbara Payton, who had acted opposite James Cagney and Gregory Peck before bringing her "bad girl" image to England. My father appears very briefly as a country solicitor in this bizarre story. The *Monthly Film Bulletin* critic sneered: "Barbara Payton seems unlikely to achieve fame for her histrionic ability, and Stephen Murray's performance was unadulterated ham."

Street Corner (1953; U.S. title *Both Sides of the Law*), a mixture of documentary and crime story, depicts the daily life of policewomen. Conceived as a female version of the popular film *The Blue Lamp* (1950), its stars were Anne Crawford, Rosamund John, Barbara Murray and Terence Morgan. My father has just one scene, playing a magistrate who sentences young mother Peggy Cummins for shoplifting. According to *Movie Review Warehouse*, "Director Muriel Box doesn't do anything terribly innovative with the camera, but she does know how to tell a story effectively, often a rarer skill in the film world."

Later she explained her thinking: "I thought *The Blue Lamp* had too long a run for its money, because it never mentioned women and how they cooperated in doing police work. It was about time women had a chance to show what they did, and the film was specifically designed to show their work." Box was virtually the only woman to direct mainstream British films during the 1950s, and the position was little better in Hollywood: "It was terribly difficult. They were prejudiced against you from

"THE MOST SENSATIONAL, ACTION-PACKED THRILLER OF THE YEAR!"

MR. DENNING DRIVES NORTH

starring
JOHN MILLS • PHYLLIS CALVERT
with SAM WANAMAKER

In the 1951 murder mystery *Mr. Denning Drives North*, he played the manservant of John Mills and Phyllis Calvert.

the start." After receiving good notices for her work in Britain, she asked her agent what her chances might be in Hollywood. "I wish I could tell you differently," he replied. "But if I mention the name of a woman as a director, they just turn away and look out of the window."

Front Page Story (1954) was a first-rate film, creating an intelligent picture of a day in the life of a national newspaper. It has a good range of journalist characters, catching their mixture of cynicism and idealism, the petty rivalries, the heavy drinking. The dialogue is sharp and often witty, while the narrative skillfully juggles three stories being covered by the newsroom. One of these concerns Eva Bartok, who is charged with murdering her husband. As counsel for the prosecution, my father has a lengthy speech, making the case for a guilty verdict to the jury with stern, convincing attack.

Donald Wolfit and Herbert Lom headed the cast in *The Ringer* (1952), an adaptation of Edgar Wallace's celebrated stage thriller.

At the center is an outstanding performance by Jack Hawkins as the tough but fair news editor, whose obsession with the paper almost breaks up his marriage; Elizabeth Allan gives a sensitive performance as the neglected wife. Under the skillful control of director Gordon Parry, a former actor, there's also excellent support from the reporters, notably Derek Farr, Joseph Tomelty, Walter Fitzgerald, Patricia Marmont and Michael Goodliffe.

It's a Great Day (1955) is a banal story of suburban life, based on the popular early TV soap *The Grove Family*, with Ruth Dunning and Edward Evans again playing the parents. My father, here a police inspector, has a few brief scenes, but has no scope to give him any personality.

He took part in a short film in the series *Scotland Yard*, narrated by Edgar Lustgarten, billed as "The Famous Criminologist." *The Mysterious Bullet* (1955) is

In 1953 he was the celebrity guest at a coronation street-party in Battersea.

introduced by a fevered American voice, announcing: "Scotland Yard! A determined body of men on an unceasing crusade against cases of crime, of larceny and murder, of greed and envy," etc., etc. The case itself is anti-climactic, a routine murder investigation revolving around a lot of ballistics details. My father's part is that of a rural police inspector who calls in Scotland Yard to solve the murder, leaving him as a mere onlooker.

The director John Gilling gave him a more substantial role in the crime drama *The Gilded Cage* (1955), the name of the painting which features prominently in this story of an attempted art heist. Complete with glasses, mustache and bow tie, he makes Harding, an art dealer involved in the scam, very believable. It was in marked contrast to the minor roles he had played recently, and it gives him the chance to develop his character properly, and even to evoke sympathy at the moment when he confesses to his involvement in the crime ("I needed the money"). American actor Alex Nicol, Veronica Hurst, Ursula Howells and Clifford Evans were also featured. The *Radio Times* noted, "[Gilling] tries to push the tale along at a decent rate, but spotting who framed Nicol's brother is hardly taxing"; *Sky Movies* described it as "a standard British thick-ear thriller of the fifties," but praised "the vigorous playing of a solid cast that sees the ingenuous story through."

Tons of Trouble (1956) was a desperately unfunny slapstick comedy directed by Leslie S. Hiscott. William Hartnell and Austin Trevor star with Richard Hearne, who appears as his popular television character Mr. Pastry. Hearne was the first performer to have his own series on British television. He's an old man with a walrus

He appeared as the prosecuting counsel in a murder case in *Front Page Story* (1954), starring Jack Hawkins (courtesy the Cinema Museum, London).

mustache and a trademark bowler hat, here playing an eccentric handyman working in a block of flats. My father has two mercifully short scenes as a doctor.

Turning to a film for children, he appeared as Mr. Hampton in *Raiders of the River* (1956), a serial in eight episodes telling of the adventures of a group of London children with a gang of criminals. The young leads are played by Richard O'Sullivan as Joey and Jenny Jones as Patsy.

He was then cast as a chief constable in the moderately gripping thriller *Eyewitness* (1956), with Donald Sinden playing against type as a killer, and Belinda Lee, Nigel Stock and Michael Craig in support. Interviewed in *British Cinema*, Muriel Pavlow, who played the witness to the killing, remembered Muriel Box as "a fine director and a charming woman, with a great knowledge of film-making." Sinden modeled his performance on the notorious murderer Neville Heath. The press reception was cool: *Variety* called it "an unpretentious thriller"; *Monthly Film Bulletin* felt "the theme was a serviceable one," but that "the melodrama is unadventurously developed."

My father played Dr. Underwood in *Alias John Preston* (1956), a mystery story directed by David MacDonald, who began his career in films by working as Cecil B. DeMille's assistant. It stars Christopher Lee, in his first horror film, as a stranger who comes to a village and falls in love with a local woman (Betta St. John), then seeks help from a psychiatrist (Alexander Knox) to exorcise his inner demons. "Is This Man the Devil in the Flesh?" asks the melodramatic poster.

Other Films

My father was an inspector in the romantic thriller *Third Time Lucky* (1948), directed by Gordon Parry, and starring Dermot Walsh and Glynis Johns. Johns gets caught up in the world of gambling, and a murder follows.

In *John and Julie* (1954), a comedy about two children who run away to London to visit the queen, he had a brief scene with the children, as an amiable police constable on duty outside Buckingham Palace.

The Men of Sherwood Forest (1954), a Robin Hood adventure, involved the

With Jenny Jones in the children's adventure story *Raiders of the River* (1956).

famous outlaw's efforts to rescue Richard the Lionheart from imprisonment in Germany. It was directed by Val Guest, with Don Taylor playing Robin. My father had a small part as a nobleman.

He played a surgeon in the crime B-feature *Johnny, You're Wanted* (1956), in which a truck driver is accused of murdering a hitchhiker. It starred John Slater, Alfred Marks and Garry Marsh.

In director Terence Fisher's crime drama *The Last Man to Hang* (1956), the story of a man on trial for the murder of his wife, he appears as a magistrate. The cast included Tom Conway, Elizabeth Sellars, Eunice Gayson and Anthony Newley.

He also took part in *To the Rescue* (1952), a short documentary about a stolen poodle, made for the National Film Board of Canada.

22

From *Quatermass*
to *Superman*

"As one gets older parts become fewer, but I remind myself that an actor's life is feast or famine. After so many years of feasting, I should be enjoying a diet."—John Stuart, in his memoir *Caught in the Act*, 1971

The second half of the 1950s was a time marked by caution on the part of many British studios. Films were too often based on West End stage successes or popular novels, or were remakes of earlier productions. But between 1959 and 1963, the landscape was transformed by the arrival of the British New Wave. Although it comprised no more than a dozen films, it marked the arrival of a new generation of writers, actors and directors.

It was influenced by two developments. One was the radical shake-up to the theater prompted by the work of playwrights such as John Osborne (*Look Back in Anger*) and Shelagh Delaney (*A Taste of Honey*) and the novelists Alan Sillitoe and David Storey. The other was the Free Cinema movement, a rebellious group of filmmakers including Lindsay Anderson, Karel Reisz and Tony Richardson, who declared their opposition to the commercial film industry.

The result was a very different kind of film. Many of them focused on the everyday working-class experience, especially in communities in the north of England. Often shot on location, they came to be known as "kitchen sink" films. Directors such as Reisz (*Saturday Night and Sunday Morning*), Richardson (*Look Back in Anger, A Taste of Honey, The Loneliness of the Long-Distance Runner, The Entertainer*), Anderson (*This Sporting Life*), Jack Clayton (*Room at the Top*) and John Schlesinger (*Billy Liar, A Kind of Loving*) brought a new freshness to the screen. A new generation of actors came to prominence, including Albert Finney, Rita Tushingham, Tom Courtenay, Rachel Roberts and Alan Bates.

The films were extremely popular, especially with the younger generation. But my father took no part in this new wave, continuing to play small roles in a steady fare of conventional studio-based crime dramas, thrillers and comedies. He also appeared in several horror movies, which were popular with audiences as a result of the meteoric rise of Hammer Films.

The company's breakthrough came when it acquired the rights to the immensely successful television science fiction horror serial *The Quatermass Experiment*, written by Nigel Kneale, which had enthralled millions. After the success of

The Quatermass Xperiment, the first film based on the story, my father appeared in the sequel, *Quatermass II* (1957; U.S. title *Enemy from Space*).

The plot of director Val Guest's film involved the threat of alien objects falling to Earth and infecting people with burn marks and turning them into zombies. "A Creeping Terror of Destruction! A Nightmare of Horror and Fear!" screamed the publicity. The story featured a secret installation, paramilitary policing, a new town, a chemical plant, synthetic food and ammonia poisoning. American actor Brian Donlevy, a film noir stalwart, was top-cast as the eponymous professor investigating the threat and its attempted cover-up. Bryan Forbes and William Franklyn are his assistants, Sidney James plays a drink-sodden reporter, and John Longden is the police inspector. My father plays a police commissioner who, having been infected by the dreaded poison, is reduced to a zombie-like state. Much of the action was shot at the eerie Shell Haven oil refinery in the Thames Estuary.

The casting of Donlevy was linked to the securing of distribution rights in America. This dismayed Nigel Kneale, who had picked Quatermass' surname out of the phone book, but had carefully chosen his first name, Bernard, as a tribute to Bernard Lovell, creator of the Jodrell Bank observatory, to suggest a pioneering English scientist. There was a further problem with Donlevy, who would sink half a bottle of whiskey while having lunch at the nearby village pub, and in the afternoon lace his coffee with brandy. Consequently he sometimes had to be reminded by Guest which scene he was about to play, and then the "idiot board" would be held up so he could read from it.

The result is a stolid and ultimately dull performance. The *Daily Herald* was dismissive: "He spends his time dashing around in short bursts,

George Sanders starred in the horror film *Village of the Damned* (1960), based on the novel by John Wyndham.

rather like somebody trying to get change for a phone call. The whole thing is quite daft and full of stilted dialogue." The *Evening News* called it "hokum," but Campbell Dixon in the *Daily Telegraph* thought it "good, grisly fun, if this is the sort of thing you enjoy." The *Daily Express* found it "eerie, exciting, and tense."

My father then featured in small roles in four more horror films. He played yet another police inspector in *The Revenge of Frankenstein* (1958), in which a scientist (Peter Cushing), having escaped execution and assumed an alias, continues to experiment with dead bodies. The film was a sequel to the previous year's box office hit *The Curse of Frankenstein*; both were directed by Terence Fisher. A conscientious craftsman, he became celebrated for his work in the horror genre.

In *Blood of the Vampire* (1958), directed by Henry Cass, my father appeared as Uncle Philippe, an ally of Donald Wolfit, who played a scientist in Transylvania put to death by villagers who wrongly believe him to be a vampire. In *The Mummy* (1959) he was cast as a coroner, in a story of three archaeologists who uncover the sarcophagus of a princess, with surprising results. Terence Fisher was again the director, while the stars were the horror regulars Peter Cushing and Christopher Lee.

And he was Professor Smith in *Village of the Damned* (1960), based on John Wyndham's popular science fiction novel *The Midwich Cuckoos*, and co-scripted and directed by Wolf Rilla.

During these years, my father also appeared in four comedies of varying quality. *The Naked Truth* (1957; U.S. title *Your Past Is Showing*) was a black comedy in which a number of well-known personalities plan to murder a magazine editor (Dennis Price) who threatens to reveal secrets of their private lives. The film also stars Terry-Thomas, Peter Sellers, Joan Sims, Peggy Mount and Shirley Eaton, with my father once more playing a police inspector. It was much liked by the critics, the *Radio Times* observing: "It's based—as the best British humour often is—on class and sex," while the critic–film historian Leonard Maltin noted, "Sellers is a special treat in this amusing satire." The film was directed by Mario Zampi, who by now had developed a talent for directing British comedies such as *Laughter in Paradise*, the top-grossing film of 1951.

In *Further Up the Creek* (1958), a classic British comedy romp, an assortment of people are duped into signing up for a supposed luxury cruise on what is actually a clapped-out frigate. Frankie Howerd is in delicious comic form as the bosun and begetter of the scam, while David Tomlinson is amusingly convincing as the ship's inept captain. Shirley Eaton and Lionel Jeffries co-star. My father, playing an admiral on shore, has a brief scene with Thora Hird, one of the passengers. Written and directed by Val Guest, the film was a hastily made sequel to the massive hit *Up the Creek* (1958), though it lacked the presence of Peter Sellers, who had by now become a big star.

My father returned to the police ranks as Inspector Jensen in the crime film spoof *Too Many Crooks* (1959), an entertaining tale about a bunch of half-witted criminals. After a series of bungled jobs, they kidnap the wife of the rich, unscrupulous businessman Billie Gordon and demand a ransom, only for him to declare that he's glad to be rid of her.

As Gordon, Terry-Thomas is in superb form, catching with panache the ultra-smooth villainy of the ultimate cad with exquisite comic timing. Brenda de Banzie convincingly makes the transition from the put-upon wife to the assertive woman, who persuades the gang of incompetents to help her get revenge on her straying husband. George Cole also shines as "Fingers," the gang leader responsible for the failure of their various jobs. My father has a couple of scenes in which he is increasingly frustrated in his attempts to question Terry-Thomas about the supposed murder of his wife. Directed by Mario Zampi, the film also featured several

The nautical romp *Further Up the Creek* (1958) was a sequel to the popular *Up the Creek*, with Frankie Howerd taking over from Peter Sellers.

popular comic actors of the day, including Sidney James, Vera Day, John le Mesurier and Bernard Bresslaw. The *New York Times* called it "a good, crazy, brisk farce."

My father also appeared briefly in the comedy *Idol on Parade* (1959), the story of a rock'n'roll star drafted into the British army. Anthony Newley appeared in the title role, supported by William Bendix, Sidney James, Lionel Jeffries, Harry Fowler and Susan Hampshire.

Mario Zampi also directed the dire comedy *Bottoms Up!* (1960), a cheap version of the TV sitcom *Whacko!* It starred the popular comedian Jimmy Edwards as the cane-wielding headmaster of a school where the boys rebel against his repressive regime. Richard Briers and Martita Hunt also appear, while my father plays a police officer called in to deal with the boys' rioting.

This was a period which saw him playing small parts in several crime films. *Chain of Events* (1958) was a taut melodrama based on a radio play by actor Leo McKern. As the publicity explained, "It started with a man without a bus fare, and ended in BLACKMAIL and VIOLENCE!" Kenneth Griffith is the nervous bank clerk whose petty crime causes the mayhem; Dermot Walsh, Jack Watling, Lisa Gastoni and Susan Shaw co-star. Playing the small part of Griffith's boss, my father conveys well the weary, irritated bank manager. "Very much a B-movie feature," noted *Cinemaretro*, "it works exceptionally well on its own merits." These include sharp, realistic dialogue and believably shifty characters. The director was Gerald Thomas, who was to take charge soon afterward of the hugely popular, bawdy *Carry On* films.

Then there was *Three Sundays to Live* (1957), a low-budget film noir starring Kieron Moore as a bandleader wrongly accused of murdering the boss of the nightclub where he works. Directed by Ernest Morris, it also starred Jane Griffiths, a regular in B-films, and the archetypal good-time girl Sandra Dorne. Basil Dignam and John Longden also feature, while my father appears as a judge.

In the spy thriller *The Secret Man* (1958), directed by the Scot Ronald Kinnoch, a young atomic physicist (American actor Marshall Thompson) allows Scotland Yard to use him as bait as they track down a leak from his research station. It's a moderately tense story with plenty of taut dialogue. My father plays scientist Dr. Warren, a reasonably substantial part which he handles smoothly. John Loder convinces as the man from the Yard, and Henry Oscar is cool and sinister as the spy.

His next film, the melodrama *Pit of Darkness* (1961), was directed by Lance Comfort who, according to Brian McFarlane's book about his career, "made some of the most entertaining films in Britain between 1941 and 1965 … but was the most unjustly neglected director in British film history." The film stars William Franklyn and Moira Redmond, with Leonard Sachs and Nanette Newman among the supporting cast. The plot concerns a safe designer who breaks up a crime ring, and in doing so recovers his lost memory. My father plays Lord Barnsford, a solicitor whose safe is burgled during the night. He appears in his pajamas, brandishing a rifle and foiling the gang of robbers.

Even with the Second World War long over, war films continued to find their audience, and my father played in two of them. In director Ernest Morris' *The Betrayal* (1957), he plays a war crimes commissioner. An Allied pilot (Philip Friend) is captured by the Germans, who blind him during his imprisonment. Realizing that one of his fellow-officers betrayed him to the enemy, after the war he vows to find the traitor despite his disability.

Sink the Bismarck! (1960) was the true story of the hunt for the dreaded German battleship, based on a book by C.S. Forester. The distinguished director Lewis Gilbert was in charge, and a big model of the ship was built in the huge Pinewood tank. Kenneth More stars as the Admiralty's chief of operations, with much of the film centered in the Admiralty War Room. My father has a substantial and interesting role, exuding authority as Ralph Kerr, captain of HMS *Hood*, which is eventually sunk by the *Bismarck*.

The film was well-received by the patriotic paper the *Daily Telegraph*, but attacked by the anti-war critics. The *Radio Times* reviewed it favorably, stating: "This fine film fully captures the tensions, dangers and complexities of battle by concentrating on the unsung back-room planners as much as on the combatants themselves. …There is a respect for the enemy that is missing in many previous flag-wavers." It became the second-best box-office draw of the year, and to Gilbert's surprise proved a success in America.

From the mid–1960s on, my father concentrated for several years on theater work and television, and made no films at all. His third marriage had been falling-

ing apart for some time now: rows were frequent, with my mother sometimes turning violent. In 1957, he left the family home in Battersea, but returned again after two years. But in the early 1960s, once my brother and I had left school, our parents separated permanently. My father rented a room in a Knightsbridge flat and remained there for most of the rest of his life. Despite his successful career, he never actually bought a place of his own.

Our mother moved to Chelsea and then Hammersmith, where she became a well-known voice coach, working with American stars Meryl Streep for *The French Lieutenant's Woman*, William Hurt for *Gorky Park* and Margot Kidder for

In the war film *Sink the Bismarck!* (1960), he was cast as the captain of the doomed HMS *Hood* (courtesy the Cinema Museum, London).

Flash Gordon. She also coached Helmut Berger for one of Visconti's films, probably *The Damned*, and Marisa Berenson for *Barry Lyndon*.

In the 1970s, she returned to her original career as an actress. On television she was in the soap *Kate* (1971–72), the story of life on a woman's magazine, with Phyllis Calvert as the titular agony aunt; the crime drama series *Public Eye* (1973), starring Alfred Burke; and the drama series *Intimate Strangers* (1974).

In films she was seen as a party guest in Peter Finch's house in *Sunday Bloody Sunday* (1971), directed by John Schlesinger, and in *Got It Made* (1974), a family drama starring Lalla Ward, Michael Feast and Fabia Drake. She played Frau Kummer, the decoy bandaged substitute for Miss Foy, in the remake of *The Lady Vanishes* (1979). Notoriously, she was the sadistic prison governor in *The House of Whipcord* (1974), which became a cult film.

Despite their failed marriage, she and my father remained in touch. He accepted the slowdown in his film career with a good grace, writing in his memoir: "I have had a very interesting and varied life, which I have enjoyed immensely. As one gets older parts become fewer, but I remind myself that an actor's life is feast or famine. After so many years of feasting, I should be enjoying a diet."

He returned to the cinema with *Young Winston* (1972). The film covers Churchill's early life and career, from his time as a war correspondent in India and a soldier during the Boer War, to his entry into Parliament, where my father plays the heavily bearded Speaker of the House of Commons, Viscount Peel. Written by Carl Foreman and directed by Richard Attenborough, the film has Simon Ward in the title role, heading a starry cast that includes Anne Bancroft, Robert Shaw,

DIRECTED BY RICHARD ATTENBOROUGH

ROBERT SHAW   ANNE BANCROFT

SIMON WARD

YOUNG WINSTON

Jack Hawkins   Ian Holm   Anthony Hopkins   Patrick Magee   Edward Woodward   and   John Mills

He played the Speaker of the House of Commons in *Young Winston* (1972), the story of Churchill's early life.

Anthony Hopkins, John Mills, Ian Holm and Jack Hawkins. This fine film won several awards, including an Oscar and a BAFTA.

My father's last appearance was in *Superman* (1978), the first in a series of Superman films. It was directed by Richard Donner, with Christopher Reeve cast as the superhero, Margot Kidder as Lois Lane and Gene Hackman as the villainous Lex Luthor. My father was involved in the early scenes on the planet Krypton, as one of the ten elders on the council alongside Harry Andrews, Trevor Howard and others, with Marlon Brando playing their leader Jor-El. When the planet explodes, Brando and the Elders are cast into space. It was a dramatic and fitting finale to my father's 58-year film career, which ended, as it began, in silence.

In his final film *Superman: The Movie* (1978) he was one of the elders on the Planet Krypton council, led by Marlon Brando.

Other Films

Five Clues to Fortune (1957), directed by Joe Mendoza, was the story of children searching for a treasure hidden in Woburn Abbey during the dissolution of the monasteries. My father played an abbot.

He appeared in two more films in the *Scotland Yard* series: *The Cross-Road Gallows* (1958), a story of a murder in a caravan park, in which he plays Mr. Simmons, a civilian, and *The Unseeing Eye* (1959), in which detectives pursue a killer arsonist. He plays Murray, a police doctor.

In *Compelled* (1960), he has a small part as a professor who buys a volume of Keats' poems in a bookshop where a jewel heist is being planned, and nearly exposes the scheme. The film, directed by Ramsey Herrington, stars Ronald Howard and Beth Rogan.

He played a prison governor in *Danger by My Side* (1962), a conventional crime thriller. Directed by Charles Saunders, it starred Anthony Oliver, Maureen Connell and Alan Tilvern.

In *Paranoiac* (1963), directed by Freddie Francis, he plays the manservant Williams to Oliver Reed's wealthy psychotic, whose brother mysteriously arrives to claim his share of the family inheritance. Janette Scott and Sheila Burrell also star.

He appears briefly in the English Civil War adventure *The Scarlet Blade* (1963; U.S. title *The Crimson Blade*), which starred Oliver Reed and June Thorburn, and was directed by John Gilling. He plays Beverly, a loyal Royalist, who refuses to reveal the whereabouts of Charles I and is swiftly put to death.

The comedy adventure *Royal Flash* (1975), directed by the American-born Richard Lester, stars Malcolm McDowell as the rogue hero Harry Flashman and Oliver Reed as his enemy Otto von Bismarck. My father appears very briefly as an English general to pin a medal on Flashman.

23

The Final Years

"What the hell are you doing here, John?"—Alfred Hitchcock's first words
to my father when they met in Stockholm in 1968

In 1965, my father met Muriel Angelus while she was on a short visit to England. It was the first time they had been reunited since their marriage ended and she had moved to America. In the intervening years, she had retired and married Paul Lavalle, a composer-arranger, and conductor of the Radio City Music Hall orchestra. In 1959, she resisted the efforts of her friend Richard Rodgers to get her out of retirement and play the Mother Abbess in the first Broadway production of *The Sound of Music*. At the end of her life, she admitted it had been a mistake to leave England: "I was caught up in the glamour, but once in Hollywood I was nothing more than a tiny craft battling in an ocean beside much weightier ships." She died in a Virginia nursing home at the age of 95.

In 1971, my father's memoir *Caught in the Act* was published. In the foreword he thanked the London Fire Brigade, "who salvaged my press cutting books, without which the following memoir could never have been written. The books were in a store in Baker Street when, during the Battle of Britain, it was partially destroyed by enemy bombing. By a stroke of luck they were only slightly damaged, and for the most part are quite legible, so that I was able to derive much information from them about my career."

Eminent film critic Dilys Powell reviewed the memoir in *Silent Picture* magazine:

It's very slim but packed with detail, and illustrated with those forgotten stills—the aquiline profile under the wavy hair looking devotedly into the face under the bob and the cloche hat—which stir in the film addict so deep a nostalgia for the innocent past.... He was the cinema hero whom the autograph hunters pursued. In a way his story embraces the story of the British screen between the wars. ...You won't find critical examination of the cinema in his pages; anecdotes perhaps, but not analysis. What he does is write modestly and confidingly about his share in making films. He has enjoyed his life; he has never lost heart. And that makes his story, too, enjoyable.

In the autumn of his life, my father met two celebrated figures from his past. In 1961, he got together with Gary Cooper at Elstree Studios, where they were both filming; the Hollywood star was making his final picture, *The Naked Edge*. "I went on to the set to see him, and we talked about the old school days, and had many a laugh," he recalled. A photograph shows the American actor towering over his former schoolmate.

With his son Stephen and grandsons Jesper (left) and Per Nicklas on a visit to Sweden in 1968.

Then in 1968, while visiting my brother Stephen and his family in Sweden, he met Alfred Hitchcock for the first time in 40 years. Stephen had discovered that Hitchcock was in town and arranged a meeting in a restaurant with a photographer present. Hitchcock left his table, and in the foyer greeted my father with: "What the hell are you doing here, John?" They chatted briefly, and posed for a photograph.

He was frequently invited to introduce one of his films at the National Film Theatre in London. I accompanied him to a screening of *Number Seventeen*, when he talked about working with Hitchcock. In 1970, he acted as compere for *The British Silent Cinema*, a program arranged by the film historian and silent-film specialist Anthony Slide. The screening was billed as "an opportunity to become better acquainted with the films and personalities involved in the British silent cinema, an area of film for too long much maligned." The program included extracts from the works of George Pearson, Maurice Elvey, Walter Summers and Graham Cutts, introduced by some of the technicians who worked with them.

A growing interest in silent films was reflected in a television program in the series *Yesterday's Witness* (1971), in which my father took part, along with Hitchcock, Michael Balcon, George Pearson, Mabel Poulton and John Longden. Extracts from

Kitty were shown, with my father talking about the impact on the critics and the audience of the historic moment when he spoke those first words on screen.

During his final years, he kept active playing bowls. He was a regular member of the Stage Eccentrics team, which played in Battersea Park and later Hyde Park; he also belonged to an indoor bowling club in Richmond. On his eightieth birthday,

Top: In Kew Gardens with Jonathan's eldest son Ben in 1968. *Bottom:* In action with the Stage Eccentrics bowl team in Hyde Park.

my wife Jan and I and our children Ben and Julius gave him a celebratory lunch at our Richmond home. At the end of the meal, recalling his silent film days, he sang "Roses of Picardy," his attractive voice still in pretty good shape. It was a poignant and touching moment.

Near the end of his life, he suffered a series of small strokes. Finally, thanks to the kindly support of Richard Attenborough, president of Denville Hall, the actors' home at Northwood in Middlesex, he moved there for his final year. He enjoyed reminiscing with other actors in residence there. He was also popular with the staff, one of whom wrote: "It was a pleasure and a privilege to have him here with us, and whatever we did was done because he really was in our eyes the greatest—and the perfect gentleman."

He died of a stroke in Harefield Hospital in Middlesex on October 17, 1979, aged 81. His brother Eric's wife Julie wrote: "He was not only my dear brother-in-law, but a gentle and kindly

"I look back with pleasure on the past." From his memoir *Caught in the Act* (1971).

man. In times of crisis in my own life he was always a good listener. I shall never forget his goodness. One never heard him utter an unkind word about anyone."

Obituaries were published in several newspapers, including *The Times*, the *Daily Telegraph*, *Variety* and *The Stage*. Their principal focus was on his years of stardom. *The Times* suggested, "He will probably be best remembered as a romantic lead in 'the weepies' of the 1920s and 1930s, first in silent films and later in the 'talkies.'" In *The Stage,* R.B. Marriott wrote: "Although he was best known as one of the earliest stars of British silent and talking films, he was also a stage actor of considerable gifts, suave yet compelling, with a deep sense of character and theatrical effect."

Epilogue

This extended voyage round my film-star father has been a revelation to me. The man I lived with in his middle age—he was 43 when I was born—had certainly not prepared me for the startlingly different person I was confronted with as I researched this book.

To my great surprise, as I examined his scrapbooks full of riches about his career, I encountered an active, ambitious, hard-working man of great physical courage. He emerged in many guises: the keen all-round sportsman, the songwriter, the concert performer, the collector of antiques, the writer of articles about his life as a star, the stage director, the articulate and untiring spokesman for the fledgling British film industry—and, not least, as I watched and re-watched his films, an actor of great charm and authenticity.

His wide range of skills, and his outgoing personality, astonished me. At home he had been essentially a passive presence, very much dominated by my strong-willed and self-centered mother. He was gentle and kind, and inspired affection, but he also seemed to be lazy and weak, and somewhat emotionally reserved. He appeared to have no strong opinions, and was generally hopeless at disciplining me and my brother Stephen, which was sometimes necessary. Nor did he offer us any guidance for life, or give us the benefit of his own experience of it.

Despite having two very keen sporting sons, he never talked about his own sporting exploits, or took us to any football or cricket matches. More surprisingly, he also never took us to the theater, nor in my case to the cinema, although he did occasionally take my brother to the Gaumont in Chelsea, where they got in free because he knew the manager. It was our mother who provided us with cultural experiences, with outings to the theater and to the children's concerts being staged at the Festival Hall. He remained a distant if benevolent father, and this was not just because during our formative years he was away touring for weeks on end, or working a great deal in television.

He and our mother had separate bedrooms in our Battersea flat, a reflection of their increasingly unhappy marriage. I picture him sitting in his room, puzzling over the *Daily Express* crossword, checking the racing form or the football results, while waiting for his agent to ring. I never saw him reading a book or listening to music. His modest, easygoing nature seemed to hold him back from actively seeking work and generally promoting himself. This infuriated our mother, and led to many furious rows. My brother recalls an incident when she threw a heavy ashtray at him, he ducked, and it made a considerable dent in the wall behind him.

One question I pondered as I looked into his long career was why, despite his early stardom, he never quite achieved his full potential. I think this was partly because he took on too many mediocre, unchallenging roles. He appears to have had no full-time agent to help him make judgments about the work he was offered. It seems to me that quality was too often sacrificed to quantity, resulting in a certain loss of status which prevented him from reaching the top of his profession.

Although he seemed to be ambitious, I think he lacked that steely, ruthless quality which many of the greatest stars possess. As my brother rightly says: "He was not basically a driven person. He was driven by other people's agendas. He also seemed to go out of his way not to upset anyone, to say favourable things about them, as if he needed to be liked."

He never spoke at home of his experiences in the First World War on the western front in France, where so many of his close friends died fighting alongside him in that appalling conflict. So it was both moving and shocking to read an interview in which he admitted that these losses affected him so profoundly. I suspect this was the cause of the frequent nightmares he experienced during our childhood, when he could be heard shouting out in his sleep. How bitterly I regret not trying to get him to talk about that traumatic time in his life. I was young of course, and it was hardly my role to do so. And yet maybe it would have made for a closer relationship between us, and perhaps also served to release some of his demons.

However, I have at least one compensation. Having built up a large collection of his films over the years, I am able at will to bring back temporarily to life the father I never really knew or understood, and immerse myself in his remarkable work during his six decades on screen.

Film, Documentary, Theater, Television, and Miscellaneous Appearances

Film

1920 *Her Son, The Great Gay Road, The Lights of Home.*

1921 *Land of My Fathers, Something in the City* ("Leaves from My Life" series), *The Stolen Jewels* ("Leaves from My Life" series), *Belle of the Gambling Den* ("Leaves from My Life" series), *The Notorious Mrs. Fagin* ("Leaves from My Life" series), *The Case of a Packing Case* ("Leaves from My Life" series), *The Man Who Came Back* ("Leaves from My Life" series), *Home Sweet Home* (song film), *Eileen Allanah* (song film), *Sally in Our Alley* (song film).

1922 *Sinister Street, The Little Mother, A Sporting Double, If Four Walls Told, The Extra Knot.*

1923 *This Freedom, Little Miss Nobody, The School for Scandal, The Loves of Mary, Queen of Scots, Constant Hot Water, The Mistletoe Bough, The Reverse of the Medal.*

1924 *Claude Duval, His Grace Gives Notice, Her Redemption, The Alley of Golden Hearts.*

1925 *We Women, Daughter of Love, Venetian Lovers, Bachelor Wives, Parted.*

1926 *London Love, The Woman Juror, Back to the Trees, Mademoiselle from Armentières, Curfew Shall Not Ring Tonight, Herne the Hunter* ("Haunted House" series), *Baddesley Manor* ("Haunted House" series), *Kenilworth Castle* ("Haunted House" series), *The Tower of London* ("Haunted House" series), *In Feudal Days* ("Haunted House" series).

1927 *The Pleasure Garden, Hindle Wakes, Roses of Picardy, The Glad Eye, The Flight Commander, A Woman in Pawn.*

1928 *Sailors Don't Care, Mademoiselle Parley Voo, Yacht of the Seven Sins, Smashing Through.*

1929 *High Seas, Kitty, Taxi for Two, Memories, Atlantic.*

1930 *Eve's Fall, The Brat, No Exit, Children of Chance, Kissing Cup's Race.*

1931 *Hindle Wakes, Midnight, The Hound of the Baskervilles.*

1932 *In a Monastery Garden, Verdict of the Sea, Number Seventeen, Men of Steel, Little Fella, Women Are That Way, L'Atlantide: The Mistress of Atlantis.*

1933 *Mr. Quincy of Monte Carlo, Naughty Cinderella, The Lost Chord, This Week of Grace, Love's Old Sweet Song, Head of the Family, Mayfair Girl, Home Sweet Home, Enemy of the Police, The Wandering Jew, The House of Trent, The Pointing Finger.*

1934 *The Black Abbot, The Four Masked Men, Grand Prix, The Blue Squadron, Bella Donna, Blind Justice, The Green Pack.*

1935 *D'Ye Ken John Peel, Abdul the Damned, Royal Cavalcade, Once a Thief, Lend Me Your Husband.*

1936 *The Secret Voice, Reasonable Doubt.*

1937 *The Elder Brother, Pearls Bring Tears, Talking Feet, The Show Goes On.*

1938 *The Claydon Treasure Mystery.*

1940 *Old Mother Riley in Society, The Big Blockade.*

1941 *Old Mother Riley's Ghosts, Ships with Wings, The Seventh Survivor.*

1942 *Penn of Pennsylvania, Flying Fortress, The Missing Million, Hard Steel, Banana Ridge.*

1943 *Women Aren't Angels.*

1944 *Headline, Candles at Nine.*

1945 *Madonna of the Seven Moons.*

1947 *The Phantom Shot, Mine Own Executioner, Mrs. Fitzherbert.*
1948 *House of Darkness, Escape from Broadmoor, Third Time Lucky.*
1949 *Man on the Run, The Temptress, The Man from Yesterday.*
1951 *The Magic Box.*
1952 *Mr. Denning Drives North, The Ringer, A Time to Be Born.*
1953 *Four-Sided Triangle, Mantrap, Street Corner, The Mysterious Bullet.*
1954 *Front Page Story, Men of Sherwood Forest.*
1955 *Alias John Preston, The Gilded Cage, It's a Great Day, John and Julie.*
1956 *Eyewitness, Johnny You're Wanted, Raiders of the River, Tons of Trouble.*
1957 *Quatermass II, The Naked Truth, Five Clues to Fortune, Betrayal.*
1958 *Blood of the Vampire, The Crossroad Gallows, Chain of Events, Further Up the Creek, The Revenge of Frankenstein, The Secret Man.*
1959 *The Unseeing Eye, The Mummy, Too Many Crooks, Idol on Parade.*
1960 *Bottoms Up!, Compelled, Sink the Bismarck!, Village of the Damned.*
1961 *Pit of Darkness.*
1962 *Danger by My Side.*
1963 *Paranoiac, The Scarlet Blade.*
1972 *Young Winston.*
1975 *Royal Flash.*
1978 *Superman.*

Documentaries

1945 *Camera Reflections.*
1952 *Introducing the New Worker.*
1952 *To the Rescue.*
1954 *Missing from Home.*
1954 *Someone Else's Child.*
1959 *This Is Your Life.*
1960 *On the Road.*
1971 *Yesterday's Witness.*
1995 *Cinema Europe: The Other Holly*wood.

Theater

The year indicates the production's opening.
1919 *The Trojan Women* (Old Vic).
1920 *The Chinese Puzzle* (Windsor and tour).
1923 *Our Betters* (Globe).
1925 *Sumurun* (Coliseum), *Courting* (tour).

1930 *The Bachelor Husband* (Walthamstow and tour).
1934 *Finished Abroad* (Savoy).
1935 *Public Saviour No. 1* (Piccadilly), *A Butterfly on the Wheel* (Playhouse), *The Limping Man* (Saville).
1936 *No Exit* (tour).
1937 *What We All Want* (tour).
1938 *Honeymoon for Three* (Brighton). **Weekly repertory season at the Empire, Sunderland:** *The Ringer, No Exit, The Lost Chord, Love from a Stranger, The Scarlet Pimpernel, The Limping Man, The Amazing Doctor Clitterhouse, The Constant Nymph, Bulldog Drummond, White Cargo, The Silent House, Mr. Wu, The Calendar, Just Married, Journey's End, Interference.*
1939 **Weekly repertory season at the Empire, Sunderland:** *Pygmalion, George and Margaret, Passing of the Third Floor Back, Busman's Honeymoon, I Killed the Count, Charley's Aunt, The Faithful Heart, The Middle Watch, Murder on the Second Floor, Accent on Youth, Tovarich, Nothing But the Truth, The Ghost Train.*
1940 *Faithfully Yours* (tour). **Weekly repertory season at the King's, Sunderland:** *Full House, French Without Tears, The Housemaster, Black Limelight, French Leave, George and Margaret, Dangerous Corner, The Sacred Flame, The Shining Hour, Tonight at 8.30, Rookery Nook, Night Must Fall, The Late Christopher Bean, Hay Fever, Bella Donna, Happy Ending, The Green Pack, The Circle, A Little Bit of Fluff, Goodness How Sad.*
1942 *Escort* (Lyric), *Jam Today* (St. Martin's).
1943 *What Every Woman Knows* (Lyric and tour).
1945 *Pygmalion, Rain, Caesar and Cleopatra, Rosmersholm, The Cathedral* (all Playhouse, Oxford), *Ten Little Niggers, A Kiss for Cinderella* (both Q, Kew).
1946 *A Doll's House* (Winter Garden and tour), *The Nineteenth Hole of Europe* (Granville, Fulham), *The Bells Ring* (tour), *The Faithful Heart* (Q, Kew).
1947 *Said the Spider* (tour), *The Bride Goes West* (Fortune), *The Poisoned Chalice, No Exit, What Every Woman Knows* (all Q, Kew).
1948 *The Unguarded Hour* (Q, Kew).
1949 *The Giaconda Smile* (tour), *The Blind Goddess* (Q, Kew).
1950 *Johnny Belinda, The Man in Grey, Mary Bonaventure* (all tours), *The Governess,*

Who Goes Home?, *If This Be Error* (all Q, Kew).

1951 *Venus Observed* (Citizen's, Glasgow), *Rainbow*, *A Pin to See the Peepshow* (both New Bolton's, Kensington), *Pick-Up Girl*, *The Heiress*, *The Holly and the Ivy* (all Q, Kew).

1952 *Lords of Creation* (Vaudeville and tour), *Tomorrow's Too Late* (Comedy), *The White Sheep of the Family* (Amersham), *Caroline* (Salisbury), *After My Fashion*, *Red Letter Day*, *The Girl from Rouen* (all Q, Kew).

1953 *Waters of the Moon*, *Housemaster* (both Windsor), *Neighbours* (Richmond), *Dead Secret*, *The Dormouse Sings* (both tours).

1954 *Let's Talk Turkey* (Windsor), *Grand National Night* (Q, Kew).

1955 *Book of the Month* (tour), *The Lost Generation* (Brighton), *Pygmalion* (schools tour).

1956 *The Final Ace* (New Lindsey, Notting Hill), *The Trial of Mary Dugan* (tour).

1958 *The Silent Inn* (Richmond).

1960 *Ross* (Haymarket and tour).

1962 *The Captain's Hero* (Royal Court).

1963 *The Tulip Tree*, *Caroline* (both Windsor), *The Judge's Story* (Worthing).

1965 *The Creeper* (St. Martin's and Richmond), *Difference of Opinion* (Bromley).

1972 *The Hollow* (Windsor).

Miscellaneous

1930 Variety Evening, Palladium, London.

1936 *Sunday Non-Stops*, Prince of Wales, London.

1936 Concert, Royal County Theatre, Reading.

Television

The year indicates the first screening.

1947 *Murder in the Cathedral.*

1948 *R.U.R.*, *The Chronicles of Ben.*

1949 *Ten Little Niggers.*

1950 *Time and the Conways*, *Mr. Bowling Buys a Newspaper.*

1951 *The Railway Children*, *The Blonde Informer.*

1952 *Joey*, *Billy Bunter: The Siege*, *Billy Bunter: The Piece of Cake.*

1953 *Joey's Burglar.*

1954 *The Lost Planet*, *A Private Room*, *Billy Bunter: Bunter Won't Go*, *The Smith Family*, *Ninety Sail*, *Missing from Home.*

1955 *Return to the Lost Planet*, *The King's Square*, *That One Talent*, *The Makepeace Story.*

1956 *Space School*, *The Fisherman King*, *Lucky Silver*, *Nom-de-Plume*, *Galleon's Key*, *The Byzantine Treasure*, *The Deserted Castle*, *The Grove Family*, *Big City*, *As Others See Us*, *Boyd Q.C.*, *Guilt.*

1957 *Uncertain Honours*, *The Railway Children*, *Operation Big House*, *The Road to Rome*, *Four Farewells in Venice*, *Decision*, *Lockhart Casts a Net.*

1958 *Slave Traders*, *The Gentle Jester*, *Shadow Squad*, *Kidnap*, *Flying Ambulance.*

1959 *Crime Sheet*, *Emergency Ward 10*, *The Verdict Is Yours*, *Sunday Closing*, *Beyond Fear*, *Dead Man's Hands*, *Decision*, *Deadline for Murder*, *Silent Accusation*, *Interpol Calling*, *The Judge's Story*, *The Man Who Lost His Trousers*, *Jo's Boys*, *Mark Saber*, *Boyd Q.C.*

1960 *Spycatcher*, *Love by Extortion*, *The Key Witness*, *Focus.*

1961 *The Case of George Peterson*, *Paul of Tarsus*, *The Frame*, *Love by Extortion.*

1962 *Dr Finlay's Casebook*, *The Minister*, *Alida.*

1963 *The Goldfish Bowl*, *I Can't Bear Violence*, *The Human Jungle*, *A Woman with Scars*, *Code-Name Murder*, *The Secret Place.*

1964 *Dr Finlay's Casebook.*

1965 *The Sullavan Brothers*, *The Minister.*

1966 *Blackmail*, *Son of the Sahara*, *Weaver's Green*, *A Man of Reputation*, *The Case of the Prominent Thespian.*

1969 *The Six Wives of Henry VIII.*

1972 *Doctors' Lib.*

1973 *Members Only*, *Mr. Calloway Is a Very Cautious Man.*

1974 *The Tattered Anarchist.*

1975 *Against the Crowd*, *Nights*, *Poor Baby.*

1976 *The Nicest Man in the World.*

1977 *Countess Ilona*, *The Werewolf Reunion.*

1979 *Ends and Ways.*

Bibliography

Ackland, Rodney, and Elspeth Grant. *The Celluloid Mistress*. Allan Wingate, 1954.

Adair, Gilbert, and Nick Roddick. *A Night at the Pictures: Ten Decades of British Film*. Columbus Books, 1985.

Armes, Roy. *A Critical History of British Cinema*. Secker & Warburg, 1978.

Balcon, Michael. *Michael Balcon Presents.... A Lifetime in Films*. Hutchinson, 1969.

Bamford, Kenton. *Distorted Images: British National Identity and Film in the 1920s*. I.B. Tauris, 1999.

Barr, Charles (ed.). *All Our Yesterdays: 90 Years of British Cinema*. BFI Publishing, 1986.

Barr, Charles. *Ealing Studios*. University of California Press, 1977.

Barr, Charles. *English Hitchcock*. Cameron Books, 2000.

Barry, Iris. *Let's Go to the Pictures*. Chatto & Windus, 1926.

Bergan, Ronald. *Eisenstein: A Life in Conflict*. Little, Brown, 1997.

Betts, Ernest. *Heraclitus, or the Future of Film*. Kegan Paul, 1928.

Blum, Daniel. *A Pictorial History of the Talkies*. Spring Books, 1958.

Bouchier, Chili. *Shooting Star: The Last of the Silent Film Stars*. Atlantis, 1996.

Bret, David. *Greta Garbo: Divine Star*. Robson Press, 2012.

Brook, Clive. *Eighty-Four Ages: Clive Brook, His Life and Times* (unpublished).

Brownlow, Kevin. *David Lean*. Faber & Faber, 1996.

Brownlow, Kevin. *The Parade's Gone By*. University of California Press, 1966.

Burton, Alan, and Laraine Porter (eds.). *Scene-Stealing: Sources for British Cinema Before 1930*. Flicks Books, 2003.

Butler, Ivan. *Silent Magic: Rediscovering the Silent Film Era*. Columbus Books, 1987.

Cardiff, Jack. *Magic Hour*. Faber & Faber, 1996.

Chamberlain, Derek. *39 Steps to Stardom: The Life and Times of Madeleine Carroll*. Matador, 2010.

Clair, René. *Cinema Yesterday and Today*. Dover, 1970.

Cocteau, Jean. *The Art of Cinema*. Marion Boyars, 1992.

Compton, Fay. *Rosemary: Some Reminiscences*. Alston Rivers, 1926.

Cook, Pam (ed.). *Gainsborough Pictures*. Cassell, 1997.

Croall, Jonathan. *The Croall Family History* (unpublished).

Croall, Jonathan. *Forgotten Stars: My Father and the British Silent-Film World*. Fantom Publishing, 2013.

Dixon, Bryony. *100 Silent Films*. Palgrave Macmillan/BFI, 2011.

Duncan, Paul. *Alfred Hitchcock: Architect of Anxiety 1899–1980*. Taschen, 2003.

Durgnat, Raymond. *The Strange Case of Alfred Hitchcock*. Faber, 1974.

Fields, Gracie. *Sing as We Go*. Frederick Muller, 1960.

Gielgud, John. *Early Stages*. Macmillan, 1939.

Gifford, Denis. *The British Film Catalogue 1895–1985*. David & Charles, 1986.

Gledhill, Christine. *Reframing British Cinema 1918–1928: Between Restraint and Passion*. BFI Publishing, 2003.

Greene, Graham. *The Pleasure Dome: Collected Film Criticism 1935–1940*. John Russell Taylor (ed.). Oxford University Press, 1972.

Hepworth, Cecil M. *Came the Dawn: Memories of a Film Pioneer*. Phoenix House, 1951.

Higson, Andrew (ed.). *Young and Innocent? The Cinema in Britain 1896–1930*. Exeter University Press, 2002.

Kuhn, Annette, and Guy Westwell. *Oxford Dictionary of Film Studies*, 2nd ed. Oxford University Press, 2020.

Landy, Marcia. "The Extraordinariness of Gracie Fields: The Anatomy of a British Film Star," in Bruce Babington (ed.), *British Stars and Stardom*. Manchester University Press, 2001.

Low, Rachael. *The History of the British Film 1918–1929*. Allen & Unwin, 1971.

Low, Rachael. *Film Making in 1930s Britain*. Allen & Unwin, 1985.

Mackenzie, S.P. *British War Films 1939–1945*. Hambledon & London, 2001.

Macnab, Geoffrey. *Searching for Stars: Stardom and Screen Acting in British Cinema*. Cassell, 2000.

Manvell, Roger. *Films and the Second World War*. Dent, 1974.

McFarlane, Brian. *An Autobiography of British Cinema*. Methuen, 1997.

McFarlane, Brian (ed.). *The Encyclopedia of British Film*, 4th ed. Manchester University Press, 2013.

McFarlane, Brian (ed.). *Sixty Voices: Celebrities Recall the Golden Age of British Cinema*. British Film Institute, 1992.

Montagu, Ivor. *The Youngest Son: Autobiographical Sketches*. Lawrence & Wishart, 1970.

Moseley, Roy. *Evergreen: Victor Saville in His Own Words*. Southern Illinois University Press, 2000.

Murphy, Robert. *British Cinema and the Second World War*. Continuum, 2000.

Mycroft, Walter C. *The Time of My Life*. Scarecrow Press, 2006.

O'Leary, Liam. *The Silent Cinema*. Studio Vista, 1965.

O'Rourke, Chris. *Acting for the Silent Screen: Film Actors and Aspiration Between the Wars*. Bloomsbury, 2021.

Pearson, George. *Flashback: The Autobiography of a British Film-Maker*. Allen & Unwin, 1957.

Perry, George. *The Films of Alfred Hitchcock*. Studio Vista, 1965.

Perry, George. *The Great Picture Show: From the 70s to the 90s*. Paladin, 1975.

Poulton, Mabel. *Cockles and Caviar: A Story of Theatre and Film Studios* (unpublished).

Powell, Michael. *A Life in Movies: An Autobiography*. Heinemann, 1986.

Quinlan, David. *British Sound Films: The Studio Years 1928–1959*. Batsford, 1984.

Quinlan, David. *Illustrated Directory of Film Stars*. Batsford, 1981.

Quinlan, David. *Quinlan's Film Directors*, rev. ed. Batsford, 1999.

Richards, Jeffrey. *The Age of the Dream Palace: Cinema and Society in Britain 1930–1939*, Routledge, 1989.

Richards, Jeffrey (ed.). *The Unknown Thirties: An Alternative History of the British Cinema 1929–1939*. I.B. Tauris, 1998.

Robinson, David. *Hollywood in the Twenties*. Tantivy Press, 1968.

Sargeant, Amy. *British Cinema: A Critical History*. BFI Publishing, 2005.

Shafer, Stephen C. *British Popular Films 1929–1939: The Cinema of Reassurance*. Routledge, 1997.

Shipman, David. *The Story of Cinema: From the Beginnings to Gone with the Wind*. Hodder & Stoughton, 1982.

Spoto, Donald. *The Dark Side of Genius: The Life of Alfred Hitchcock*. Ballantine Books, 1983.

Stock, Francine. *In Glorious Technicolor: A Century of Film and How It Has Shaped Us*. Chatto & Windus, 2011.

Stuart, John. *Caught in the Act*. The Silent Picture, 1971.

Sweet, Matthew. *Shepperton Babylon: The Lost Worlds of British Cinema*. Faber & Faber, 2005.

Taylor, John Russell. *Hitch: The Authorised Biography of Alfred Hitchcock*. Faber & Faber, 1978.

Thomson, David. *The Big Screen*. Allen Lane, 2012.

Thomson, David. *Have You Seen? A Personal Introduction to 1,000 Films*. Allen Lane, 2008.

Truffaut, François. *Hitchcock*, rev. ed. Simon & Schuster, 1983.

Warren, Patricia. *The British Film Collection 1896–1984: A History of the British Cinema in Pictures*. Elm Tree Books, 1984.

Webb, Paul. *Ivor Novello: Portrait of a Star*. Haus Books, 1999.

Winchester, Clarence (ed.). *The World Film Encyclopedia*. Amalgamated Press, 1933.

Wood, Linda (ed.). *British Films 1927–1939*. BFI, 1986.

Wood, Linda (ed.). *The Committed Imperative in the British Film Industry: Maurice Elvey, a Case Study*. BFI, 1987.

Wright, Basil. *The Long View: An International History of Cinema*. Secker & Warburg, 1974.

Works on VHS, DVD, and CD

Brownlow, Kevin, and David Gill, *Cinema Europe: The Other Hollywood*. DVD, 1995.

Dickens Before Sound. DVD, with booklet notes by Michael Eaton, BFI.

Gifford, Denis, Interview with John Stuart. CD, 1964.

Oliver, Jane, and Stephen Peet. *Yesterday's Witness*. BBC, VHS, 1971.

Silent Britain. DVD, with booklet notes by Bryony Dixon, BFI.

Silent Shakespeare. DVD, with booklet notes by Nicci Gerrard, BFI.

Index